Texas Hold'Em

Tournaments, Cash Games and Embarrassing Social Gas

by

Tony Korfman

DNA evidence has proven beyond any reasonable doubt that this book is the baby of Hold 'em Investments, LLC 806 Buchanan #115-315 Boulder City, Nevada 89005. It has been Registered, Trademarked, Copyrighted, Baptized and Circumcised. This was all done in 2007. It was a very busy year.

Table of Contents

If there is a word in the book you are not familiar with, chances are it's in the Glossary. Actually, chances are it's **not** in the Glossary. I figure, what the fuck you doing reading this shit if you don't already know the terminology? But that's not the type of attitude I should have toward a nice person like you who gave me your hard earned money to read what I made up. So I apologize profusely. Want to know what profusely means? Look it up in the Glossary. But I'll tell you now- It's not in there, Bucko. You want definitions? Buy a fuckin' dictionary.

Warning! Warning! Warning!

A Warning Note From the Author

Kids under 17 should not read this book unattended. One or both parents should be present along with a priest or someone that says he's a priest. Actually, any holy fuck will work, but I said a priest because I'm Catholic and my mom gets pissed if I don't mention the word "priest" whenever I write something. Thank you for your understanding and cooperation. Especially you kids under 17.

Tony Korfman

The Author

For Your Information:

When I began to write this book I decided to give all the proceeds to charity. I wanted to be a Barry Greenstein clone, only 5 feet taller and 200 pounds heavier. The charity thing sounded like a great idea. Then I said, "What am I? fuckin' nuts?" I'm the one who wrote this crap. I'm the one who plagiarized a bunch of shit. I'm the one who could go to prison. I'm the one who will have to put up with a cellmate named Vito. But I care about people. So I wanted to give part of the proceeds to the tired, the poor, those yearning to be free. So what I decided is, I'm not going to pay the printer. Fuck the printer. He charges a fortune for some low-grade paper. People don't buy the book because of the paper. If they did, they would just buy a notepad. So I'm going to donate the money I would have paid the printer to the Imus Ranch for Kids with Cancer. The Imus Ranch is in a small town in New Mexico. They do good work. It's a win-win for almost everyone. Except the printer. Oh well. Fuck the printer.

Endorsements

These endorsements are certified, notarized, and fantasized and kept in a hermetically sealed mayonnaise jar on someone's fuckin' porch. Anyone who would like to see the original documents can go fuck themselves.

"This book is fuckin' funny."

A local Parish Priest

"I laughed my fuckin' ass off."

Las Vegas Mormon Bishop

"I haven't had this much fun since my last circumcision."

Las Vegas Rabbi

"This book is tremendously entertaining, unbelievably humorous, historically fascinating and endlessly interesting. I have no fuckin' idea what I just said. I was told to say it."

A Gnome-Like Elvis Impersonator

"I couldn't believe it! My John was reading this book and laughing while I was blowing him."

Mustang Sally

"Never before have the Ninjas endorsed a book- let alone a book about Texas Hold 'em- let alone a book by Tony Korfman. But Korfman is holding one of our own hostage. We have no choice. This book is endorsed by Ninjas. Now please let my husband, Ninja Fred, go. He needs his meds."

Ninjess Ethel- Ninja Fred's wife

"The National Ninja Organization for the Preservation of Ninjas Past and Present, or the NNOFTPONPAP for short, does not endorse any publication, movie or showtune, no matter who is being held hostage."

Ninja Garth

President of the NNOFTPONPAP

Dedications and Thank You's

A special dedication and thank you to David Letterman and Oprah Winfrey. Why? It can't hurt. And thank you to Bernard on the Imus program. Why? Fuck- I don't know. I just think he's funny.

Thank you to the 7 year olds in China who helped assemble this book. Thank you to the tennis shoe industry for allowing me to use them.

Thank You Barret Garrett-

Whoever You Are

Thank you to Barret Garrett of Las Vegas, Nevada- a small town near my town of Boulder City, Nevada. Actually, his real name is Barret Thomson, but I can never remember if it's Barret or Garrett so I call him both names. Barret designed the cover and spent many countless minutes doing it. Actually, I think there were 10 of them. If he wouldn't have spent so much computer time trying to make me look younger, he could have cut his time in half. Five minutes in computer time is like 7 months in dog years. If I wouldn't have changed the cover 14 times, he says he could have done the cover in less than 2 minutes. But I couldn't help it. I change my mind a lot. I'm old. So I also thank Barret Garrett for his patience. And for the camaraderie we developed. And someday I hope to meet him. Maybe at a book signing. If he buys my book.....

Provocations, Inspirations and Must Reads

-Doyle Brunson's "Super System 1 & 2"

-"Harrington on Hold 'em 1 & 2"

-David Letterman and his Top 10 Lists

-George Carlin

-David Sedaris- Everything he writes

-Dave Barry- Everything he writes

-Mitch Albom

-Steve Allen

-Billy Crystal- "700 Sundays"

-Steve Forte- "Casino Game Protection" and "Poker Protection"

-Richard Marcus- "Dirty Poker"

-Jay Leno- He makes people laugh. God bless anyone that does that.

Before You Buy A Book

Before you buy a book you should ask yourself many questions. First and foremost of course is the question "Can I afford this fuckin' thing?" Some books are very expensive. Fortunately most bookstores and book clubs have mortgage brokers they work with. They offer government loans insured by FHA and HUD so that normal people with normal incomes can afford to read the works of Dr. Phil and other authors that are designed to give us great advice, and of course add rooms to the palaces they already live in with the proceeds. But remember it's all done for the greater good. The more rooms the authors add on, the more staff they need, and more people then have jobs. But I am not here to judge. Most of the time I am not even here. So before you buy a book, look at affordability- monthly payments, interest, tax, service charges and the like. Don't forget the tip. The next question is, will the book entertain you? And is it informative? And will it make you grin, smile, laugh? Is it fully constructed? Good binding? No blank pages? Many authors publish 300 page books with 150 blank pages for notes. I know this for a fact. I've done it. In fact, I'm doing it right now. The pages in the rear of this book are for your notes. They are also a ploy to make you think the book is bigger than it is. It's called ingenious marketing. It's called "selling the sizzle". It's called fraud. But who am I to judge? I'm just a poor, lowly writer trying to add a few rooms to my mansion. Excuse me for a minute, my pool boy Raul needs to consult with me…

This is the Top of the "Very Important Shit" Page

No part of this book may be reproduced, copied, read aloud or fondled under penalty of intense, and I mean fuckin' intense pain. Unless of course you get permission from me, my wife, my mother or anyone I like or pretend to like. This book may not be used in a court of law against a husband or wife unless one of them is an asshole.

This is the Middle of the "Very Important Shit" Page

All names, characters and incidents written in this Shakespearean type work are true. Except for the parts that are fictitious. And the parts I made up. No identification with actual persons living or dead or almost dead, is intended. Any coincidence of any event or person who thinks he was the person I am talking about just because I used his name has a big fuckin' ego. Right now I can't deal with big fuckin' egos. I have a book to write

This is the Bottom of the "Very Important Shit" Page

A book isn't something that you just sit down and write in 20 minutes. This book took almost an hour. And I was standing. But the feeling you get when it's finally finished is amazing. You feel so fulfilled. You feel so angelic. You feel so nauseous. That's why I'm a fan of the purple pill. Especially after "bad beats". Is there really even a "good beat"? Aren't they all bad beats? If you get beat, it's bad. Pure fuckin' simple. Mike Tyson never said in his endearing whiney voice, "I got beat, man. But it was a good beat. It felt really fuckin' good. It humbled me. It made me rethink my contribution to society and the difference I'm making just being on this big fuckin' rock." Actually, out of those 38 words, he's probably never said or knows the meaning of 35 of them. But I like Mike Tyson. I think he's just surrounded himself with the wrong people. If he had made some good investments in rental properties he wouldn't be in the boat he's in now. Right now I'm in a similar boat. I can't figure out how to get out of this bit. I guess I can take an easy out and do what I was taught in my high school theology class.

Yours in Christ
(it always works)

One of Many Disclaimers

I did not write this book alone. I say that in case there are lawsuits. There's always lawsuits. It seems like everyone sues. Everyone. A little old lady started it all in 1847. She bought a cup of hot coffee at the local General Store and was drinking it in her horse and carriage. She took her eye off the road, the carriage hit a rut, the horse reared and the coffee spilled on her lap. The rest is history. She sued the General Store owner for serving hot coffee. She claimed the coffee was hotter than the hot coffee that she thought she was going to get. Anyway, she went to court with her stained dress on. No one thought she still had the dress. The coffee DNA match was perfect. The General Store had no outs. It was their coffee. The old lady won the case. Big time. She wound up owning the general store. Today that General Store is called WalMart. Sam Walton married her and took all the credit. What a prick.

What People Say About Tony Korfman

"I think he's great. A great writer, a great guy. The $50 check he sends me every month never bounces. I love him like a son."

        Mrs. Millie Korfman- Tony's mother

"He's an asshole."

        Other family members

"Tony who?"

        Mike Caro

"Tony loves kids. He gives them his time- his money. Whatever it takes to get them into the van."

        Ernie Cabral- Action Magazine owner

"Ernie is an asshole."

        Connie Cabral- Ernie's wife

To Err is Human...

There are mistakes in this book. Some are really mistakes and some are there on purpose. Why would anyone put mistakes in a book on purpose? Because there are some people out there that look for mistakes. Their goal in life is to find mistakes in books. They are very lonely people. And I want to please everyone. Well, not everyone- but almost everyone. I don't want people to anguish and have to read and reread this drivel not finding a mistake. By putting them in on purpose, I have ensured the fact that I will get letters telling me about the typos and that I am an ignorant fuck. That's O.K. The people that write those letters need to vent. And I make a good vent-ee. I think I just made up a word. Maybe it's ventee. Now I'm questioning my own mistake. Please, no letters that I am a sick fuck. I already know. And sometimes I am redundant. I repeat myself when I write. When I write I forget what I write sometimes. I guess that's why writers hire editors and proofreaders. They look for redundancy. They look for mistakes. They look for misspellings, they look for the proper usage of participles and dangling participles and anything else that might be dangling. Fuck the proofreaders and the editors. I'm not perfect.

A Quick Quiz

I love quizzes. Especially quick ones. Long quizzes would be called tests. No one likes tests. When you go to a doctor he always wants to do tests. That's why no one wants to go. If he would say, "We're going to do a quick quiz today Mr. Korfman," then it would seem like a fun thing. It reminds me of school. When the teacher came in and she would say, "Class, today we are going to have a quiz. Nothing serious- just a fun quiz to start off your day and then treats for everyone. Big giant Oreo's for all. Except for you Korfman. Your mom called and said you're getting so fat you can't see your penis. NO COOKIES FOR YOU!" The fuckin' cookie Nazi. Just my fuckin' luck. But I'll have fun anyway because of the quick quiz that Mrs. Ratchett is giving us. What a nice old cunt (end of dream sequence). Tests on the other hand are a different animal completely. Same scenario- same class- same cunt. "Class, today we are going to have a test. A long, hard test. A test that will make you wish you brought an extra diaper to class. A test that will be 50%- no 60%- fuck it 90% of your grade. That's if you do poorly. If you do great, I probably won't count it at all. I am Mrs. Ratchett. You will have nightmares about me until you are in your 40's. I own you. I deliver bone crushing, soul crushing, testicle crushing river cards!" See the difference? So this is a quiz. A quick quiz. And Mrs. Ratchett had no input. Except in my dreams.

Take this quiz before you read the book. Then take it after you read the book. 4 out of 5 dentists do better **after** they've read the book. 3 out of 5 people who have voices in their head telling them to kill, do better **before** they've read the book. There was no difference in the other 12 people who helped us in our mass research project. The 9 to 17 year old age group did exceptionally well before and after they read the book but they weren't supposed to read the book (see "Warning! Warning! Warning!" page at beginning of book). Apparently there is a huge market for the 9-17 age group for poker instructions so my next book will be "Mr. Rogers Teaches Hold 'Em in his Neighborhood" which hopefully can be transformed into a daily TV show for kids starring Phil Hellmuth. It could be huge. And scary. Mostly scary. OK, so here's the quiz as it almost appeared on pokerletter.org, a great free online newsletter. I added my own twisted sense of humor to it plus the swear words. Let's face it- a quiz without swear words just isn't a fuckin' quiz. God, I love this country.

1.)   You've got the dealer's button. You look down at 10♠-10♣. The pot is raised 3x the big blind before you get to act. You are on the short stack with about 10x the big blind in chips. You should:

    A-   Throw your cards into the muck and lay a hellacious fart.

    B-   Call the raise.

    C-   Double or triple the raise.

    D-   Push all-in and say, "I own you mother fucker."

2.)   You're in a tournament heads up. You're in the big blind and have 4x as many chips as your opponent who has exhibited himself through the tournament as being a real asshole. He limps in and you look down and see A♠-A♥. You begin to climax but get control when you realize you're being televised. The right move to make is:

    A-   Check your option with the big blind and make a sucking noise.

    B-   Make a large raise.

    C-   Make a callable raise.

    D-   Go all in and scratch your scrotum (I love that word- scrotum).

3.)   You have A♥-7♠ in the big blind. The pot is raised and then re-raised to 12x the big blind before reaching you. You have about 20x the big blind in chips. You should:

A- Muck your cards aggressively.

B- Call the raise.

C- Re-raise the re-raiser all-in, subtly giving him the finger.

D- Spill your Bloody Mary into the dealer's rack and say, "I'm really fuckin' sorry."

4.)   You're on the button with J♥-J♠. Two players ahead of you limp in and you raise to 5x the big blind. The big blind calls your raise and everyone else folds like a Sam's club lawn chair. The flop comes J♦-9♦-5♦ and your opponent checks. You should:

A- Push all-in yelling, "I got the fuckin' nuts!"

B- Make a substantial bet- whatever "substantial" means.

C- Check by pounding the table in an explosive manner.

D- Make a small teeny weeny bet and say, "I'm betting a teeny weeny bet- like your penis."

5.)   You're playing heads-up against the chip leader and table captain at the final table of a tournament. Your opponent raised from the button and you called with 9♠-10♠. The flop comes 7♠-J♦-8♥. You should:

A- Check the hand, hold your breath and fart.

B- Push all-in and fart.

C- Make a small bet and fart loudly.

D- Make a big bet, do the dance of joy and pass gas.

6.)   You are in the early position of a hand in a tournament and
       are dealt 7♥-7♠. There are seven players behind you and
       you are on the short stack with 11x the big blind left in
       your stack. You should:

       A- Call the big blind with a smirk.

       B- Muck your hand at the dealer's forehead.

       C- Bellow out "RAISE!"

       D- Go all-in using one of the pro's all-in hand
          motions. Hand motions are very intimidating.

7.)   You are on the button and you pick up a pocket pair of
       Kings. Three players ahead of you limp in and you raise.
       Two players call and the flop comes 10-4-A. The first
       player bets 5x the big blind and the second player calls.
       You should:

       A- Call the bet and look for a reaction.

       B- Muck your cards at the player's face and cause a
          reaction.

       C- Re-raise- gently, softly.

       D- Push all-in, put your sunglasses on and chew gum.

8.)   The term in poker "He's on tilt" means what?

       A- He's on a hot streak and idiocy runs in his family.

       B- He's playing like a fuckin' idiot.

       C- He's really lucky and playing like a fuckin' idiot.

       D- His wife left him because he plays like a fuckin'
          idiot

Answers to Quick Quiz

(Peeking at the answers is illegal in 5 states. If you are a peeker, just hope to God you are not in one of those 5 states.)

1.) D- Push all in. The "mother fucker" part is optional. You want to force out all the mediocre hands that can beat you and go head to head with the initial raiser. I think. Fuck, I don't know. I just make this shit up.

2.) C- Make a callable raise (sucking noises are optional). Pocket Aces is a great hand- a monster hand- any fuckin' time you get it. Especially heads up. Your main goal here is to keep your opponent from throwing his cards away while you extract as much money from his bankroll as possible. You don't want him to have a free flop, but you also want him to stay in the pot. So you do whatever you have to do to keep him in the pot. Handjobs are allowed in this example.

3.) A- Muck the muckin fucker cards. Ace-small isn't going to get it this hand. Your tournament life is on the line and by mucking the cards you live to fight another day. Bloody Mary's are really sticky and cause chaos when spilled. I love chaos.

4.) B- Make a substantial bet. Any flush beats you and right now you need information. If he calls a substantial bet he's probably on a nut or close to a nut Diamond flush draw. You need to make him pay to get that card he needs. Even if he calls and gets the flush, you could pair the board or get quads and make his tournament life cease to exist. And if he's suicidal, his entire life might cease to exist. Then you would feel guilty. Or maybe not. You won the hand. Life is good.

5.) A- Check the hand. You have the fuckin' nuts with a Jack high straight and this is a great time to set a trap. The more he gets involved with the pot, the more likely he is to call you on the river when you put him all-in and crush his spirit, his soul, his being. This is what you live for. Along with family, friends, religion and other bullshit that's never there for you.

6.) D- Go all-in. What the fuck. Small pairs are really tough to play. You're short stacked. Not that many chips. Time to make a move before you get blinded out of the game. At some point you've got to gamble. This happens in all tournaments. Always be ready to make a graceful exit. You know. Stand up, salute the players, wish everyone good luck, tip your chair over and mother fuck the dealer. You know it's his fault. It always is.

7.) B- Time to say goodbye to your Kings. A tearful goodbye is allowed. Chances are one of these guys in the pot with you has an Ace. Kings are tough to lay down, but sometimes you have to. It doesn't take a fuckin' genius to figure out that this is one of those times. Tearing them in half sometimes makes saying goodbye easier.

8.) **B-** Maybe. But his wife could have left him because he doesn't spend any time at home with her and the kids and she is fuckin' whining all the time about poker being more important than her. Altogether now- can we all say the word "PRENUP"!!!

Poker Playing as a Business

If you are going to be a professional poker player you still need to file an income tax statement every year. So you need to keep records. Your accountant will love and adore you and maybe even promise to buy one of your books (wholesale of course) if you ever write one. When you play for a living you can accumulate tremendous wealth in a short period of time. This is especially true of tournaments. Let's take a look at Jamie Gold's incredibly detailed accounting of his tremendous payday at the World Series of Poker

Accountant Style Notebook	$9.49
Hire Driver to go get notebook	175.00
Parking	10.00
Beer Stop for Driver	12.00
Lunch for Driver	27.00
Tip for lunch	5.00
Damage to fender from running over pedestrian after beer stop	912.00
Damage to windshield from running over pedestrian after beer stop	230.00
Bail for driver	5,000.00
Attorney for driver	67,500.00
Support driver's family while he does 3 years	105,000.00
Stitch up bullet wound in fight with driver's brother	27,500.00

More legal fees	25,300.00
1/2 of proceeds of WSOP winnings to guy who said Gold promised it to him	6,000,000.00
Tip Gold said he would give dealers if he won	1,000,000.00
Income tax on $12,000,000 check he received	4,000,000.00
More legal fees	508,319.00
Donation to Catholic Church (in case they're the right one)	100,000.00
Donation to Morman Church (you never know)	50,000.00
Donation to Jewish Temple (why take a chance?)	50,000.00
Donation to Muslims (there's a ton of them. Why create bad karma?)	50,000.00
Buy-in for next years WSOP	<u>10,000.00</u>
Total Costs	$11,999,999.51
WSOP Winnings	$12,000,000.00
Net Profit	$0.49

OK, so $0.49 may not seem like a lot. But how do you put a price on having fun? How do you put a price on being on the cover of magazines that will be collectors' items in 20 years when they don't exist? How do you put a price on the friendships and relationships you develop when you go on tournament breaks and share urinals with other men? What does the commercial say? Priceless. I say fuckin' priceless. Especially the urinal part.

Random Thought

For most of us, the dream of becoming a champion poker player is a fantasy. For a special few assholes, that dream is a reality. Most of them are overweight, smell badly and couldn't do 5 sit-ups if their life depended on it, but we cheer them, we live through them and we want to have sex with them. It's hard to fuckin' believe. God, I love this country.

The TV Loser's Speech

When people lose in TV tournaments the announcer always interviews the guy that just got busted. They are humble, they are thankful they got as far as they did, they are polite, they are usually in shock. I know one of these days I'll be interviewed and because of my demeanor I plan to be very calm, very humble and all the other bullshit adjectives I used a few sentences ago.

Announcer: Mr. Korfman, how do you feel?

Me: I'm happy to have come this far.

Announcer: This is your first time at the final table.

Me: Do you have a point?

Announcer: No, it's just an observation.

Me: Well, aren't we fuckin' observant!

Announcer: Mr. Korfman- Be Nice.

Me: I'm happy to have come this far.

Isn't that what all the losers say? "I'm happy to have come this far." Why don't they speak the truth. From their heart. From their soul. A "tell it like it is" interview. Like Howard Cossell would do if he would be interviewed.

Announcer: Mr. Cossell, "How do you feel?"

Cossell: How do you think I feel you pompous ass prick?

Announcer: This was your first time at the final table.

Cossell: And I would still be there if it weren't for that fuckin' idiot asswipe kid who called me with a 6-7 offsuit. But it's a big parking lot and that young fuck still has to go to his car.

Has anyone checked his I.D.?

Announcer: Wow. Mr. Cossell, we have never had such a candid interview. Thank you for your time.

Cossell: I'm happy to have come this far.

I Love Interviews

I do a lot of interviews. It's easy to get to the stars when you're popular and represent a major publication. Unfortunately, I am neither. But representation is everything. Well at least 80%. Like Hold 'em- 80% betting, 20% cards. When I got Sam Farha's personal phone number I was excited. There were only 3 rings when a man answered.

Me: Sam?

Sam: Who's this?

Me: Sam?

Sam: Who's this?

Me: Tony

Sam: Tony who?

Me: Tony Korfman from People Magazine

Sam: Who? From where?

Me: Tony from Cardplayer Magazine

Sam: Who?

Me: Barry Shulman from Cardplayer Magazine.

Sam: Hi Barry. My pool boy Raul usually screens my calls.

Me: How nice.

Sam: What do you want?

Me: A very short interview.

Sam: No.

Me: I only say positive things about people. That's how I know this interview will be very short.

Sam: We seem to have a lot of static. I think my cell phone is going dead.

Me: But I called your landline.

Sam: Oh.

Me: May we continue?

Sam: Click.

Me: Asshole.

Sometimes interviews don't go as planned. In fact, come to think of it, none of them have gone as planned. Actually, none of them have gone anywhere. Maybe it's me. Maybe it's me.

Random Thought

I love to laugh- except when it makes Perrier come out of my nose and makes me fart at the same time.

An Offer I Couldn't Refuse

I was very fortunate recently. I was one of 3 billion people who received a great offer from my Chase credit card company to visit Disneyland, "Where dreams come true." It was billed as, "a very special offer just for me." I was excited. I was thrilled. I had to pee. The brochure was colorful. It was attractive. It was sticky. I think the mailman accidentally spilled a sticky substance in his bag. Or in his truck. Or on his yacht. Depending on where he sorted my mail. But I was ready for my dreams to come true. Nothing could stop me. Except the offer. And the asterisk. But it was a real classy asterisk. No ordinary asterisks for Chase. No ordinary asterisks for Disneyland. No ordinary asterisks for Pluto. But the planet Pluto doesn't exist anymore. It's not a planet. It's been erased from our solar system. So where does that put Pluto from Disneyland? What's his position on the elimination of his namesake planet? What if the scientists decide to eliminate him from the Disney Characters just so we're not constantly reminded of our missing planet. Especially during an election year. Whenever Disneyland would mention Pluto in an ad there would have to be a special asterisk. Much like the offer I got from Chase had a special asterisk. And because of the asterisk, my "Absolutely Free" room offer also has a small catch. Well, not real small. I have to pay for the first few nights. 37 Of them. But I ask you- Isn't it worth it- where wishes are granted and dreams come true? Doesn't everyone want to get away to a magical place? A place with dream makers. A place with Disney characters? A place with asterisks? But the asterisk clearly defined why I was selected for this great offer. And I quote. Well, almost quote. This is actually taken from the offer. Except for the parts I made up. In very very tiny tiny print at the bottom of the offer, as near as the human eye can tell, it says the following:

> * You were selected to receive this offer because you have been identified as meeting certain criteria, for example, you are in a certain age or income range or if you are jobless, your cardboard sign meets our dimensional standards. By responding to this offer you will effectively be disclosing to us that you meet these certain

standards, no matter how low they are, or how embarrassing. Other restrictions may apply that are far too long and detailed to explain here. And they could be too personal. Or they could be construed as sexual, racist, or just plain not nice. Our offer is seasonal and is subject to change without notice so even if you called ahead and drove 4 hours it could change while you're in line. It goes without saying that this offer is subject to availability. Advanced reservations are suggested but not required, just like shirts and underwear.

I need some time off. I'm going to Disneyland.

Random Thought

     When I write, I write to have fun. When I write, I enjoy it. To take a blank piece of paper and pick up a pen or pencil and create words that will take someone on a journey, is a feeling I enjoy. Whenever I wrote anything in high school I had one of two objectives. Make the teacher laugh or make the teacher cry. Sometimes I made my mom cry with some of the terrible grades I got, but that was not the objective. I go off on tangents when I write. I'll get hung up on something but then somehow I'll get us back on track to the subject matter at hand. Sometimes. Actually, I do remember the time… (dream sequence) O.K. I'm back. I use the word "fuckin'" a lot when I write. I don't know why. I don't talk that way. But I write that way. That probably explains some of the bad grades in school. Mrs. Hopkins in the third grade just didn't fuckin' get it. Come to think of it that was probably her problem. She never got it. Anyway, I just can't fuckin' help it. Be prepared to have some fun. Be prepared to learn some good shit about Hold 'em poker. Be prepared for some surprises. Be prepared.

Tournaments and Stress

Playing tournaments is extremely stressful. There are simple tips that if used correctly may get you to the final table. If they don't work, then use performance-enhancing drugs. Steroids seem to be the favorite of many. You may not get to the final table, but every one of your opponents will envy the size of your arms.

Tip #1- Take Deep Breaths- very slow, deep breaths de-stress the body. Tournament play is long and grueling. Deep breaths are very affective. The good news is that by taking deep breaths you can remain very calm. The bad news is if you can't take deep breaths you are probably dead.

Tip #2- Think Good Stuff- A simple way to de-stress your body is to think good thoughts. Think of how beautiful life is- think about the new car you're buying- think about spending a night in bed with Gavin Smith. Thinking good thoughts will send a chemical message throughout your body that life is good. And don't forget to smile. And wink. Some people love smilers and winkers. It makes them feel like they're in Hollywood.

Tip #3- Slow Down- There's nothing wrong with slowing down. We all go too fast. Slow down. Ponder your hands more before you commit to a pot. Ponder long and hard. Even if you have 2-7 offsuit pre flop. Slow, deliberate, Gandhi-like moves will slow the game down and make everyone feel peaceful and tranquil. Remember- if the whole table plays slow enough, it will be the final table.

Tip #4- Be Positive- We will have a lot less stress if we are positive about things. Look at the glass of water as always being half full, never half empty (I have no fuckin' idea what that means but I've heard it a million fuckin' times and I'm sick of it). You may get a really really bad beat and lose all your chips and your rent money to some punk prick, but you must look at the bright side. He drove to the game and it's a big, dark parking lot and he still has to get to his car. Positive thinking will give you less stress and make you a better person. It will also add years onto your life and make your penis harder.

Tip #5- Let it Go- Sometimes you cannot change what has happened. It happened and you have to make a conscious decision to let that event go. It may be the worst bad beat you have ever encountered in a game that will probably affect your life and your children's lives, but you have to let it go. It may be a devastating disaster that you can't stop thinking about, but you have to let it go. It is the right thing to do. It is the Christian thing to do.

Tip #6- Totally ignore Tip #5- I must have been drunk when I wrote it.

Random Thought

Next year at the WSOP I want the hemorrhoid cream concession. You play 15 hour days on a 2 hour chair. Most uncomfortable. Next year the cushion concession that Harrah's will own will take in over 2 million dollars.

Harrah's and The Venetian Team Up

It's nice to see the Venetian following in the footsteps of Harrah's Entertainment Corp. to help problem gamblers. Their campaign is a solid one. They recognize the obsession and the addiction that can control lives. Gambling is a great form of entertainment. But like anything else, it is abused by a small percentage of people and many times those people or their families don't know where to turn. Harrah's stepped up to the plate many years ago. Now the Venetian is climbing on board. Someday I'm sure the Internet sites will also get on track. I'm sure they will contact Harrah's so they can mirror their program because of its success. My guess is that the conversation will go like this:

Phone Operator: Harrah's Entertainment. May I entertain you?

Poker Site Marketing Genius: Hi. This is a poker site marketing genius. May I speak to someone regarding your problem gambler program?

Phone Operator: Yes sir. I'll connect you to our Problem Gambler Marketing Genius. Have a nice day.

Poker Site Marketing Genius: Don't tell me how to live my life.

Phone Operator: Please hold sir while I rub the phone on my crotch. Connecting sir.

Problem Gambler Marketing Genius: Hello, this is Harrah's Problem Gambler Marketing Genius. Can I help you?

Poker Site Marketing Genius: Hi. I'm a poker site marketing genius. We want to copy Harrahs' Problem Gambler program.

Problem Gambler Marketing Genius: We are honored that you would pattern a program after ours. It has been very affective. We have helped tens of thousands of people overcome their addiction. Just by calling 1-800-522-4700.

Poker Site Marketing Genius: You've cured tens of thousands of people from their gambling addiction?

Problem Gambler Marketing Genius: That's correct.

Poker Site Marketing Genius: And there was no charge? You didn't make any money doing that or have a hidden agenda or a plan to actually have them bet more?

Problem Gambler Marketing Genius: That is correct. The plan has been very affective and Harrah's is very proud of the fact they are at the forefront of the industry to show that we are concerned about problem gamblers and their families.

Poker Site Marketing Genius: Never mind. Click.

We Are a Product of Our Leadership

I worked at the Dunes in 1971 and 1972. In the dice pit. I lasted 2 years. I say "lasted" because I knew from day one that it was not a "career move" when I went there. Most of the shift managers and pit bosses were fuckin' miserable. And nasty. It was like the old Chinese laundries use to be. In the Chinese laundry, there were three people sitting on stools waiting to go to work. If your productivity fell, they would fire you and send over the one on the end stool. Then everyone moved down a stool and a new person sat on stool number 3. Much like the Price is Right. But at the Dunes, there was no threat of people on stools to take your spot. Just a 2-foot stack of dealer applications stacked on the pit stand to remind you that you were expendable. The "old" Dunes was old when I went to work there and it was real real fuckin' old when they finally blew it up. Or down, depending on your perception of it. Yes, they imploded it Virginia, but the explosives still had to "blow up". But who the fuck cares. The main thing is, it's gone. And most of the miserable old fucks that fired so many dealers, and made the dealers' families cry and worry about how they were going to pay the rent and make ends meet, are gone too. Good fuckin' riddance. How I lasted there 2 years is somewhat of a fuckin' miracle.

Finally, on that fateful day, the Casino Manager, George Duckworth or "Slick" as I use to call him, called me to the rear of the pit and even though I had been there 2 years and never missed a shift he said, " I gotta let you go." I said, "What? What for?" He said, and I'm not making this shit up, "You're too friendly to the players." I said, "Mr Duckworth, give me another chance. I can be nastier." He said, "Too late." I was in shock. I realized I had committed the cardinal sin of the Dunes. I was not a product of my leadership. I was not a product of my surroundings. I was not a prick. But you learn a lot as you go through life. You pick up bits and pieces from experiences and from people you know. Your value system starts when you're a toddler and your parents teach you to say "please" and "thank you". I have never missed a please or a thank you. Whether it's a waitress bringing me coffee or someone doing something for me, however small, however mundane, I say thank you. It shows good upbringing. It shows respect. It shows that the beatings I got as a child worked.

And I continued the tradition. I still spank my kids once a week even though the youngest one is 26. Of course I'm only kidding. I wouldn't have the strength to spank my kids once a week. I'm way too old and too tired. Once a month is all I have the strength for. The Dunes actually created the saying "The beatings will continue until morale improves". They created a lot of stuff. They created Junkets from New York. Big ones. Big Julie brought in a weekly junket from New York, every Thursday night. A plane full of players, no wives, flew into Las Vegas Airport and were brought to the Dunes every Thursday evening and stayed until Sunday when the plane left. Unless of course, someone was a big winner. Then the plane was delayed due to "engine trouble", and as we all know, no one wants to get on a plane with a bad engine, a bad tire or a drunk pilot. Well, maybe a drunk pilot is OK, but the other 2 are unacceptable. So the players would be notified that they would have to wait and keep playing at the Dunes until the guy winning lost all his money or the engine was repaired- whichever happened first. And the engine was never repaired first. Sometimes it took forever to order the phantom part and have it driven from Des Moines by horse and buggy. But the Dunes motto always came first: The safety of our players will never be compromised as long as they are winning. And big Julie was all about safety. Because he was on the fuckin' plane too.

The Dunes poker room was one of the hottest spots in town. You could borrow money at a very reasonable 5% a week rate or buy a really nice piece of jewelry or get your asshole ripped out and handed to you by playing poker with the poker parasites of that era. Major Riddle who was part owner of the Dunes also owned the Silver Nugget and also bought the old Thunderbird. When he died, the poker players he played with sobbed uncontrollably for days. He was responsible for their wealth and as we all know, enough is never enough. Never. A book could be written about everything that went on at the Dunes during the 70's. The joint made a ton of money. Especially from Big Julie's junkets. If it had been run by good leadership, caring leadership, friendly leadership, it would have made 10 tons instead of 1 ton. But they lived for the day. They lived for the moment. Most of them don't live anymore. Neither does the Dunes. It is a distant memory for some and a distant nightmare for others. I didn't like the

Dunes when I worked there, but I had to make a living. I didn't like it then- I don't like it now. I'm glad it's gone. But from the ashes and the rubble came the Bellagio. And the Monte Carlo. It's good to see that something so good came out of something so shitty. The mob should be ashamed of themselves for how they allowed the Dunes to be run. When I left the Dunes I left for good. I never set foot inside that shit box again.

The Las Vegas Hilton was my next stop. The Dunes to The Las Vegas Hilton was like going from sandlot baseball to Yankee Stadium. I was there for 5 years and never once, not for one day or one hour, worried about my job or paying my mortgage or feeding my family. Jimmy Newman ran a great joint. He was one of those guys that looked great in a suit. Not a speck of dandruff on the collar, not a wrinkle on his suit, not a nose hair out of place. His white hair looked like he had a hairdresser in his office to make sure no hair was ever out of place. Ever. He was a class act. Good leaders surround themselves with good people. They are a reflection of their leader. And Jimmy picked people that got the job done without sacrificing anyone's dignity. The pit bosses and shift managers treated everyone with respect and they took good care of the customers. Bob Barry, Walter Heinz and Val Roulette were the best role models a guy could have. The dealers could talk to the customers and the customers kept returning because of the Hilton's friendly atmosphere. And no one fucked with Newman. Barron Hilton hired some German fuck that thought the hotel ran the joint but he found out in a hurry that Jimmy Newman was the man. People came to the desert because of the fuckin' gambling not because a hotel was parked in the middle of it. The German pulled in his horns and tiptoed around Newman so he could keep his job. The Hilton was sold many years ago but Jimmy Newman was retained because of his rapport with the casino personnel and above all, the customers. If Newman would have left, a lot of good customers would have followed him. That's why casino executives, especially casino hosts are so important in the industry. They have a tiny black book full of customers' names and addresses that really isn't too tiny. When they leave a joint to go somewhere else, they notify the people in their book. And many times the customer will follow them. They're already a known entity to the host. They don't have to prove themselves to a new host or a new owner or a new casino manager.

Lately, the landscape of proving yourself has changed with the
inception of players cards. Players cards are the ultimate tracking
system. If you play a lot, the computer will track your play and you
will be amply rewarded. So who needs a host anymore? All the joints
do. A good host is still worth his weight in gold. Computers can give
you the facts about players but they have one big inherent problem.
They have no fuckin' personality. None. Zero. Zip. People want to
deal with a host that's assigned to them. They develop a rapport. They
develop a friendship. They develop the same aches and pains. They
have lunch. They have dinner. They have sex. Well, they probably
have sex but not together. The mailing lists, the player tracking and the
players club cards are great tools for the 21st century. But human
contact is still needed. Humans are still the greatest and most
important tracking device in gaming. There are many customers that
don't want a players club card, even though they know they get a lot of
perks and offers in the mail because of their play. They just don't want
a card. I've heard many reasons why a player doesn't want a players
card. When I was at the Edgewater in Laughlin, Nevada for 4 years as
General Manager, our casino hosts tried to get players cards into as
many players pockets as we could. We had aggressive campaigns and
finally got to the point where 55% of our players at any given time
were using a players club card when they played. But 45% didn't or
wouldn't use a card. They thought the machines were tighter if they
used their card. Or that the government was tracking them. Or that it
was plain unlucky. And the reasons went on and on. The players that
used their cards made it so much easier for us to determine their level
of comps. Most casinos are very liberal with their comps to guests who
play. So it's really nuts not to use the cards when you play. It's
actually **fuckin'** nuts. You can get great room deals even if you're not
a high roller. And food. Maybe not in the steakhouse but many of the
buffets on the Las Vegas Strip are fuckin' great. The players often
ignored are the ones not playing with a players club card for whatever
reason. That's where a good host comes in. A good host watches the
slot machines that are getting a lot of play from players that don't have
a players club card inserted into the machine they are playing. Then
there is the foreplay period. The introduction, the bullshit, the sales
pitch. The object is to make the customer that doesn't want a card
become a steady customer and have a host he or she can contact. Since
there is no players club card involved, there is basically no computer

record of the customer's play. The host would then record the customer's play manually and give the player his business card. When the customer wanted to make a return visit, the host would arrange everything based on their play. Many good players who don't use a players club card fall through the cracks. A good host recognizes these people. The host is a very important link between the customer and the casino's bank account.

All slot departments have the latest and greatest slot machines. International Games Technology or IGT is the "nuts" in slots and video poker machines. The table games have such an array of side games, called carnival games, that the title "21" pit is a misnomer (I love using a word once in a while that makes me look smart- see the Glossary if you don't know the origin of the word "misnomer"). Poker rooms have expanded in the past few years due to one simple reason. The young have become involved and they have a ton of fuckin' money. Hold 'em has gone fuckin' nuts. The poker boom was recently born, and it looks like it's here to stay. For a while anyway. Hopefully until I sell out of these fuckin' books. I can't stand having books stacked up to the ceiling in my bedroom fuckin' up my view. And creating darkness. And I don't like the dark. The stacks of books hide the light. I'm not too fond of the light either, but I hate the dark. Because in the dark things go bump in the night. Especially when I trip over a fuckin' stack of books on my way to the bathroom. And I pee a lot. I'm diabetic. And diabetics pee a lot. So if you are thirsty all the time, and you pee a lot, and you have diabetes in your family, you shouldn't be eating that chocolate bar you're dripping all over my book. Sugar is a diabetic's enemy. Actually, sugar is everyone's enemy. But it's so fuckin' good. And it's legal. And it's addictive. Chocolate and poker have so much in common. I have to end this chapter. I just heard a strange noise in my fridge and it could be that chocolate cake asking to get out. And the next time you get out and go to your favorite casino, make sure you get a players club card. Poker rooms now give you credit for playing, so you can use the card in the poker room also. The leaders of the industry have finally recognized the importance of the poker community by trying to give us "comps" based on the hours we spend in their poker rooms. We thank the casinos for that recognition.

Random Thought

There were tons of stories about Kerry Packer who was a multi-multi billionaire from Australia who played at the MGM whenever he came to town. Mr. P was known to tip the dealers millions of dollars. Yep, I said millions. It was not unusual for a cocktail waitress to get a $25,000 tip when she delivered him a drink. Anyway, the story goes that Mr. P was playing at one of the tables and a blow hard Texan looked over at Packer and said, "I like to bet real big too." Packer was annoyed at the guy's pompous behavior and loud demeanor. He said to the guy, "How much you worth guy?" The guy said, "About 100 million." Packer looked at him straight in the face and said, "Let's flip for it. Double or nothing." Every dealer and pit boss within earshot was wildly applauding in their mind.

A Happy, Healthy Poker Player is a Sickening Thought

Playing tournaments and even cash games puts you in contact with a wide variety of poker players. I have always been one to profess health and happiness. Especially happiness. After that 3rd piece of chocolate cake, health kind of goes out the window. But happiness abounds. I don't think I've ever used that word before. Abounds. I've used inbounds, out of bounds, rebounds, mounds, which is almost like bounds, but never abounds. Sometimes I amaze myself by my insight. Anyway, it was obvious to me that if I was going to write about healthy and happy, I would need outside help with healthy. So I interviewed healthy-looking poker players. Out of the 450 players in a tournament, I quickly narrowed the "healthy" field down to 3. The first one I approached talked in a very mumbled gruff tone that sounded like Leon Spinks. I think he said he gave the commencement speech when he graduated from high school. When he was 42. It was an honorary graduation since he was older than most of the teachers. And healthier. So they asked him to speak. I think that's what he explained to me. It was like he was talking in tongues. Or without one. I excused myself and went to find my second choice. A really good looking kid-blond, muscular with a big smile. If there was anyone who could give me great information about healthy and happy poker players this was my guy. I said to him, "Excuse me, I'm writing a humorous book on Hold 'em and I'm including some serious stuff about being healthy. Can I ask you a few questions?" He said, "I'm not gay." I said, "No, you misunderstand me. I'm not questioning your sexual preference or your manhood. You look like you are very healthy and work out and I just need some information on how you maintain your healthy look." He said, "I just want you to know I'm not gay." I said, "OK, I believe you." He said, "I need another $500 to enter this tournament. Would you sponsor me?" I said, "I'm sorry kid, I'm just trying to interview someone who looks healthy." He said, "Would you sponsor me if I blow you?" I then looked for candidate number 3. He was an older guy. Looked to be about 32. I was getting frustrated. I was getting depressed. I just had to get to the bottom of this health issue. I know people want to be healthy. Everyone wants health, wealth and happiness. Not necessarily in that order. And of course, occasional sex. So here's what I learned about health from "Ashton". Not once did

Ashton say he wasn't gay. In fact, he kept putting his hand on my knee.

Tip #1- Eat a red grapefruit for breakfast regularly. If grapefruit is not available, then any fruit will do. Except Michael Jackson.

Tip #2- Drink peppermint tea. If you don't like to drink tea, try smoking it. Or rubbing it on your body.

Tip #3- Floss. Flossing can add about 3 years to your life. Floss. Floss. Floss. Floss between hands. Floss on your tournament breaks. Floss while standing at the urinal. If you are over 90 and you're lucky enough to have gotten this far in the book without keeling over, you may want to think about starting to floss immediately. If you can pick up a quick 3 years, why not?

Tip #4- Cherries are great for heart disease, cancer and arthritis. Eating large amounts of cherries can give you those 3 diseases almost immediately. Or maybe they fight those diseases. I took bad notes during the interview.

Tip #5- Stock the fridge with some yogurt. Fancy named yogurts are preferred. Like Yoplait. This way if anyone goes into your fridge they will think you're rich and sophisticated. And of course, life is about image.

Tip #6- Leave a few bites on your plate while you are eating at the poker table. Or any table for that matter. Research shows that leaving a few bites will reduce your caloric intake by 20% and provide the bus boy and his family a nice meal.

Tip #7- Garlic helps to lower your cholesterol. The smell also irritates the shit out of your opponents and makes their eyes water. This makes it more difficult for them to see their hole cards and a misread is more likely. I love garlic. It makes me smell so "Italian".

Tip #8- Eat the skins of fruits and vegetables. Along with the fruit or vegetable, of course. Fire your grape peeler. You don't need him anymore. The skins of fruits and vegetables aids digestion. It also provides you with incredible smelling farts that might cause some players to leave the table and get "blinded off" while they're gone. It's a strategy that the amateurs have been using for years. There are so many fuckin' pros we had to come up with something.

Tip #9- Researchers have found that instead of eating potatoes or pasta, you should eat a chicken breast. Chicken breasts have very few calories. If you are on a very strict diet and really really want to limit your calories, a *hooker's* breast is even better. Calorie intake is almost zero.

Tip #10- Two 20-minute walks a day is great for your heart. It's much better than one long workout. 3 Out of 5 dentists agree with this research. Researchers agree that the other 2 dentists were assholes.

Tip #11- Cuddling with your significant other releases oxytocin, the hormone associated with emotional closeness. If you don't have a significant other, a blow up doll will do. All in the name of good health, of course. Thank God for research.

Tip #12- When you go to bed, breathe deeply for 10-15 minutes. This will restore balance in your nervous system and make your penis hard. The light-headedness you will experience from this exercise will make your penis look bigger than it really is. This may also be a good exercise for your bedmate.

Tip #13- Lemon tea is excellent during tournament play. It's good for your memory so you can remember every bet and every card when you get a bone crushing, soul crushing river card shoved up your ass.

Tip #14- Yoga should be practiced at least once a week. This is not to be confused with yogurt, which should never be eaten. Yogurt should be kept in the house though, in case there is an emergency and you need some penicillin. Yogurt, when mixed with one-month-old bananas, creates penicillin. If the bananas are more than one month old, you get electricity.

Tip #15- Plan a vacation. Credit card research has shown that people who take more than 3 vacations a year owe a ton of fuckin' money! And 3 out of 5 credit card counselors agree that people are not as stressed when they realize there is no fuckin' way they can pay off the credit card company. Ever!

Tip #16- It's hard to relax if you have on a watch or have a clock with a cuckoo next to your bed. Research shows that people are less stressed if they aren't constantly reminded that time is running out and they are going to die.

Tip #17- Your social life can improve your attitude and your health. Next time you want to be recognized at a party, stand in the center of the room and take your clothes off. Then order a dirty martini. Or a Dirty Harry. See if I care.

Tip #18- Your sex life is an important part of your overall health. Hire hookers whenever possible. But I emphasize this: Don't, and I can't be more emphatic about this, don't tell your wife. She may not understand. Then all these healthy tips will be for naught if you get shot and die. But if she is not a good shot, you will heal quicker if you're healthy.

Tip #19- Eat a piece of chocolate whenever you can. Researchers from the Hershey Chocolate Foundation have shown that chocolate makes us healthier and wealthier. No one has ever disputed this research.

Tip #20- This is almost the last one so bear with me. Maximize your workout. Start out with low-intensity activities like watching porn, then graduate to Richard Simmons workout tapes where people are screaming and jumping and vomiting. Much like they were at my wedding. I bought the Richard Simmons diet package. The exercise video, the wallet and the deck of cards. The cards had all the food groups listed on them. You arranged the cards on one side of the wallet in compartments. As you ate during the day, you would remove the card with the item you ate from the left side of the wallet and put it in the compartment on the right side of the wallet. When you were done removing all the cards from the left side, you were done eating for the day. I was done eating by 8 A.M. So I bought 3 more decks of cards.

Tip #21- Salmon is the healthiest fish you can eat. The omega 3 fatty acids that the salmon provides does wonders for our health and actually alleviates depression. I wonder if it makes the salmon family less depressed when we take one of its own. Research isn't in yet. I'll keep you posted.

So remember- Healthy poker players play healthier cards. Here's to your health.

Meat and Potatoes-

Well, Almost

The kid that's typing this thing for me is named Grant Turner. Real handsome kid. Funny too. Everywhere he goes he has women fawning over him. Anyway, he has a computer program that literally performs miracles, especially for a writer like me who writes shit on a yellow legal pad and is always changing stuff. Grant and I meet a few times a week and I give him the stuff I've written and he sits about 20 feet from me at a desk in my office. I'm at my desk and I can see him in the distance staring at the computer screen, pounding on the keyboard, adjusting his headphones and smiling with great satisfaction. This whole scenario begs the question, actually it screams the question- is it the keyboard he's pounding on? About 30,000 words ago, he looked at me and said, "Hey Tony, when are we going to get into the meat and potatoes of the book?" Now don't get me wrong. Grant is a nice kid. He's not a smart ass, so I didn't take any offense to his comment. In fact, I felt he had a point. There's a picture of me choking Grant at a poker table somewhere in this book. That was taken right after his comment. He handles being choked well. Maybe that didn't come out the way I intended. We are talking strictly about being choked around the neck. No chickens involved.

Grant's computer program fuckin' amazes me. When I wrote a series of books many years ago called the "Playing to Win" series, which were "Playing to Win Craps", "Playing to Win Blackjack", "Playing to Win Roulette" etc. there were 6 of them- I wrote as I do now, in longhand. I keep a pad and pen next to my bed and a lot of times I write at 4 in the morning. My wife has gotten use to the bright lights. Grant has managed to decipher my 4 A.M. doctor-like penmanship and type it into his computer. I proof it and make a few corrections and add or delete a line or two and we would repeat the process again and again. So one day I realized we should have capitalized the word Hold 'em. I told him when we go through this thing in the final read, we need to change every hold 'em to Hold 'em. He said, "OK" and looked at me 1 minute later and said, "Alright, it's done." Apparently the program he is using allows you to do magnificent things without going through the entire manuscript. He tells me periodically how many "fuckins" I've got written and how many variations of the word "fuck" I've used. When I wrote the "Playing to Win" series, I hired a girl to sit at a typewriter and she would type the stuff I wrote and she would have to painstakingly retype a whole page when I changed something. The process took forever. Then when I took the books to the printer, I would get proofs that I would have to reread to find any errors the typesetter made (the typesetter was Mormon and every "fuckin'" was deleted- a far cry from Grant who adds additional "fuckins" whenever he feels I am slacking a bit). Man, things have really fuckin' changed. TIVO, OnStar guidance systems in your car, computers- for a guy these are great things. Of course, poker and blowjobs are still on the list, but maybe not one and two anymore. But none of these things were on Grant's mind when he questioned me about meat and potatoes. He was looking for substance. He was looking for knowledge. He was looking for strategy. Something that would help his poker playing abilities. Something that would get his picture not in a book like this, which will probably only be seen by family members, but on the cover of *Card Player Magazine*. Or the cover of *Bluff*. Or the cover of Meat and Potatoes.

My problem with the meat and potatoes thing-and I didn't have the heart to tell Grant- is that I don't eat meat very often. I have nothing against the meat eaters of the world. But meat is very very hard to digest. It takes about 10 days for it to get out of your colon. And some little tiny pieces stay with you a lot longer. I recently had a colonoscopy, which is highly recommended by doctors everywhere who make their living giving colonoscopies. This is a procedure whereby your friendly doctor rams a 60-inch plasma screen television up your ass and entertains everyone in the building with a travel feature starring your fuckin' colon. They look for things like polops, cancer, and of course, meat fragments. My last one revealed an old piece of a Zims hamburger I had in 1965. Man, that was a good fuckin' hamburger. Zims was the best. It was on 19th Ave. in San Francisco. Today, my favorite is Fatburger. The Double Fat with double cheese is pure fuckin' Heaven. I only have one every few months, but it's an orgasmic event when I do. So meat isn't my first choice when I have dinner. It's usually fish or chicken. A delicate fish.

Like sole. Or orange roughy. And I enjoy quiche (Holy fuck- did he say quiche? The fuckin' Q word? Is this fuckin' guy gay? He eats quiche?). Well, I don't exactly enjoy quiche. I sample it periodically when my wife orders it (Whew! Thank God he doesn't order it himself. I'd never be able to explain to my buddies that I'm reading a book by a guy who eats quiche. Let's face it- all manly men know that if you eat quiche, you're just one step away from giving someone a blowjob). And usually when my wife does order it, I taste it because she **forces** me to. Then I misdirect her attention to something else and I spit it out in a napkin, which, of course, is always a pleasant experience for the surrounding tables. Because I want to make sure that it is fully documented that I spit it out in case any manly men are watching, and at this point in my life I don't want to do anything that could affect my reputation, or book sales, in a negative manner. In fact, for dinner tonight I think I'll go to Ruth's Chris Steak House and order $300 worth of meat. I think you can get a 6-ounce filet for that. Of course, the potato and vegetables are extra. I made Grant a promise that I would start talking about the meat and potatoes of the book. And my word is my bond. But I've got to tell you- I've just had an incredible fuckin' urge for quiche…..

Random Thought

He got into poker because he's virtually unemployable. During job interviews he asks the wrong questions. He always asks, "When is payday? How often do I get a break? Do you ever press charges? Maybe it's these questions that never have other applicants view him as a threat.

The Marines Have Landed At The Venetian

Along With Accordions, Bagpipes and Hasselhoff

For years, the Bellagio and Caesar's Palace have been my two favorite places. I have another favorite place. That's three. That's enough. Here's the skinny, the lowdown, the down under. I don't play in cheap tournaments, but if I did my buddies tell me The Sahara, Sam's Town and The Orleans are the places to go. They are not at all expensive and it gives you a chance to experience live action tournament play at a reasonable price and interact with people that you've never met before and for the most part, hope you never meet again. These are the type of tournaments where everyone has a nickname. There's "Skid Rowe", "One-Eyed John", "Smelly Kelly" and of course my favorite "I Once Beat an Opponent to Death and That's Why I Have This Scar" Fred. So getting back to my original sentence, which I am sure some of you have forgotten, but I am not allowed to since I am writing this shit, I have another favorite place. The Venetian. The first thing you notice when you walk into The Venetian is the spacious lobby and long rotunda leading to the casino. The tile floor looks like a giant checkerboard and you try not to stare at it but it draws your eyes to it like a hypnotist's watch. And nobody likes hypnotists. Or their fuckin' watches. So while I'm staring at this floor from Hell, I hear an unmistakable irritating sound. I'm thinking, "I must be hypnotized. I looked at the fuckin' floor too long." But the sound grew louder. It was coming closer. You're not going to believe this, but I swear I'm not making this shit up. It got louder and louder and finally the noisemaker came right up to me, smiling. One of my least favorite sights. A smiling accordion player. I'm thinking, "What the fuck is the ghost of Lawrence Welk doing in the Venetian lobby?" To me, nothing says we don't want your business more than accordions in the lobby. Except maybe a lobby with bagpipes. Accordion music and bagpipes should be banned. They should be illegal. We should ask congress to designate them as weapons of mass destruction. The more I think about it, the more I came to realize that we have the answer to war. We have the answer to strife. Whatever the fuck strife is. We have the answer to world peace and domination. Mostly domination, of course. No bullets. No more bombs. No more guns. The answer has been right under our noses. Actually to the right and left of our noses. The answer has been our ears. Whenever there is a threat of war in the world or any civil unrest anywhere, we send in accordion players. Thousands of them. If the unrest isn't settled in 8 hours we give the pricks causing the unrest a final warning. Then we send in ten thousand bagpipers. With accordions, there's always the chance that after 8 hours all the accordion players may play the same song- "Lady of Spain". And people might think they sound pretty good. There's always that chance. It's a long shot, but every once in a while 2-7 offsuit does beat pocket Aces. But the odds of ten thousand bagpipers playing the same melody is incalculable. It can't happen. You can't play a melody on an instrument that was designed to give off a shrieking shrill noise. Instrument? Did I say instrument? How the fuck can an instrument be designed to look like an octopus on steroids? Unrest would end. Wars would be history. The world would be passive. Except probably Scotland. We couldn't threaten them with bagpipes. They like bagpipes. They have bagpipe bands. And parades. And contests. Like Scottish Bagpipe Idol- a very popular show where young people go on television, play the bagpipe and people vote for their favorite. There are 3 judges who criticize their bagpiping abilities and one of them is a very nice girl, Paula Abdul McFadden, one is a fat black guy named Randy McFaddin and the other is an asshole, Simon McFaddan. So as you can see, bagpipers are very popular in Scotland. We would need something else to send Scotland if there was unrest. Something so horrible that the unrest would stop immediately. Like a Miss America Pageant. Hosted by David Hasselhoff. For 30 hours straight. And here's the best part- Hasselhoff would sing. Have you ever heard David Hasselhoff sing? No one else has either. His last album sold 6 copies. To bagpipe players. He caters to a very specialized group. Tone-deaf bagpipers. They love him. As you can see a lot went through my mind when I entered the Venetian lobby on my way to the poker room. But it's a fairly long walk from valet parking. And I can write as I walk.

The card room hasn't been open very long, and they literally struck out twice in the past, but this time I think they are there to stay. The room is a no smoking room of course. It's very open and spacious, attentive food servers are there whenever you're hungry, gorgeous cocktail waitresses are there whenever you even **think** you're thirsty and the staff is very pleasant. They have excellent tournaments. They give you some fuckin' chips to play with and they have numerous live games at all levels. I look for them to give my other two favorites, Caesar's Palace and Bellagio, a run for their money. The nice thing is, with the explosion of tournament poker, there is room for everyone. If they treat the customer right. And they don't get too greedy. So last night I was at the Venetian and enjoyed their Saturday tournament, which starts at 12 noon. That was my only beef. 12 Noon. I asked the kid taking my money, "What's with this 12 noon shit? You guys catering to dairy farmers? I mean, who the fuck gets up at 12 noon in Vegas?" The very polite young man who I am sure has gone to the Venetian school of "What to say and do when you have a really old man who looks really grumpy yell at you" just looked at me and smiled and said, "Sir, go fuck yourself." I gave him my $540 and I was entry #62. Table 37 seat 4. I thanked him and we gave each other the finger. My kind of guy. Anyway, the place is extremely friendly. From valet to buffet. Well, if they had a buffet. They are one of the only places on the Las Vegas Strip without a buffet. But if they had one, I know it would be great.

I always park in valet and when I came out to get my vehicle after the tournament, I walked toward the valet desk with my ticket. Actually I hobbled. I'm on a crutch right now as I broke my right foot in five places and it's taking forever to heal. "Forever to Heal" could be a good title for a book on bad beat stories. I have got to stop going off on these tangents. If only Betty Ford had a clinic for tangent wanderers. So I'm hobbling towards the valet desk and standing near the desk is this kid that couldn't be more than 21 dressed to the nines in his United States Marine uniform. Perfect fit, perfect shoes, perfect posture, perfect smile. He looked like he just stepped off a Marine poster. The Few- The Proud- The Marines. You've got to admit- The Marines have fuckin' great looking dress uniforms. I didn't look anywhere near that good in a tux for my senior prom. But then I didn't look good in anything back then. Now either. Some things don't change. Next to him, even more gorgeous than he was, stood a girl in a long white bride's gown. The both of them together actually took my breath away. They were obviously just married and I'm surprised the crowd wasn't chanting, "U.S.A., U.S.A." while they were standing there. I do spontaneous things. If I feel like doing something, I do it. Nothing illegal. Just little things. I stopped my hobbling right in front of this kid and his bride and said, "You just get married?" Now if I'm the kid, my response probably would have been "No, you fat fuck. We're here for the Elvis impersonator contest." Instead the kid says, "Yes, sir.". I pull out a hundred dollar bill and said, "Buy your bride the biggest box of candy you can find." He says, "Thank you, sir," shakes my hand and I proceed to the valet desk about 5 feet away. About 10 seconds later a guy walks up to me and says, "My grandson just told me what you did. He just got back from Iraq. We are really glad he's home." I said, "So am I," and I almost lost it. So I'm waiting for my vehicle and I realize I have my wife's truck. It's a big Dodge dually and we had it painted by Russ Gerner in Las Vegas who does mostly car shows. The truck is a one of a kind. It has a giant eagle on the hood with huge claws and the rest of the hood is the American flag. And it goes all around the truck and ends on the tailgate with a smaller eagle with part of the flag in its mouth. Russ did a great job. He had the truck for over a month and for a while it worried me. I thought he sold the fuckin' thing. So I'm waiting for the truck and I saw the Marine's grandpa and the family waiting for their vehicle about 40 feet away. I hobbled over to them and asked them if they had a camera. They said "sure" and I told them about the truck and they might want to take a picture of the kid in front of it. Well, valet arrived with the truck, they took pictures and the last thing I said to the kid was, "I'd give you this thing, but my wife would really be pissed." The family laughed and was very thankful for the time I took to do something special. They seemed as nice as a family could be. I didn't even ask the kid's name. I really didn't want to know. I knew he was going back to Iraq and over three thousand kids just like him had already died. Just like him. Bright, young, polite- over three thousand. Too many to name. Too many to forget. I couldn't get that off my mind. On the way home, I cried. A lot.

Random Thought

A small article recently appeared in our local Las Vegas paper. Not a big deal. I don't think the casino wanted it to be a big deal. MGM-Mirage has a program that affects a few people. And their families. Especially their families. MGM-Mirage Chairman Terry Lanni put a program into effect in 2003 that simply says whenever a member of the MGM-Mirage team, which spans a ton of casinos, gets deployed, they don't miss a paycheck. Companies are not required to do this. A few make up the difference between an employee's military pay and their civilian pay. That's nice. That's really nice. But MGM-Mirage went straight to the head of the fuckin' class. They pay their employees in full regardless of what they earn in the military. When a soldier is deployed, the financial and emotional effect it has on him and his family is usually devastating. Lanni and company have taken the financial effect out of the equation. Kirk Kerkorian picked the right guy to run his huge company. A small article recently appeared in our local newspaper. Not a big deal. But it was a big deal. A big fuckin' deal. A huge, caring, kind, compassionate deal. For a lot of families. I'm glad I spent my life in the gaming industry. Thank you Mr. Lanni. Thank you very much.

Tournaments and

P-L-I-B

Your tournament life depends on **PLIB**. For the dyslexic, it's **BILP**. If you're confused it could be **BLIP**. If you just smoked a joint, it's probably **ILPB**. But for the serious, sober, studious tournament player, it's **PLIB**. The letters stand for Patience-Luck-Intuition- and Balls. You need all four to win a tournament. Before we get into PLIB, let's talk about tournaments in general. Tournaments are work. I mean pure fuckin' work. You don't sweat- you don't get blisters- and thank Christ, there's no heavy lifting. If you play tournaments, you hate heavy lifting. That's a given. The heaviest thing you will probably lift is your water bottle. And maybe your wallet if you win the tournament. But tournaments are not easy to win. If there are 300 people in a tournament, it will probably pay 30 places. And 30th place isn't going to be a lot of money. It all depends on the entry fee. There are tournaments to fit every pocket book, every bankroll, every budget. I live in Las Vegas and we are on tournament overload. Can't sleep? It's 2 A.M.? There's a fuckin' tournament going on somewhere. The Las Vegas Strip, Downtown, an outlying area- somewhere there's a fuckin' tournament that has just started or is getting ready to start. The back pages of *Card Player Magazine* have page after page of scheduled tournaments. There are so many to choose from that you will probably need an extra Prozac to keep from having an anxiety attack.

Tournaments have taken on a life of their own. Many people I have talked to just play tournaments. Others just play cash games. And then further down the food chain is the tournament AND cash player. Tournament play is grueling. There is an intensity to tournaments that is quite different than the intensity of a cash game. Once in a while, in a cash game, the atmosphere gets intense when there is a really big pot. But that type of atmosphere prevails at a tournament from the start. There's not a lot of laughing or conversation during tournaments. It's like a funeral without the flowers or the casket. There's a lot of bodies- but no caskets. And as the hours pass and the antes and blinds keep going up, the fatalities increase. And the awareness and intensity level of the people who are still in the tournament keeps increasing. One eye is constantly on the television screens scattered around the poker room letting everyone know how many people are still in the tournament. And how much time is left before the blinds go up again. And how much time is left before the next break. And of course, it also tells you the prize breakdown. When you get to the final 20% to 25% of the field, everyone is aware of those numbers on that television screen. Most of the pros you see on television don't play in small tournaments. Why should they? Tournaments, even at the smaller buy-in events, are grueling. They are time consuming, intense, frustrating events that take tremendous concentration. So if you're going to put forth the tremendous effort to win, you would want a big payoff at the end. A giant carrot at the end of a long long stick. That is the attraction to the tournament mindset. Tournaments are definitely work. And to win a tournament, the following ingredients are necessary:

Patience: My son David asked me one day to teach him to play Hold 'em. We played around for a while and he said, "I want to play in a tournament." I said, "OK, that's fine. But first you need to get in condition." He said, "OK, dad. What do I do?" I said, "Go in the back yard. Get a chair. Sit down. And watch the grass grow." He said, "For how long?" I said, "Come back and see me in a month." A month later he came back to me and was really excited. He said, "OK, dad. I've watched the grass grow for a month. What's next?" I said, "Go watch the grass grow again." That, in a nutshell, is tournament play. Patience-Patience-Patience. Patience is an absolute requirement to get through the first 3 or 4 levels of any tournament. I'm beginning to wonder if Phil Hellmuth has the right idea to show up to a tournament late. He's blown a few bucks to the blinds, but so what. The first few hours of a tournament seems to reduce the field by 20% to 30%. So if 500 people are in a tournament, about 150 are gone if you come in 2 hours late. I've read that Stu Unger never played a hand for the first 2 levels of any tournament. He waited until the antes started. I think the same thing can be accomplished by playing only very premium hands until the second break. The only deviation would be if you're the big blind and there has been no raise. My son seems to always make it through the first and second break because of his patience. I guess watching the grass grow helped a lot. His starting hands are A-A, K-K,

Q-Q, J-J, 10-10, A-K, A-Q, and A-J. He will play a small or medium pair only if there has been no raise. Even in position he won't raise with a small or medium pair. He just limps in and calls the big blind. If he's in good position, he will raise with a premium hand. He's extremely cautious for the first 4 hours, which takes him to the second break. The important thing to remember about card selection is that mediocre hole cards lead to mediocre flops, which result in mediocre hands, which leads to bad calls, which end in bankroll crushing defeats. It's always harder to get off a hand once you've caught a piece of the flop. Plus, you've got money in the pot so you feel compelled to win the pot to get your money back. A small kicker is usually what does you in at the showdown. The showdown is like the old time gunfight only it's not held in the street. And mediocre doesn't cut it in a fuckin' gunfight. You lose your life. And in Hold 'em you lose your tournament life. So remember that when you play K-9 or A-6 or any other hand that would be classified as mediocre. Especially at the first 3 or 4 levels of a tournament. At tournaments, there are 3 words that should be your mantra- Survive- Survive- Survive. And you won't survive with mediocre whether it's in a tournament or a gunfight. You must ask yourself one very simple question whenever you enter or raise a pot or call a raise- am I willing to lose all of my chips on this hand and cause my Tournament Death? If the answer is yes- ask yourself the same question again emphasizing the words "Tournament Death". The most important decision you will make when you play Hold 'em tournaments is whether or not you will play your first two cards. Most players lose because they play too many hands. Your strategy changes as the tournament progresses. Look at it this way- you're actually playing three different phases of a tournament when you play any tournament: The first phase is the beginning of the tournament where very very tight play is required. The second phase is the middle of the tournament when the blinds are starting to climb and you still play tight but not as tight as the first phase. A-10, A-9, A-8, K-Q, K-J, K-10, Q-J, and Q-10 are hands you can play before the flop. Small pairs are good hands to limp in with. I wouldn't stand any big raises with any of these hands, but I would limp in with all of them and hope for a decent flop. The final phase is the end of the tournament, which includes the final table. The game, at this point, is not about prior accomplishments. It's all about the cards you get at that time.

The blinds come into play big time at the final table. Anyone can win a tournament at the final table if the deck cooperates. That brings us to the "L" in PLIB.

Luck: Is poker luck? Fuck yes it's luck! Of course there is lots of skill involved. But in the short term, luck will pound the shit out of skill. If I played Doyle Brunson for 20 hands, I could get really lucky and beat him 14 or 15 hands. But if I played him for a thousand hands, he would absolutely crush my ball sack in a car door. It's just like flipping a coin. It's 50-50. Flip it 5 times, it may be heads all 5 times. Flip it 5 million times, it's a different story. So why read books on poker strategy? Because learning to play strategically and sensibly will heighten your awareness level at the game and better your chances of being a winner. It's not enough to get the right cards. You also need the right situations. And for the right cards to hold up. A lot of things need to happen a lot of times for you to win a tournament. You need to get lucky. Luck is timing. We've all experienced being at the right place at the right time and being at the wrong place at the wrong time. The best hand pre-flop is pocket Aces. The worst hand is 2-7 off-suit. Yet 2-7 will beat pocket Aces 11% of the time. That's not a common occurrence. But coin flips in a tournament are very common. A guy goes all-in with a pair of 9's and you have A-K. Badda Bing- Badda Boom. Someone is going to be called lucky. In a tournament, you will have to survive a lot of coin flips to win. When a tournament starts out, it might have 500 players. It usually pays 10% of the players, which means 50 people will get something. The top 5 will get the "lion's share" of the prize pool. Out of the 500 players, there are only a few who have never played in a tournament. The last survey I saw said that a poll taken at a large tournament recently, said the average player's experience in tournaments was 3 years. So when you get down to the final 100 players out of the 500, those people definitely know what they are doing. When you get to the final 50, those people have made the fewest mistakes. And got lucky. Any one of the final 50 people out of the original 500 could win the tournament. A player needs to win key hands and coin flips to be the winner. So play tough, play your game and never give up. And practice holding your breath. You'll be doing that a lot towards the end of a tournament. In fact, you'll be doing it every time you get into a pot. The important thing to remember is that you're almost to the final table. You lucky fuck.

Intuition: The brain is a 3-pound mass of pinkish-gray tissue comprised of over 10 billion nerve cells, which are linked to each other and are responsible for all of a human being's control of his or her mental functions. Over 10 billion nerve cells! That is fuckin' unreal. Every movement and every emotion we have is controlled by the brain. It is our absolute control center. From the outside of the brain, it appears as three parts that are distinct but connected. These parts are known as the Cerebrum, the Cerebellum and the Brain Stem. The Cerebrum makes up about 85% of the brain's weight. It accounts and stores all of our intelligence. It also is responsible for many other functions that make us human. The Cerebellum controls our movements, our posture, our balance, our ability to do everything from kicking a football to picking up a small penny from the ground. The Brain Stem is divided into the Thalamus and the Hypothalamus. All sensory input to the brain, except the sense of smell, passes through the Thalamus. It's like a relay station. The Hypothalamus regulates or controls many of our daily activities like eating, drinking, sleeping and also our temperature. This is just a basic overview of the brain. There are many, many other parts to the brain, including the Midbrain, the Pons, the Medulla Oblongata, the Cerebral Cortex, the Limbic System and on and on and on. So your question has to be, "How the fuck can this have anything to do with intuition?" And my response is, "How the fuck can it not?" The brain never sleeps. It is always awake, gathering information consciously and subconsciously. When we are sitting at a poker table, we are in a state of constantly gathering information in our brain. With over 10 billion nerve cells comprising our brain, we all gather the same information, but I believe we disseminate it and use it differently. Drinking alcohol at the table definitely distorts our play because we can't think as clear as someone who hasn't had a drink. This results in mistakes, which have a direct effect on our bank balance. The number and type of functioning neurons in the brain determines our level of intelligence. When we play poker, it is absolutely imperative that we exercise our brain so that we can better perform in the game. By observing every pot, whether or not you're in it, the brain is gathering information. And information is key to success at the table. Your conscious and subconscious are picking up bits and pieces of everyone's play, and when it comes time to make an important decision, your brain will be ready to help you. Your subconscious may have picked up a "tell" from a player that you are not even aware of, and your gut, or intuition, is telling you to fold the hand- that it's beat. I always go with my intuition. It's not 100%, but it's gotten better since I've become more aware of it. A good exercise when you're playing is to try and assess what other players in the pot have as their hole cards. I've played with some people who are very good at this. When the hand is over, even though they're not in it, they'll look at the player and say "A-Q?" or "7-8?". And if you are not in the pot, you don't come off as being threatening by asking the guy what his hand was. But by getting that information, you just strengthened your read on the guy and improved your intuition. I'm amazed how many times these people come real fuckin' close. What a great exercise. Of course if there's a showdown, you don't have to ask. You see the cards. Over the course of time, you gain additional information that will give you an advantage over your opponents. When you watch poker on TV, you will notice that Daniel Negreanu is one of the best at assessing a hand. He nails the fuckin' thing a lot of the time. But he won't always trust his intuition and his instincts. His gut tells him that he's beat and he winds up talking himself into calling the bet. It is so hard for any of us to lay down a good hand even though our brain is fuckin' screaming at us to throw the fuckin' thing away. I am totally convinced that your "first read" of a situation is going to be right 80% of the time. And if you do throw the winner away and the guy gloats and shows you his bluff- so what. So fuckin' what. By the end of the night, you'll own him. You just can't fuck with an 80% success rate. You just can't.

Balls: The final letter in P-L-I-B. You need fuckin' balls to win a tournament. You need balls to put your chips in the center of the table and risk being eliminated from the tournament. You don't have to **have** balls. You just need balls. I played with a young girl about 25 years old a few months ago who had balls. She wasn't afraid to put her chips all-in and made the guys at the poker table pucker up real good. She said she was married for just 8 months and they were getting divorced. They were fighting over custody of the wedding cake and the trailer. I didn't make any comments because she looked like she was a pretty tough broad and could kick my ass. She looked like she'd been around the block a few times and that her head had been on more hotel pillows than a chocolate mint. She could make you feel minty and slutty at the same time. But she could play fuckin' poker. She was alright in my book. If you want to win tournaments, you can't be afraid to lose them. You should never be afraid to put your chips in the pot when you think you have the best hand. And sometimes you have to put them into the pot knowing you don't have the best hand. At that point, all you can do is hold your breath. It takes balls to bluff. And big lungs. But you have to learn to bluff because in tournaments there is a point when the blinds get so big that if you don't bluff, you will "blind off" all your chips and lose the tournament. It is much easier to bluff a strong player than a weak one. Your rate of success with a bluff will also be more effective if you don't bluff often. Bluffing too often early in the tournament will eliminate you very quickly because most people in a tournament will be playing strong hands before the flop. If there are too many people in the pot, your bluff will fail most of the time. The best type of bluff is against one other person. The key to any tournament is survival. The bluff is a key weapon against small stacks. You should identify the more passive players at your table so you can put pressure on them when you are both in a pot. Position is extremely important in tournament play and especially when running a bluff. As you get deeper and deeper into a tournament, stealing antes and blinds becomes crucial for survival. Bluffs can extend that survival or limit it drastically. Aggressive position betting and raising in a tournament will definitely make you known as a tough tournament adversary.

P-L-I-B is the key to winning a tournament. Any tournament. The blend of Patience- Luck- Intuition- and Balls will hopefully extend your tournament life to the final table. And maybe beyond. Where no man has gone before. Just maybe.......

Random Thought

Life is about survival. Tournament poker is about survival. Survive- Survive- Survive. When in doubt, throw the fuckin' hand away. There's another one coming in a few seconds. Make sure you're there to get it.

Tournament Overview:

This is one of those chapters with good advice that you should "earmark" and review periodically. Like every time you go to the bathroom. The human brain needs constant repetition to learn. This is about money- so learn this shit.

- ♠ Running bad and playing bad are two entirely different situations. Play your game all the time.
- ♠ To avoid tournament death, you must avoid mistakes. Protect your chips. Do not take unnecessary risks. Don't throw chips in the pot with a weak hand just to see the flop. Forget paying to draw to a straight or a flush if it costs a lot. Set aside a small stack of your chips (maybe 20%) to use as your "Attack Stack". Attack the weak. Attack the cautious. Attack the short stacks. When your attack stack is depleted, play very tight to build it back up.
- ♠ Poker is a game in which you will succeed only if you make good use of the information you gather as you play.
- ♠ One bad poker day can destroy a lot of good poker days. You need to feel good to play good. Some days it doesn't pay to get out of bed.
- ♠ Playing A-K is not playing "Big Slick". It's playing "Big No Pair". Which means a pair of deuces beats you. Play A-K cautiously before the flop. Narrow the field with a raise if you're in late position. If you're in early position and are on a short stack, you need to move all-in.
- ♠ Saying "I'm sorry" to an opponent after crushing his ball sack is ridiculous. I know it was a tear jerking line in the movie Love Story with Ali McGraw and Ryan O'Neil, but tournaments aren't the fucking movies, Bucko. Tournaments are all out war. No "I'm sorry's".
- ♠ Any style of play can win a tournament, but my vote is for the aggressive player who plays premium hands. I love to fire bullets with a premium hand, wait for the flop, fire more bullets and then hold my fuckin' breath on the turn and the river. That's what I call fun.
- ♠ As long as you have chips, you can still win a tournament. No matter how few.

- ♠ You need to make good decisions over and over again.
- ♠ On breaks I always wash my face and give myself a little pep talk. If there's time, I watch a Vince Lombardi movie and my mantra becomes, "Win one for the Gipper." Whatever the fuck that means.
- ♠ A poker player is the only animal that ponders. If you ponder more than 45 seconds, throw the fuckin' hand away.
- ♠ Beware of team play. Teams can give each other chips when they are in the pot together.
- ♠ Use the past to forge the future. Observe what is happening, even when you're not in the pot.
- ♠ Survive and advance. Another hand is 2 minutes away- be there to play it.
- ♠ When you have a good size stack of chips, always keep the pressure on the smaller stacks. Leave the big stacks alone. You can deal with them later. Attack the players that can't bust you.
- ♠ If you're in a tournament and your stack isn't getting bigger, it's getting smaller. And small stacks are like small penises- they don't get the job done.
- ♠ Missed opportunities means you will have less chips. Chips are needed to survive the bad beat you will eventually get in almost every tournament. You can survive a bad beat if you have made enough correct decisions, and in the process, accumulated chips.
- ♠ Winners pay more attention. Winners learn from experience. Winners are more determined. Winners set attainable goals. Winners don't play tired or drunk. Winners maintain their focus and intensity. Think like a winner. Be a winner.
- ♠ Each tournament is an experience that you learn from. It's not a bad idea to carry a small notebook and take notes each tournament break. It is hard to remember everything you learn, and if you are going to take the game seriously, you should follow this advice.
- ♠ Tournaments take physical and mental stamina. You cannot win a tournament in the early stages, but you can sure as fuck lose one.
- ♠ Survive- Survive- Survive- Eliminate others- Move up the prize pool ladder- Get to 1st place.

♠ Blinds drive the action. No question about it. You need to adjust your game as the blinds go up. Hands you might not ordinarily play at the beginning of the tournament become playable hands. The higher the blinds go, the more imperative it is for you to play hands and bluff.

♠ Early tournament play is a good time to practice reading your opponents. It will keep you busy so you don't become so bored you play hands you shouldn't be playing. There is too much emphasis by too many players to build up a huge stack at the beginning of a tournament. When I am moved to a different table, I can tell right away who the looser players are. They usually have the most $25 chips, which are used for the blinds, in front of them.

♠ Even at the beginning of a tournament, the bad players aren't as bad as they use to be. There is so much information available on tournament strategy, that even the poorest players absorb it. And they become stronger.

♠ You need to learn to be very selective on the cards you play. And when you've decided you're playing the hand, play aggressively.

♠ Poker is all about deception and making good decisions on incomplete information.

♠ Remember- A-K is no pair. If it is suited, it's no pair suited. Don't go busted with A-K before the flop. Give yourself a chance.

♠ A tournament is a mini war. And just like with all wars, there's usually an escalation process that sometimes comes very rapidly. Tournament play always escalates with the blinds. The blinds go up. The antes go up. The play gets intense. The play escalates. It happens very quickly. You're calm- collected- you've just peed- break's over- water bottle full- your ass is fully rested in your seat- dealer deals- you look down- pocket Kings- your heart starts beating a little quicker- you raise- there's a re-raise- you go all-in- there's a call. Cards go face up- your Kings- his Aces. No help. You're out. Sometimes things happen quickly. Very quickly. Slow down. Slow way down when a situation arises that would force you to bet all your chips or call a bet for all your chips.

♠ I have a turtle for a card cover that I use for tournaments. It tells me to "Slow down. Take it easy." It's therapeutic. Especially after a bad beat. Buy a turtle for a card cover. Not a real one. You don't need another mouth to feed until you play better.

♠ When is a hand not a hand? When you're on a draw. Paying a big raise to draw to a flush or a straight is pure fuckin' tournament suicide. What's worse is how many players pay to draw to a flush without the Ace. You could be drawing dead if you're chasing a flush and it's not even the nuts.

♠ Unlucky players seem to make more mistakes than lucky players. Go figure.

♠ We are all measured on results. And when you play in a tournament, results are all that counts.

♠ When you're playing Hold 'em, time has a way of disappearing quickly. It's meaningless.

♠ No matter how good you play or how good you think you play, you need to get lucky when it counts. Luck is a huge part of the last hour or two of tournament play. Survive and catch a rush at the end of a tournament.

♠ When your table "breaks" and you're moved to a new table, the entire process of getting a read on all of your new opponents starts again.

♠ Most poker hands are played in a 5'' arena. The space between your ears.

♠ Always, and I mean always- actually I mean **fuckin' always**, respect, and I capitalize RESPECT, the guy who comes into the pot in first position. This guy is "under the gun"- the first to act before the flop. In tournaments, when someone comes in under the gun, they have something. Don't forget that.

♠ Lose a big pot? Take a bad beat? Take a fuckin' walk. Go to the bathroom. Pee in the sink. Get it out of your system. Calm down. Then return to play the game that you play best. A tough game. You're in control again.

♠ Every situation is a unique one. There are a ton of variables. There are no set answers for any particular hand. Play your opponents, play your position, play your game. Gather all the information you can while playing. Eventually you will get in a pot where you will have to make a very expensive decision. The more information you have, the better and more educated your decision will be.

Random Thought

Playing good poker takes management. Money management, skill management and confidence management. To play you're "A" game you must be well rested, you must be feeling good and you must be thinking clearly. Tournament play leaves no room for errors unless you are the dominant chip leader. Then you might be allowed an error or two- tops.

A Sure Way to be a Winner

There is a sure way to be a winner in every poker game and every tournament you play. No bullshit. Absolutely 100% legal. Absolutely 100% legitimate. Absolutely 100% foolproof. Can you do it? I don't know. Maybe. Just own a card room. That's right. A lousy fuckin' card room. Every game takes a rake. Just a small itsy bitsy piece of the pot. Or in tournaments, a "service fee add-on" that you barely notice. Barely. Some games rake $3 from the pot- some $4, some $5. Then there's time games. It's only fair that you pay for time. The casino supplies the table, the ambiance, the dealer, the ambiance, the drinks, the ambiance, the cards, the ambiance, and did I mention, the ambiance? I just like saying "the ambiance". I know- I'm sick. Anyway, the average dealer deals about 30 hands an hour. And the average penis length of a man is $5^1/2$ inches (I have no idea why I threw that in). So at 30 hands an hour X $3, that totals $90 an hour coming off the table. Gone. Can't be won. Goes into that nice little box that gets carted away by huge, muscular humanoids with wires dangling out of their ears. These humanoids also appear whenever there is a "problem" and quickly solve it by crushing the problem maker's testicles. This doesn't work for female problem makers. First of all there are none of those, and if there were, the casino would call their husbands who would come down to the cardroom and, in front of everyone, crush her credit card. The credit card submission hold is used widely by men who are married and have bigger testicles than their wives. This is by no means for everyone, so please, I beg you, please don't try this at home unless you have conferred with someone who is familiar with the technique. Meanwhile, back at the subject matter at hand, while we were just sitting around bullshitting about credit card crushing, another $9 was raked from the pots. So, at $90 an hour, if you play 5 hours (just $1/2$ inch shorter than the average penis) there would be $450 gone from the table. GONE! If the rake is $4 a hand, it's $120 X 5 hours = $600 gone. Green Valley Ranch is owned by the Station Casinos group. They have very nice joints- great buffets, very user-friendly, very well laid out. Very nice local facilities. They are owned and operated by the Fertitta family who does a lot of nice things for the locals and are involved in a lot of community stuff. Both are very important ingredients in a local's market, and they do it well. They have this huge jackpot that poker players share in whenever there is a "bad beat" at a table. If you are playing at any of the Station Casinos, and at last count I think there were 4 million of them, then you share in the "bad beat jackpot" if a bad beat happens. So, if a bad beat happens, say in Sunset Station-Japan, and you are playing in Green Valley Ranch, a person would walk up to you at the poker table and give you your share of the jackpot. One time it was 47 yen and a nice rice bowl with chicken dumplings. This is a great perk for Station Casinos poker players because you never know where, you never know when, someone is going to come up to you and say, "Smile, you have just won a teriyaki bowl." For this tremendous "you never know when" surprise, the dealer takes $1 out of each pot. All day. And all night. "It's only a dollar. Lighten up," I thought I heard someone say. Since they have beautiful casinos with great ambiance (I love that word), they usually rake $4 from the poker pot. Plus the $1 for the bad beat jackpot. So for a total of $5 a hand, a mere pittance, you get to enjoy all that the casino has to offer and more if you happen to pick up a hooker. So $5 X 30 hands = $150 an hour X 5 hours = $750. Did I say $750? Never to be seen from again? Oh well. Someone has to pay for the ambiance. "So I'll show them. I'll only play high limit time games. $7 for a half hour. I piss $7 when I get up in the morning. No big deal." Let's see now, $7 for a half hour, that's $14 an hour X 9 players = $126 X 5 hours = $630. So you see folks, that's why I stick to tournaments mostly. Tournaments? Did I hear someone say tournaments? Tournaments are fun. They're exciting. They're exhilarating. Did I mention they're fun? How about expensive? Did I mention expensive? Every tournament has an entry fee. Someone has to pay for the free drinks. Right? Of course. By the way, free drinks cost the casino about $0.30 each. On the average. And the nice thing about poker players is we don't fuckin' drink when we play. We drink water. Or coffee. Or Pepsi or Coke. So it's even less than $0.30 a drink. The entry fee is usually about 8%. Sometimes a little less. Sometimes a little more. So, when you're in a $500 tournament at the Bellagio, you pay $540. If there are 100 people in the $500 tournament at the Bellagio, the prize pool is about $48,000. "Wait a minute," I thought I heard a math major say, "100 players in a $500 tournament equals a $50,000 prize pool." Yes, Virginia. That is correct. So what happened to the missing

$2,000? It went to the dealers and the floor staff. And that's fine. I have no problem with that. But you have to understand that in the scope of things, if you plan on playing a lot of tournaments like I do, it will be costing you a lot of money. So out of that $500 + $40 entry fee and the $2,000 from the prize pool for the casino workers, everyone collectively paid a total of $6,000 for the privilege of playing in a tournament. These numbers were huge at the World Series of Poker. Service charges alone were about 5 million dollars. That was just for the main event. There were tons of mini-tournaments, second chance tournaments, cash games and satellites leading up to the main event. This fuckin' thing went on for over 30 days! And at the same time, the Bellagio jumped on the bandwagon and held a 12 day event that was actually a lot better, in my humble opinion. All of my opinions are humble. My "whole being" is humble. That's why I have a very small entourage. And no more than 3 bodyguards at any one time. And believe it or not, only two airbrush technicians were employed for the cover on this book to make me look as youthful and slim as humanly possible. I would acknowledge them by name, but it would only result in them turning into pompous airbrushers. And pompous is a non-humble trait. And I only surround myself with humble, weak people, yearning to be free. But nothing is free. Cash games aren't free. Tournaments aren't free. So a sure way to be a winner is to own a card room. Own a casino. The casino industry is thriving. It has always thrived. Through good times and bad. The industry is fed with money. Your money. And it has an insatiable appetite. Never to be satisfied. Never.

The Karate Kid

When I play tournament poker I sometimes think of the movie "The Karate Kid". The basic premise is so much like tournament poker. The kid's teacher, a Japanese instructor of martial arts named Mr. Miyagi, took the kid to a world he had never been to. A world that allowed him to rise above his opponents. He got to that world by discipline, patience, practice and of course blowing his instructor once in a while. I can't help it. I try to be nice, I really do. I try to be serious. And poker is serious business. I know that. My 4-year-old granddaughter keeps telling me that. She says, "Papa, no cashes, no dinner," and, "Papa, I need to eat. So Papa, don't go all-in unless you have the fuckin' nuts. Please, Papa, please." I said, "Mikalina, you're not suppose to talk like that. We had a deal. You're not suppose to say 'fuckin' until you're 5." She said, "I'm sorry Papa. I won't do it again. But you get me so fuckin' upset when you don't cash." Oh well, she should do just fine in public school. Especially during lunch time when Hold 'em is played. She'll have her teachers begging for fuckin' mercy.

Random Thought

3 Out of 5 dentists agree that poker players think they will win with pocket Aces. 4 out of 5 poker players hate dentists.

Everyone Plays Poker

Everyone plays poker. Men, women, gays, lesbians. Those who want to be gay, those who want to be lesbian. Those who don't know they're gay, those who don't know they're lesbian. Black, white, Asian. Those who want to be black, those who want to be white- you get the picture? Everyone plays poker. The tired, the poor, the huddled masses. The unhappy, the slow, the sad, the miserable. Those who drive too fast, too slow, too erratic and those who never turn their blinkers off. Those who never return phone calls, who have bad penmanship, who have bad breath, who have shortness of breath, who have no breath at all. Those who never brush, never bathe, never wash, never comb, never nod, never wink, never laugh, never hug, never care. In other words, any dysfunctional slob who can sit in a fuckin' chair and wear sunglasses or earphones and never wear after-shave, after-bath or after-birth cologne. Everyone plays fuckin' poker. My mother plays it. She's 88. My grandson plays it. He's 12. Even Doyle Brunson plays it. Do I make myself clear? Everyone plays fuckin' poker. Some poker games are more popular than others. When I was a kid we use to play a game called "Tripoly". The family would gather around the kitchen table and we would play. Some money was involved. Not a lot. We didn't have a lot. But it was a form of poker. Poker is definitely here to stay. Hold 'em has evolved to be the game of choice. It's exciting, fun to watch, easy to learn and takes forever to master. Someday there will be the Masters of Hold 'em. The best of the best will come together, get a free buffet, have back massages available and- wait a minute. We already have that. It's called the World Series of Poker. But let's go farther. Let's go where no man has gone before. Let's have an invitation only Masters tournament with a $100,000 entry fee. We will limit the entries to 100 of the best players and they have to live together in a Big Brother house with 100 cameras. Whenever they are eliminated from the tournament, they are evicted from the house and shrouded. And the people left in the house will vote on whether or not they should first be castrated. Or worse- cremated. It will pay to get along. I wonder how Phil Hellmuth Jr. or Mike "The Mouth" would fare. And maybe a gay version for gay poker players. Maybe that would be called Really Really Big Brother. These shows would be reality TV at its best. Coming to your living room soon... Everyone plays fuckin' poker. Everyone. What a country. What a great fuckin' country.

Diabetes and Sculptures

I have diabetes. It's not good. It's not even close to being good. My blood sugar levels are sometimes as high as my S.A.T. score. That's not good either. Then I broke my foot. But I didn't know it. I have numbness of the feet because of the diabetes. Since I didn't know I broke my foot, I kept walking on it and it got worse. Now I have what's called Charcot Foot. It takes about a year to heal. Leave it to the fuckin' French to come up with something that takes a year to heal. My doctor says I have about another 10 months to go before I can throw away my crutch. I asked him how he could be so precise on knowing it will be 10 months. He said two reasons: #1- He has read extensively on the research that has been done on Charcot and my case is a classic case, and the past 2 months my foot has responded exactly the way the book said it should. And #2- He has exactly 10 payments left on his Mercedes. Now I have to hope he doesn't buy a fuckin' boat. Charcot Foot was apparently discovered by a Frenchman named Freddy Charcot. He is no relation to Freddy Deeb. Apparently, as the story goes, Charcot had diabetes and his feet were numb. He was doing some yard work and his neighbor John-Paul Francois needed help to move this huge sculpture from his garage. He was sending it to the U.S. as a gift and Charcot went over to his house to help him put it in the back of a pickup truck. Well, it fell on his foot and broke the shit out of the top of it. Charcot Foot was born. And the sculpture wasn't broke. Charcot was the proud recipient of Charcot Foot and we were the proud recipient of the Statue of Liberty. It was a good day for everyone.

Random Thought

I have friends that have living wills that specify that they don't want any extraordinary means done to keep them alive. DNR- Known as Do Not Resuscitate. Fuck that. I want every means possible to keep me alive. Pull the plug? Fuck you. I want my wife to station a security guard next to the plug. I don't want someone accidentally tripping over it. Plus I want a generator in my room in case the power goes out. And keep my relatives out of the room. They might try to pay off the guard.

Jamie "I Want All The Gold" Gold

Jamie Gold won the WSOP. 12 Million bucks. He had a rush
that wouldn't quit. He couldn't lose a hand. Huge chip lead. Before the
tournament he made a deal. He would split his winnings with Bruce
Crispin Leyser. I know what you're thinking. Why would anyone
name their kid Crispin? That was my first thought too. And Bruce. I
could do 20 minutes on that also. Well, maybe not 20, but at least 10.
Anyway, Gold woke up with pocket Aces numerous times on his way
to victory. The day after his victory he woke up to the fact that he had
made a deal to give up half his winnings. Then those immortal words
came into his head that so many have said after we make a bad call,
"What am I? fuckin' nuts?" So Goldie gets an attorney or two and
decides he isn't going to play nice. "Poker players lie all the time," and
"Deceit is part of the game," will probably be the cornerstone
arguments by Goldie's law firm- Scumbag and Sons. The last part of
the Review Journal article had a humorous line. It said, "It's unclear
why Gold is challenging the payment; his representatives have refused
to comment." Mmmmmmmmm… I wonder if it has something to do
with MONEY! Lying at the poker table about your hand is different
than doing a deal. Deals are done all the time in poker tournaments.
Gold is either a fuckin' idiot or has had some very very shortsighted,
bad advice. I would have given my left nut to be this kid's advisor.
First off we would have 6 million in cash sitting on a poker table and
Gold would have been giving it to the guy he made a deal with. We are
talking huge coverage. ESPN, Fox News, NBC, ABC, CBS, Travel
Channel. Everyone would be there. If there was life on other planets,
they would also send representatives to film this historic event. The
headlines would scream, "When Jamie Gold Gives His Word, He
Keeps It," or "His Word is Gold." Give that to some marketing genius
and watch him run with it. Large corporations would clamor for his
endorsement. $6 Million? Fuck, he'd make that in the first month. It
could have been absolutely fuckin' huge. Instead we have a court case.
And a recording in Gold's voice making a promise. A promise not
kept. No matter what the outcome you can't unring the bell. Gold's
word is not gold. Not even close. He says most of his money is going
to help his dad who has Lou Gehrig's disease. He also says he will
start a foundation for Lou Gehrig's disease research. How nice. Unless

he's bluffing. Or lying. You did a deal, Jamie. You could have been a super star. Instead you're a super prick. In my opinion- of course.

Random Thought

Every now and then lady luck smiles on her followers. Sometimes they're nice people, sometimes they're assholes. Oh well, at least it's only now and then.

Santa Thanks His Elves

I am required by law to acknowledge the people that helped me with this book. There were so many. Where do I start? If I leave someone out they will be pissed and not talk to me anymore. Or even worse, they won't help me with future projects. You know- the books to follow, the movie rights, the book tours, the talk show circuit. You know- all the things that come with a billion seller. Just like "Doyle Brunson's Super System". It's like $100 a copy. When I went to buy one of his books I asked the price and when the clerk told me I grabbed my chest and reached for my defibrillator. Then I asked the clerk if it came with some land. Maybe a small lot? He said, "Listen you fat fuck, (I seem to get that a lot) if you don't want the book, put it back." Apparently he didn't see the mustard stain I had accidentally put on the cover. I was eating a hotdog at the time. So I was really buying "uper System". The "S" was missing. Well, not missing, just kind of covered with mustard. So I bought the book. It didn't come with any land, and because of the steep price, little Jimmy wasn't able to have that operation. When I mentioned little Jimmy to the clerk he said, "Fuck little Jimmy. No one likes him anyway." The sad part was he was right. Little Jimmy has always been a pain in the ass. I've even loosened the lug nuts on his wheelchair a few times myself. But I'm glad I bought Doyle's book. I've bought all his books. My favorite was his first one. I believe it was called The Book of Genesis. Adam took a bad beat. My favorite chapter is "Let There Be Light". And in every one of Doyle's books he acknowledges all those who have helped him. It's the law. So I have decided that in the interest of the time space continuum, I refuse to spend any more precious time and space in listing all of the people that have contributed to the immense success I expect. Fuck the law.

Yours in Christ,

Tony Korfman

Random Thought

What's the difference between a skunk being run over by a car and a bagpipe or accordion player being run over by a car? There's skid marks in front of the skunk. *Badda Bing Badda Boom.*

Survived By His Wife

Alan King use to do a comedy routine that was taken from the obituaries. Yep. The obituaries. There's comedy everywhere. It was called "Survived by his wife". When you read an obituary, it always shows who the person is survived by. It seems that no matter how old a guy is when he dies, he is survived by his wife. I don't know if any in-depth analysis has been done to see how the guys who play poker fare against the guys who don't. But all in all, it seems that no matter how old the guy is, the magic words "survived by his wife" appear in the obituary. Fred Arnold, 72- survived by his wife. Danny Sullivan, 87- survived by his wife. Arthur Santiago, 97- I figured, fuck we've got to have a winner here! Nope, survived by his wife. Today I read about the oldest guy in California who just died. He was 112. The autopsy showed that his organs were those of a 60 year old. He ate junk food. His diet consisted mainly of sausage and waffles. His name was George Johnson. He lived in Richmond, California. He drove until he was 102. He had no children. He was not survived by his wife. She was 92 when she died. We finally won one. God bless George Johnson. I wonder if he played poker...

Random Thought

There's an old saying, "What you see is what you get." With rare exception, that is true. I'm a firm believer that to achieve success you must be sincere. Once you can fake sincerity, you've got it made.

Tired of Poker? Want Some Great Jazz?

Call the Child Protective Services Hotline

You're not going to believe this. I needed to reach the Mohave County Child Protective Services and I didn't have the number. I called City Hall in Mohave County. They didn't know the number and told me to call Justice Court. They didn't know the number either and gave me the number of the Administrator's office who gave me the number of what they thought was the Child Protective Services department. After numerous "Press 2 if you're looking for the nearest 7-11," and "Press 3 if you ate at Joe's and are feeling nauseous" messages, the recorder finally said, "Press 4 if you are reporting a child that needs our immediate help." I pressed "4" and you won't believe this; you just can't make this shit up. I listened to a message with background jazz music for almost 25 minutes. There were numerous recorded apologies while I was waiting. "The hotline is experiencing high call volume so please tell the little whippersnapper to calm down. Help is on the way right after this next song by jazz great Harpo Marx." I just couldn't fuckin' believe it. It was a hotline for Christ's sake. Can you imagine calling the fire department and getting a 25 minute recording? We're sorry, but the fire department is experiencing a high volume of calls from the firemen's families and girlfriends. Please be patient. While that flame is licking at your ass, we hope you enjoy one of Jerry Lee Lewis' albums, "Come on Baby Light My Fire." So, I'm on the phone waiting and waiting for Child Protective Services and we were closing in on 30 minutes of hold messages and jazz. They mixed up the messages nicely. Alternating between the jazz music was a man's gentle voice and a woman's voice and it almost made the call a candidate for a Saturday Night Live skit.

SNL Hotline- Thank you for calling the Child Abuse Hotline. Your call is very important to us. But first a few jazz albums that I'm sure you've been wanting to listen to, but haven't had the time.

Phone Caller- (Yelling to wife) You won't fuckin' believe what the hotline just said. It's a fuckin' recording.

SNL Hotline-   Sir, if you're going to get the full enjoyment
               from a jazz album you can't be yelling and
               swearing.

Phone Caller- Hello. Hello. I want to report a child abuse
               problem. It's very important. It's almost an
               emergency. Hello.

SNL Hotline-   We hope you enjoyed that latest rendition of
               "Joy to the World" in jazz. Next is something
               that will have your toes tapping and your groin
               itching. Hit it Satchmo!

Phone Caller- I've got to write this down. People won't
               fuckin' believe it when they read it.

SNL Hotline-   Your call may be recorded for quality assurance.
               Your swear words will be deleted because the
               person monitoring the call is a strict Mormon.
               We thank you for calling the Child Abuse
               Hotline. Let the kid know that help is on the
               way. We are concerned. We are sympathetic.
               We are gassing up the car as we speak. But first
               a great song by legendary jazz musician Ozzy
               Osborne.

Phone Caller- Honey, come listen to this song. It's great!

SNL Hotline-   We hope you've enjoyed today's featured
               albums while you've been waiting. Our quality
               assurance operator had to go home because the
               babysitter was spanking the kids. Please call
               back tomorrow when we will feature Elvis
               Presley's top 5 albums. If you still have an
               emergency situation after being on hold for 45
               minutes, please call FEMA. If you enjoyed our
               recordings, you will love theirs.

-    Dial tone.

A Memo of Love

Trouble was brewing at the World Series of Poker. Dealers were calling in sick, they were quitting, they were walking out. They weren't getting any breaks, their tokes were being fucked with. They were pissed. Harrah's Corp and the Rio, with their tremendous 6th sense, felt that a memo that conveyed a feeling of caring, a feeling of love, a feeling of- well you get the picture- needed to be written to the poker dealers. I suggested the following:

To: All WSOP Dealers

From: Management

Subject: A Memo of Love

We have not succeeded in solving all of your problems. The solutions we have found only seem to raise a whole new set of problems. We are as dazed and confused as ever, but we believe we are dazed and confused on a much higher level and about more important things. Our goals are similar to yours. To make a huge amount of money from all of these fools who play. Did I say money? I meant long term customers. Did I say fools? I meant kind souls who gave us their hard earned money. So, our company thanks you for the work you do and we thank you for not having to drink a sip of water or go to the bathroom for 5 and sometimes 6 hours. I know that some of you are diabetic and need to urinate with more frequency. "That's really too fuckin' bad. Get a job selling magazine subscriptions." Did I say, "Too fuckin' bad?" I meant, "I really feel fuckin' sad." I'm really sorry you have diabetes and will probably die a horrible, painful death in front of your family and friends. But this memo isn't about you. It's always you, you, you. This memo is about me. Actually, it's about Harrah's. We know Bill Harrah would be so proud. His company has become a huge, monster company. Thank you Bill. And of course, thank you to our leader Gary Loveman. And of course, thank you to you, the little people that make everything happen. We love the little people. We love **you**. Harrah's is all about love. And of course, money.

Yours in Christ,

The Management

Harrah's didn't like my memo.

In Memory Of

Steve lost his life, and to this we honor him. We honor his memory. We honor his place at work. We honor the coffee cup he used to drink his coffee from. We want to honor him in other ways, but we don't know how. We're not idiots- we just haven't thought of other idiotic ways we can honor him. We had no services. Because there was no body, there is no grave. Steve lost his life to poker. We think. Steve went out to play one night and he hasn't been seen since. He likes to play tournaments. Maybe the tournament isn't over. He hasn't called. But cell phones aren't allowed to be used in tournaments. He hasn't texted. Text messaging is forbidden. Sometimes tournaments are very long. His family and friends understand that. They understand that people have visibly aged during tournaments. And they didn't even cash. That's what everyone is worried about. Steve has been gone for so long. Weeks? Months? His family has lost track. What's foremost on his family's mind is his safety. And if he came in the money. Not necessarily in that order. Tournaments are grueling. And it's only the few, the lucky, the dedicated that get to cash. The weak, the tired, the meek- they go home early. So we are all hoping that Steve is safe. And of course that he cashes. And if he's not safe and he hasn't cashed, then Steve's family hopes his body will be found. So **they** can cash. On his life insurance policy. Steve would want this. We all would. Then we could honor Steve the way honoring someone was meant to be. With pomp and circumstance. Lots of pomp. Whatever the fuck pomp is. And plenty of circumstance. I have no fuckin' idea what that is either (I don't think you're suppose to end a sentence with "either". Oh fuck, I did it again). Circumstance? Could they have meant circumcision? Pomp and circumcision? That makes as much sense as circumstance. So anyway, hopefully we hear from Steve. Or someone who has played with him. He looks like a typical poker player. He's ugly. And fat. And never changes his clothes. He doesn't have to, it's a tournament. No one cares. It's not a fashion show. For Christ's sake, Jim. I'm only a doctor, not a fuckin' runway model. Steve will always be remembered. And loved. And missed. And honored. For as long as it takes...

Random Thought

Kids who grow up having family dinners are 50% less likely to get involved with drugs and alcohol. They will still chat in chat rooms, play Hold 'em online and masturbate 3-5 times a week, but they won't be drunk when they do them. Three out of five psychotherapists totally agree with the numbers that I just made up. The other two wouldn't return my calls.

Undaunted By Avalanches

I bank with Wells Fargo. They had a recording when you phoned them and they put you on hold that told about Billy Bartlett. He was a Wells Fargo agent who rode through the sleet, the snow, the heat and the rain to deliver the mail. When a pass was unpassable, he would strap on his snow shoes- all in the name of "on time delivery". The recording goes on to say that Billy was "undaunted by avalanches". I wish my morning newspaper boy would listen to the recording. He's undaunted by alarm clocks. He use to throw the paper on the lawn and the sprinklers would come on at 11 AM and get the paper sopping wet (I think in all my years of writing I have never used the word sopping). 11 AM for Christ's sake. I told him if I wanted an evening paper, I would order one. When I was a paper boy yadda yadda yadda. I droned on and on. I like to drone. Anyway, I asked the paperboy very politely, very nicely, in a kindly, fatherly manner to put my paper in a dry place. Very simply, I said, "Hey you stupid fuck. Put my paper where it won't get wet." He said, "Yes sir." The next morning my paper was on my roof. He obviously was undaunted by my request. I too am undaunted by things. One thing is bad beats. I am totally undaunted by bad beats. If I talk about them it's usually in a humorous way. Because I try to find humor even in pain. I know, I'm a sick fuck. I am never looking for sympathy. A bad beat story and 5 bucks will get you a cup of coffee at the Mirage. Without a tip of course. I hate bad beat stories. No one cares. That's all you hear during poker tournament breaks. When I'm on a break I want to pee. And wash my face. Not necessarily in that order. When I get back to the table I announce to everyone, "I peed and washed my face, but not my hands. Players beware." While walking to the bathroom you see all the clusters of people telling bad beat stories. And of course every cell phone in use is someone telling a bad beat story to someone on the other end who is trying to act like they give a fuck. For every bad beat story, there's someone telling the story from the other side. The guy that won the bad beat hand is telling his "miracle card" story. For once I would like to hear something on a tournament break that doesn't start with, "You won't believe," or "The flop came 3-7-9 rainbow." I have enough trouble remembering my hole cards let alone a hand I played an hour ago. Of course, there are some hands you remember. Good and bad. Like events in your life. You remember some good ones and some bad ones. But the detail that some people remember in the hands they played hours, days or weeks ago is remarkable. They must have a photographic memory and be incredibly fuckin' lonely. And have nothing else to talk about. And no one else to talk to. Their life is comprised of bad beats and beating off. And it's not just me that thinks that way. Three out of five dentists agree. The other two are just drifting aimlessly through life. I think I saw one at a poker tournament telling a bad beat story. The other one is missing and we are trying to organize a search party to look for him. But why the fuck would anyone look for a missing dentist? I know I wouldn't.

Random Thought

How bad does a bad beat feel? It burns- It stings- It puckers your asshole. But then it's over. Sure you talk about it ad-nauseam for about a day or two. But then it's over. And by then there's a new bad beat story to talk about. Like anyone gives a fuck. But people fake looking sympathetic. We all do.

No Wonder Everyone Loves Chocolate

You know, there's some shit you just can't make up. In this morning's paper was an article about a girl in Fountain Valley, California who works at a chocolate factory that makes- what else? Chocolate. Anyway, a worker, according to the article, spotted a lump of chocolate while cleaning the chocolate drippings, that had a striking resemblance to (you fuckin' ready for this?) the Virgin Mary. Now things like this really piss me off! Six months ago when I had the flu and threw up the bean and cheese burrito I ate, I could have sworn I saw Jesus. And then I saw God. By the way, she's colored. Not Jesus. God. What color? Kind of a Klingon Green. I called the same Las Vegas newspaper that had the "chocolate miracle" article in it and they hung up on me. Then about 3 weeks later, a potato chip I was about to eat bore a striking resemblance to Regis Philbin. I was really hungry so I ate it anyway. I know, I know, I should have called a press conference. So now, this 2-inch column of "miracle" chocolate drippings of the Virgin Mary is on display in front of the company gift shop in a plastic case. And according to the article, the discovery came "just in time" for the lady who "discovered" the drippings. Raising a son on her own, she has struggled with marital problems for months and said she was about to lose her faith. Hey lady, I've been struggling with marital problems for the last 40 years. And the Regis Philbin potato chip didn't do a fuckin' thing to help. "Miracles" are around us all the time. I discovered one while reading a proof of this book. Stare at this page intensely while slowly rolling your right eye toward the middle of your face. Now slowly, and I mean slowly, insert your middle finger into your ass. If you are looking at the correct part of the page you will see an image of an ear of corn. If you look closely at the top 4 kernels you will see what looks like Elton John fucking a gorgeous, blonde-haired female model. Now that, my friends, is a fuckin' miracle.

Random Thought

I played at a tournament in the Venetian with Joe Hachem. It was nice to see that success hadn't changed him at all. Well, at least not too much. Except for the silk scarf. And the skipper's hat. And the pipe. And the body guards. Still the same old Joe. With the open shirt. And the hair hanging out. I could go on and on and you know I probably will. It was good to see Joe. He brought a lot of things to the event. He brought excitement. He brought warmth. He brought laughter. Thank God he didn't bring Taylor Hicks. Or Liza Minelli.

Another Fuckin' Disclaimer

When Will They End?

This book will explore every fact of life. It will "cut to the chase", get down to the "bare bones" and be as actual and factual as any history book you have ever read or thought about reading. Every fact in this book is either based on intense, and I mean fuckin' intense research, or I made it up. I can't help making up facts. A guy once told me you can take an ordinary Kleenex, say that Elvis or Liza or even Cher sneezed in it, put it in a little glass case with a nice plaque in front of it and you have credibility. You have net worth. You have an eBay auction item in the making. You have fuckin' fraud. In a good way. Who's to know? You, my friend, have an eBay auction item in your hands. Providing both hands are on this book. Or on the wheel. Always drive with both hands on the wheel. No one does. Except when you first learn how to drive. For about 3 hours. By then it's time to call someone on your cell phone. And put on makeup. And sample that Carl's Jr. Superstar "dripping good" burger you're suppose to be taking home for lunch. Let's face it. You're an experienced driver. You've had about 3 hours real time experience. And you haven't been stopped or cited yet by anyone in law enforcement or anyone who "says" they're in law enforcement. So the proof is in the pudding (Now what the fuck does that mean? The proof is in the pudding. If something was in the pudding why would you eat it? Who eats pudding anyway? We all eat Jell-O). So we will explore. We will investigate. We will probe, look into, search out, inspect, scrutinize, examine and research the game of Hold 'em as we know it. As our forefathers knew it. And as our foremothers knew it when they tried to get our forefathers to come home from the local Indian casino they were playing at. Just remember one very important fact- There are no fuckin' refunds. And Virginia, I'm sorry to be the one to tell you, but there is no fuckin' Santa Claus. I felt you had to know. And when I use the term "extensive research has shown", there's been no fuckin' research. I made it up. The only thing I know for sure is that pocket Aces are suppose to win 80% of the time. I think.

2 Out of 10 Are Offsuit-

And There's Nothing Wrong With That

It's a proven fact that one out of five guys is either gay, wants to be gay or has been gay at some point in his life for at least one year. So when you are at a full table of 10 guys, at least 2 of them qualify for this award. A gay poker player who writes a tell-all book about himself might have trouble coming up with titles for his chapters. I came up with a few to get him started.

Chapter 1-   Poker Players That Would Look "Hot" Oiled Up

Chapter 2-   How To Pretend To Like The Cocktail Waitress

Chapter 3-   At First I Thought I Was Bi-polar

Chapter 4-   How To Make the Guy Next To You Think You're a Tailor While You're Playing With His Inseam

Chapter 5-   Doing a Reach Around Without Causing Suspicion

Chapter 6-   An All-In Bet Takes Balls

Chapter 7-   Poker Dealers Who Left a Bad Taste In My Mouth

Chapter 8-   He Rivered Me Without a Condom, Then With a Condom, Then Without a Condom Again

Chapter 9-   Is That a Wad of Cash In Your Pocket or Are You Just Happy To See Me?

Chapter 10-   If I "Raise" You, Will You "Re-raise" Me?

Chapter 11-   When The Tournament Director Says "Shuffle Up and Deal" I Get Aroused

Chapter 12-   He Beat Me With His 9 High

Chapter 13-   If Only This Chapter Was In Inches

Chapter 14-   Getting Beat With "The Nuts"

Cell Phone Explosion

Cell phones are not allowed to be used during tournaments for one simple reason. It was rumored that somewhere in the universe, while talking on a cell phone, a tournament player's head caught on fire and exploded causing chaos and a misdeal. We all know how tournament participants hate misdeals and an easy fix was to ban cell phones. Since this rumored event happened during a tournament and not a cash game, cell phones are OK in cash games.

Phil Hellmuth's Daily Prayer

Dear Lord, so far today I'm doing pretty good. I have not gossiped, lost my temper, mother fucked anyone, been nasty, selfish or self-indulgent. I have not whined, cursed or kicked any poker dealers. However… I am going to get out of bed in a few minutes, Lord, and I will need a lot of help after that.

You Can Call Me Johnson

Bad beats are a way of life. And of poker. If you play poker you will have bad beats. It's a simple rule of the game. When it happens you need to regain your composure and take 5 minutes to adjust your focus and your thoughts. This is an absolute fuckin' Star Fleet directive. You must go to the bathroom and wash your face and when you come back to the game you need to have a completely fresh state of mind. When you experience a bad beat, you have a tendency to go on tilt. Your emotions kick in. You must take a break just to break the cycle you are experiencing. There's no better way than by going to the bathroom and shaking your Johnson and washing your hands and face. Especially your face. Fuck the hand-washing thing. Those cards are Petri dishes anyway. If you feel this ritual hasn't helped you, then change it around a little. Shake someone else's Johnson and **don't** wash your face. Do whatever it takes to get your frame of mind back to a stable state. Then go back to the table and bust the prick that gave you the bad beat!

California- Disclaimer Hell

I am watching TV on a California channel and this ad comes on for some type of mortgage company. It's called Greenlight Financial Services. The commercial was about 10 seconds long. Real quick. The final "screen" has a disclaimer. Well, actually it has lines of disclaimers. Line after line after line. I think there were 26 lines. 26 Lines of disclaimers! I'm not making this shit up. I couldn't. I'm not that good. The print is so small I couldn't read it. None of it. What you need is to tape it. Then enlarge it. Then have an attorney translate it for you. It could be a fun class project for you school teachers reading this shit. Actually, there should be a course in school called disclaimers and asterisks. Every deal has an asterisk. Or a disclaimer. Or both. The company that is advertising the deal wants you in their store or car lot. That's why they spend millions and millions of dollars advertising. They need to grab your attention. They need to grab you by the balls. So they advertise the fantastic price on the item they are seducing you with, and next to the price is a tiny tiny asterisk that you think is a piece of dust that landed on your paper. If you're a new customer, they want you in their store. If you're a good customer already, they want to entice you back. My wife likes to shop at Macy's. Actually, she likes to shop at any store that has an Open sign, but Macy's is one of her top one thousand favorite places. Her credit card bill is huge every month. Our mailman has threatened to quit if her credit card bill isn't shipped U.P.S. He said it's so heavy it hurts his back. She likes Macy's because it has really nice clothes for the grandkids. Every time she goes in there it costs me $500. Last month Macy's sent her a $10 gift certificate. Ten fuckin' dollars. Here's what the gift certificate said, "Just for you, here's your $10 in-store certificate*." No, that wasn't a piece of dust that landed on the paper next to the word "certificate". That was the dreaded asterisk. For a lousy 10 bucks. To a great customer. The bottom of the certificate had 10 tiny lines of disclaimers. It read as follows:

*Valid for a one-time use in-store September 9, 2006, only. Limit one per customer. $10 minimum purchase required; no change will be given. EXCLUDES: Cosmetics and fragrances, fine and fashion watches,

Lacoste, Impulse, bridge sportswear, Coach, kate spade and Dooney & Bourke handbags, designer and bridge shoes and handbags for her, selected men's designers, Baccarat, Lalique, Waterford, Frango, All-Clad, furniture, mattresses, and area rugs. ALSO EXCLUDES REGULAR-PRICED: selected women's designers. Not valid on Everyday Values, fine jewelry super buys, Macy's Gift Cards and Gift Certificates, special orders, previous purchases, restaurants, or nonmerchandise-related services; on purchases from macys.com, macysweddingchannel.com, thisit.com, Gift Registry kiosks, gift wrap or leased departments; or as payments on credit accounts. Federated employees not eligible. Discount will be deducted from the current price (regular, sale or clearance, as applicable). **Cannot be combined with another savings pass or discount offers.**

Asterisks and disclaimers. I fuckin' love them.

Carrot Sticks With No Ranch Dressing

There are very few who turn into celebrity personalities on the poker circuit. First of all they have to **have** a personality. That eliminates 95% of the poker players that win tournaments. And it **has** to be a big tournament. You have to win a "big one" to become a spokesman for a gaming site to help suck out the spendable dollars that our youth has. The "personality" is the carrot and the computer is the stick. A very long, long stick. Winning online tournaments is just the beginning of your road to riches. An online tournament is the vehicle that helps excite you and propel you into a live tournament and then of course you have to reach the final table. Oh, and did I mention you then have to win. Then you get the carrot. Sometimes you get the carrot stuck up your ass. But when you get to the final table you have all of the gambling sites clamoring for you to wear their gear. Their visible gear. Wearing Party Poker underwear doesn't count. And if you are the first one knocked out of the final table, no one wants to talk to you. Online sites have been known to rip the T-Shirt off your back and grab your logo'd cap and have David Sklansky stare at your knees (whatever that means). Online sites want representatives that are winners. Not sniveling 10th placers that have just been eliminated from the final table and are sitting in the corner sobbing uncontrollably. And if you happen to be wearing their gear, and you win the event to which you have invested your life savings and your parents' home, then you are their celebrity. Their hero. Their marketing tool. Did I just call you a tool? Sorry. I get carried away sometimes. OK, most of the time. So then, and only then, are you on the road to becoming a "celebrity personality". You have reached out, stretched out, and grabbed the carrot. But of course, all roads are fraught with bumps, and grinds, and curves, and potholes, and pockets of a quicksand-type gooey puss. But that's the highway of life. So be careful what you wish for. You might be allergic to carrots and not know it.....

Random Thought

I enjoy playing in tournaments. They are fun. But I have noticed one troubling aspect of the game. I see lots of kids playing. A lot of the same kids. And more and more of them are looking for a stake- someone to a buy a piece of them for a certain percentage. Their money and their resources are starting to show signs of strain. That is not a good sign. Some of these kids are very very good, solid players. But the game is tough to beat consistently. They all want to be in tournaments and make the final table, and wake up to "pocket Aces". I'm just worried that 5 years from now they'll be "waking up" to no career. I'm hoping I'm wrong, but the signs are there.

Foot Tells? At The Bellagio?

The Bellagio has really great tournaments. I'll say that a lot in this book. Because they really do. And as you already know, this book is all facts. "Fact filled" I like to call it. Except for the parts I make up. Which will probably be the parts I'll be questioned about in a court of law. Hopefully not by my wife's attorney. I don't do well under cross-examination. And that's what I like about the Bellagio. No one ever cross-examines me. Or crosses me. There are a few that would like to see me dangling from a cross. But not at The Bellagio. Not yet. I think. When you play at The Bellagio, they have every kind of limit your heart desires. And tournaments. I love their tournaments. You meet so many other lonely people who don't change their shorts either. What camaraderie. What male bonding. What bullshit. When you play tournaments, you see a lot of the same people. A lot of the same faces. A lot of the same sweaty T-shirts. There's a lot of youth that plays. There's a lot of middle aged people. And a lot of the"I'm just trying to get to fuckin' lunch" crowd. We smile at each other. We nod at each other. We can't stand each other. Actually, most people are likable. To someone. Somewhere. I think. They smile, they nod, they wink at you. The wink is kind of a defining moment. It's like the winker is saying, "Remember the time I knocked you out of the tournament right before you cashed. And it was on the river? And I crushed your hopes and dreams of getting to the final table? And I crushed your soul? Remember that?" Wink wink. I hate winks. I hate winkers. But I'm not a hateful guy. I like most things. I like most people. I hate winkers. David Sklansky is not a winker. Neither is Rene Angelil. I love saying his name. Angelil. It's so Italian. It's so French. It has just the right amount of vowels and consonants. Rene plays a lot of tournaments. At The Bellagio, of course. He wears sunglasses all the time. So I don't know if he's a winker or not. I don't think he is. When I first played with him, someone came up to me on a break and said, "Do you know who's sitting next to you?" I said, "No. I wasn't there during the introductory phase of the tournament." (You see, my sarcasm extends way beyond my writing.) (That probably explains why I'm loved by men, women, children and clergymen everywhere.) (Now I'm wondering whether or not it's proper to have two parenthesis sentences in a row.) (Holy fuck, now it's three.) (I've got to stop this now! My

OCD is kicking in.) (I love Monk). And he said, Rene Angelil is sitting next to you. He's Celine Dion's husband. Now, that's another thing I hate. When people identify themselves or someone else identifies them by a relationship.

Officer stopping traffic violator: Sir, you were doing 110.

Traffic Violator: Don't you know who I am.

Officer: No, sir. I don't. Would you please give me your license and registration.

Traffic Violator: I am a distant friend of Jerry Seinfeld's nephew.

Officer: Sir, Mr. Seinfeld doesn't have a nephew.

Traffic Violator: That's true copper. But if he did, I would be his distant friend.

Officer: 110 Miles per hour in a school zone is totally unacceptable. Please don't do it again.

Traffic Violator: I thought I was only doing 100.

Officer: Say hello to Mr. Seinfeld for me.

Traffic Violator winks at the officer. (Fade to black)

We are a society mesmerized by celebrity. I am mesmerized by the fact that I used two big words in the same sentence. If you play enough poker you will eventually rub elbows with a celebrity. Or someone who knows a celebrity. Or someone who wishes they knew a celebrity. And my strong suit, if I do say, is rubbing elbows. I have great elbows. My hopes and dreams of being a foot model have been dashed because of my "broken in 5 places" foot. And the warts on my hands rule out hand modeling. But I have great fuckin' elbows. I actually wear long sleeve shirts because when I wear short sleeves, people stare at my elbows and become aroused. And then they wink…

So I'm playing a tournament at the Bellagio and the final table is comprised of me, Rene Angelil (Celine Dion's husband), David Sklansky (Mrs. Sklansky's husband), Marco (who probably has 15 paternity suits pending from women that want him to **be** their husband), and another kid who looks like he has his life savings in his right hand pocket (either that or he was excited about my elbows). There were also 5 other people that I'm sure had famous wives. Or knew someone who had a famous wife. Sklansky is like the world's greatest math guy. When a teacher in Brazil can't figure out what 12x9 is, she calls Sklansky. And he calls Homework Hotline. He knows how to get the answers. That's why he's great. The Shell Answer Man was patterned after him. And rightly so. He looks like a gas pump with a beard. So three of us get involved in a pot, and I figure I'm sucking hind tit, so I muck my hand after a short pondering session. After the hand, which Sklansky won, the kid politely asked Sklansky why he just raised and didn't go all-in. An all in bet at the time would probably have been the appropriate move and the kid was hoping to further his poker knowledge by asking the question with dignity, respect and politeness, all attributes that I find annoying and disgusting. Sklansky has written numerous books on the "math" of poker and is an authoritative figure in the world of poker. And probably other worlds too. And other solar systems. Anyway, the table went silent to hear the response by this poker guru. The entire table and bleachers were astounded by his response. A hush fell over the poker room. The crowd was silenced. The room was silenced. The Bellagio was silenced. It would be hours before the poker room had a normal "poker room hum" to it. Sklansky looked at the kid right in the foot (he doesn't make eye contact well) and said, "I don't answer questions about how I play hands to anyone." Or something like that. And then he glared at the kid's knee. He was working his way up to his eyes. I was shaking. I was trembling. I had to pee. The kid apologized and we all looked at each other and I know our thoughts were the same. Please Lord, let David Sklansky's next bowel movement be square. Thank you, Lord. A few hours later we decided to chop the prize money. There were four of us left to figure out fairly, or what seems to be fair to most of us, except the guy getting screwed, how much to give each of us based on the amount of chips we had at the time. David Sklansky was one of the guys involved in the chop.

Have you ever tried to chop prize money with a mathematician? Have you ever tried chopping prize money with Einstein? Have you ever tried chopping money with the Marx Brothers? Negotiations were chaotic. Negotiations were fierce. We realized we needed help. We called the floorman over. We called the card room manager. We called Henry Kissinger, Henry Fonda and Henry Aldrich. We needed decisions. Finally after what seemed like hours and hours (it was actually 12 minutes by Pacific Standard Time) we came to an agreement. David Sklansky would get all the money and we would get a copy of his next book "I Never Met A Man I Liked Or Wanted To Like". With a chapter on "Foot Tells". Tournaments are fun. The Bellagio is the funnest. I like the Bellagio. But I think I already said that.

Random Thought

He was always a leader and we all felt that besides being the table captain, he had the ability to take over a small size country.

Lord- Send Us Another Kid

E. Pluribus Unum. The Latin motto on the Great Seal of the United States translates as, "Out of many, one." And one emerged out of the World Series of Poker. Just one. Out of 8,700. But why in God's name did it have to be Jamie Gold? Why Lord? What did we do to you? Poker players pray constantly. We are always praying to you. Your good name is used in poker rooms all over our great land. Before and after the flop. And you give us Jamie Gold. Maybe you thought his name was what we were looking for- Gold. So you gave us a name we all yearned for. You sent us your only son Jesus to die for our sins. Lord, it's a huge sin that Jamie Gold represents every poker player in the world. It's a giant sin. Lord, it may be time to send us another kid. Maybe you could send us a daughter. I don't think the son thing worked out too well. Maybe it's just me, Lord. Maybe it's just me.....

Glory Glory

There are actually some Glory, Glory, Hallelujah moments at tournament tables. You can't yell Glory, Glory, but you can think it. You can't yell it because it would be improper and many people might think you are a religious fanatic and burn your lucky crucifix card cover. Smoking is prohibited at the table but I don't think "burning" has been addressed. There's nothing like covering pocket Aces with Jesus. God would be proud. So would his Son.

A Small Gesture

Small gestures in life are important. When you're driving and someone lets you in a lane, a wave is a small but friendly gesture. It's always appreciated by the person you're waving to. If he won't let you in the lane, the finger is an appropriate gesture. This could provoke the guy to pull out his concealed weapon and fire a few shots at you. He would then be charged with attempted murder and do at least 5 years in the penitentiary. This will accomplish 2 things: It gets the prick off the road thereby making the road a better place, and I'm sure the next time he drives 5 years later, he will be a friendlier driver. Anger management classes in prison should also help him contain his anger so he can shoot straighter and hit his target with more accuracy. A lot of good can come out of an incident like this. Small gestures in life are important.

WSOP- Top 11

Results just in: The 2006 World Series of Poker top 11 winners- A top 11 list? Unheard of. Next to their name is the amount of money they won. Real money. Real U.S. currency. Minus, of course, tax and tip.

11) Lief Force		$1,154,000
10) Fred Goldberg		$1,154,000
9) Dan Nassip		$1,566,000
8) Erik Friberg		$1,979,000
7) Doug Kim		$2,391,000
6) Richard Lee		$2,803,000
5) Rhett Butler		$3,216,000
4) Allen Cunningham		$3,628,000
3) Michael Binger		$4,123,000
2) Paul Wasicka		$6,102,000
1) Jamie Gold		$12,000,00

I just **had** to put in the 11th place winner. With a name like Lief Force you have to bend the rules. My top 11 list. It might not work for Letterman, but it works great for me. May the Force be with you. And me. Out of the 11 winners that I posted above, there is a tremendous overweight of the first 7 letters of the alphabet. Force, Goldberg, Butler, Binger, Gold, Cunningham and Friberg. 7 Out of the eleven winners had last names that started with the first 7 letters of the alphabet. There were 873 winners. All the way from $12,000,000 for first place to $10,600 for 873rd place. The 37th Annual World Series of Poker is over. Thank God. Thank fuckin' God.

Mr. Lonely

When we get busted out of a tournament, the lonely walk through the room to the exit is the loneliest walk you will have. Heads turn to see who got busted out so that they are one notch closer to the top prize. When we take that long walk, and we all do, we must focus on the future. We must focus on tomorrow. We must focus on the mother fucker that busted us and hope his kids are born with warts on their asses. No, no, no. That's not nice. And you all know by now how nice I am. What I meant to say is we must move on. Actually, we can't move on. We can try but we never get past it. It's unrelenting. All we can do is live out the remaining days we have, alone, in hopeless, quiet desperation. Until, of course, the next tournament. Then the whole process starts all over again. And we can look for the prick that nailed us last time...

Random Thought

I was looking out from the tournament room at the Bellagio, which overlooks their fabulous fountains. The pigeons around the fountain are very smart. Sometimes they taunt you when you lose a hand. I thought I saw a Robin Redbreast walking around the patio area. Turns out it was a pigeon with a chest wound. And the Bellagio is in such a good neighborhood. What's Las Vegas coming to. Poor fuckin' pigeon.

Doyle's Day- 2006 Style

It was Doyle's day. His 30th World Series of Poker Main Event appearance. And Doyle really looked good. But that's one of the 3 phases of life. There's youth, middle aged and boy you look good. And Doyle looked good. They cheered him. They applauded him. They honored him. He was awarded the title of "Godfather of Poker" many years ago. The only award I ever got was in high school. The award read "Most likely to have someone whacked". My senior year was almost a repeat. I was voted as "Most likely to take a life". I guess it was better than Henry Simkin's award of "Most ugly". Kids are cruel. Especially if you're ugly. Or fat. Or have a small penis. If you hit the bad beat lottery and are all three, you enter into a zone where not many have gone before. High school can be miserable. Except for the few, the chosen, the quarterbacks. But then, of course, we all graduate. And everyone goes their separate ways. Until that dreaded notice comes in the mail. The 5-year class reunion. But a lot of the class is still in school. College for some. Still high school for others. Especially the fat, ugly fucks with small penises. They are way behind the curve. Then comes the 10-year reunion. Things are settling down. You've been out of school for 10 years. You're married with 2 kids. Your career in magazine sales is taking off. You think about going to the reunion. Then you say "fuck it", you'll wait for the 20-year reunion. When the 20-year reunion comes around you accept the invitation. You're 38 years old, divorced, kids are grown and you've aged well. You're slim, still have your hair, and you've invested in a penis extender operation. Life is good. Mom and dad have finally died and have left you with 2.5 million in stocks, gold and real estate. Did I say finally? I meant unfortunately. For them, of course. Not for you. You look great, you feel great, and the hot babe from "A Hot Escort for You" from page 235 of the phone book, looks fuckin' fantastic on your arm. The yellow Hummer completes your look. Time to meet with the assholes you went to school with. I wonder if the Godfather of Poker ever went to a class reunion. I wonder how popular he was in high school. I wonder if he was fat. I wonder if he had a small penis…

Random Thought

Relative to its size, the barnacle has the biggest penis of any animal. Relative to its size. So size does matter. I thought it did.

The Memo

For years I was part of the Mandalay Bay Group, which owned
a ton of fuckin' casinos. About 16 of them, including half of the Las
Vegas strip. I was the Vice President and General Manager of the
Edgewater Hotel and Casino in Laughlin, Nevada. Laughlin is about 2
hours from Las Vegas and gets about 15 degrees hotter than Las
Vegas. We had some days that were 130°. 130 fuckin' degrees. That is
fuckin' hot. But it's a dry heat. Small animals are bursting into flames.
But they're dry flames. Company wide we had over 35,000
employees. I was responsible for 2,000 of them. I believe out of the
2,000, about 1,990 of them had company computers. There wasn't an
office or a cubbyhole you could walk into that didn't have a computer.
Companies rely heavily on computers. How we managed to run these
huge companies 20 years ago, I'll never know. I believe computers
have their place in society, in business, in the home. They are a great
source for information. They are great for accountants. They are great
for the computer or IT department. The computers keep them working.
The problem I have is that every department head and every
department supervisor are in front of their computer screens most of
their shifts. There should be a 2-hour rule. You can be in front of your
computer for 2 hours and then it goes off. The rest of the shift you
should be interacting with the staff in your department and with the
customers. Yes, the casinos have hosts. But hosts take care of the high
rollers. The bread and butter of the casino industry is not the high
roller. We didn't build this city on high roller play. We built this city
on the average player. And, of course, Rock n Roll. Love that song.
We built this city, we built this city on Rock n Roll. For the life of me
I can't recall the name of that song. Or who sings it. Definitely wasn't
Sinatra or Tony Bennett. How the fuck did they get so popular without
computers? One word my friends. Interaction. Interaction with their
fans and the American public. And self promotion. I'm a firm believer
in self promotion. Many of our motivational speakers thrive on self
promotion. I am planning a huge self promotion campaign as soon as I
publish this. I'll start out small. Maybe a local 7-11 book signing. And
then I'll hire 100 people to go to the local Barnes and Noble and ask
for this book. And cause a scene when they're told they don't have it
in stock. And they'll buy other books on Hold 'em and burn them in

front of the store. That always works. Book burnings get national press. Barnes and Noble will be begging me to have book signings. And I'm sure I'll get a few calls from Borders. And I wouldn't be surprised if one or two psychic bookstores jumped on the bandwagon. We use to have a psychic bookstore in our local shopping center. But it went out of business. You think they would have known before they blew all their fuckin' money. Barnes and Noble weren't psychic. But they are doing great. The psychic bookstores should have followed their lead. Open your bookstores next to Starbucks. It was a natural. It doesn't take a psychic to figure out what you do when you order a cup of coffee. You read books! I guarantee that 3 out of 5 copies of this book that are returned, will be returned with a coffee stain on it. Or on the returner's shirt. Or on his shorts if he happened to spill the coffee in his lap. While reading. Trying to sip coffee while laughing hysterically is difficult to do. He'll stop laughing when he gets to the counter and realizes that there are no fuckin' refunds. The girl behind the counter has one simple line to say that I have sent to every bookstore in very legal, very important, very professional memo form. It reads:

To: All Bookstore Employees

From: The Author of the Very Funny, Very Informative, Very Cheap "Tournaments, Cash Games and Embarrassing Social Gas"

Subject: Refunds

All,

There will be no refunds for this very funny, very informative, very mediocre product. When the customer tries to return it, just be kind and polite. Most of this author's readers are borderline psychotic. Not psychic. Psychotic. Do not panic. Relax. Look the person in the eye and say in a very polite voice, "I'm sorry sir, there are no refunds for this literary piece. Now please get out of my fuckin' face so I can serve our next customer." And then with authority, yell, "Next!" Eye contact with the subject is imperative during this conversation- or confrontation, depending on your point of view. If the subject's eyes start getting a "glazed look" and he adjusts his backpack, and the small device in his hand looks less and less like an iPod and more and more like a detonator, call your manager. The no refund policy will still stand, but buying him a latte at Starbucks isn't out of the question. End of memo.

Yours in Christ,

Tony Korfman

These are the kind of memos that people read. And re-read. They are simple. They are direct. They are terrifying. But they get the job done. They convey to the low-ranking, $7 an hour employee how to handle a situation when it arises. And they let the reader know that you, as the all powerful, all knowing, all loving executive, have their best interest at heart. And that you care for them. Hence, the ending. Yours in Christ. Just in case of a worse case scenario. There's nothing safer and more calming than to read or say "Yours in Christ" right before you're blown to smithereens. But that's worst case. There's like 100,000 bookstores that carry this book. And worse case, maybe 4 or 5 that will have a psychotic person return this book. Thousands of psychotics may *want* to return it, but only 4 or 5 will remember where they bought it. And out of those 4 or 5, maybe 2 will have detonators (the other 3 will have forgotten them at home or lost them). Out of the two that brought the detonators with them, I guarantee one of them won't work. I mean, we're talking about a psycho wiring a detonator. Come on folks. Some of the wires have to be backwards or the wrong color. And we all know from watching numerous movies that colors on wires are very important to allow the bomb squad the opportunity to disarm the device with 7 seconds left. And no detonator maker worth his salt would think of using the same color wire for the whole project. So the bottom line is one and only one detonator will work. And it's just possible that that guy forgot his backpack. But if he didn't, and he has the detonator- well, bucko- you just hit the lottery. One out of a hundred thousand. I guess you should have stayed in school. I wish I had stayed in school. And at least took a computer course. So I could decipher one of the memos I received when I was at the Edgewater. It was from "Corporate IT". Let's all say this together. Big fuckin' deal. Corporate memos from the IT- the computer geek part of a company- are never fun, are never clear, are never understandable and are never read. Here's an actual memo from an actual person:

Subject: CMS Account Merge Issues- Response Requested

Importance: High

All,

CIT is working toward a fix for the Merge issue that all properties are experiencing, in the meantime we would like to ask for your input on a temporary solution to eliminate customer inconveniences due to incomplete merges.

We have two issues happening:

1) Once a customer was issued a One Club Card, that OCR # went to CDS as a recognized and accepted OCR

due to the prefix. CMS users have been merging duplicate accounts at properties when the customer is not in front of them to turn in their cards and receive a new card, which is attached to the surviving account.

Resulting issue: This allows the customer to play on the card that was attached to the now deleted account but has an acceptable prefix so the Slot system will not show on the reader Invalid Card. The ratings are not posted to the customer account because the OCR # is not attached to the surviving account.

2) A property finds two locally enrolled duplicate accounts, and merges one account into the other. Another property has the now deleted account locally enrolled, but not the surviving account. The merge process currently enrolls the surviving account, but does not merge the existing account, which is deleted at the Central Server into the newly enrolled surviving account. We have found cases where the survivor was not locally enrolled when it should have.

Resulting issue: This causes the existing account that has been deleted at the Central Server to give a "Customer # Not Found" or "Amount Exceeds Available Cash Value" message the first time a user tries to update it, but you can print a card from it without knowing the account does not exist at the Central Server.

Our thoughts are should we hide the F9 Combine Accts function key from Option 14 Update Existing Customer to prevent merges until the merge issue is fixed. It is possible to hide the F9 key on certain

Menus such as Player Club and Marketing, but leave it on Credit for emergency merges. This would not mean the Club calls Credit to merge customers but for emergency Credit Acct merges. These may also fail so CIT would still need to be notified if problems exist on accounts after a merge is performed. Please respond with your thoughts on this subject.

Thank you,

My immediate thoughts were that: 1) The writer of this memo needed a fuckin' enema- STAT! and 2) The writer of this memo needed a fuckin' enema- STAT! I actually read it twice trying to understand even one line. I'm thinking, "Are the person that wrote this and I from the same species?" If you're ever near a computer tech while they are saying the Pledge of Allegiance, they say, "One nation under Google, with liberty and justice for all." That's the reason I've never had a computer in my office. Many people have asked, and now everyone knows. They have their place in business, but not in my office. Not on my watch. No fuckin' way.

Random Thought

There are two poker sites that can keep you busy for many hours for no charge. They are fun because they have a ton of information and you can learn all the percentages of certain hands to improve your game. The sites are:

Cardplayer.com

Lasvegasvegas.com

Write those down on the palm of your hand so you'll have them tomorrow when you're sitting in your cubicle at work looking for a diversion. You won't be disappointed, and they are both free! I know it's hard to fuckin' believe. Finally, a free lunch.

The Really Big Fuckin' Kahuna

David Sedaris is a very funny writer. He writes funny shit and has quite a few books out. He talks about a device called a "Stadium Pal" in one of his essays, and it's a hilarious piece. I actually bought one just to see the fuckin' thing. It's a bag you strap to your leg and a tube runs up your leg and the end of it is like a condom and you attach it to your "thing" or your "Johnson" as it is commonly referred to. By doing this you are able to watch a complete ball game in a stadium without missing a pitch. Thereby, the name "Stadium Pal". David writes about his experience using it. It's really fuckin' funny. He writes these types of essays in his books. Another one is about the time he was at a backyard picnic at a friend's house and numerous people were there. He had to go to the bathroom to pee and he announced it to everyone before he left the picnic area. When he got to the bathroom, he locked the door and turned around to face the toilet. He was shocked to see this absolutely fuckin' enormous turd floating in the bowl. It was the size of a huge burrito or a small howitzer. It looked like "The Incredible Hulk" had lost one of his arms. He obviously did what any one of us would do and he flushed the toilet. The water filled up and this huge, pulsating turd floated to the top and the water receded down the sewer, but the turd stayed in place in all of its turdy splendor. And then the inevitable happened. An "Oh my God" moment, or a "Holy Shit" moment depending on how you look at it. Someone was trying to turn the doorknob and come in. Then they knocked and said, "You almost done in there?" Well, panic set in. There weren't many options, but he entertained them all. The bathroom was in back of the house facing the picnic and patio area, so bundling that Great Dane up and throwing it out the window would have definitely brought the line of people waiting for their BBQ hamburgers and hot dogs to an abrupt halt. It was obvious by the next knock on the door that the person waiting on the other side was also in distress. The options had narrowed after discovering the exit via the window strategy wouldn't work. Anyway, he wound up unscrewing the handle of the plunger and stabbing it until it broke up, constantly flushing and reflushing until it all disappeared. It's a hilarious story by a hilarious writer, David Sedaris.

I bring this story up because I was at Caesar's Palace playing a tournament a few weeks ago and the Poker Room bathroom only has one handicap stall, which I use since I broke my foot in 5 places and am temporarily handicapped. I hobble around on a crutch and when I take a piss I need to hold on to a rail, which the handicap stall has, since my balance is not good. It's break time during a tournament and of course there is the usual mad dash to the men's room. I hobble in and make my way to the handicap stall. I locked the door, turned around, and instantly felt David Sedaris' pain. There was a dump in the bottom of the toilet that can only have been put there by a group of farm animals. It was incredible. No four humans collectively could have carried this much waste around in their colon. It was impossible. It trembled. It pulsated. It actually winked at me. It was fuckin' huge. Think breadbox. Think African python. And it was full of corn. Yes, Corn! The human body does not digest corn and it looked like this mother fucker ate a cornfield. Plus a load of corn dogs, corn flakes and corn nuts. I've never seen so much fuckin' corn. I was in awe. I was mortified. I was mesmerized. I was circumcised (well, many years ago). I've been naturalized, criticized and fortified. And let's not forget stupefied. As you can see I've been "fied" numerous fuckin' times (I must ask my therapist about these tangents). Then it fuckin' came. I couldn't believe it. A rattle at the handicap stall door. "Anyone in there?" someone said. "Fuck yes there's someone in here." Do I flush, or run? Or both? Or leave a note (I am a good note leaver). WWDSD? (What would David Sedaris do?) Fuck Sedaris. What would Jesus do? I wonder if they had corn at the last supper. This was like all the disciples took a dump in the same toilet. Back then they didn't have to worry about plumbing capacity or flushing. Most of them probably didn't wipe. Or wash their hands before making the pita bread. Oh God! I am a sick fuck. Back to Caesar's. I had to think fast. Running was out of the question. I had broken my foot in 5 places and was on a crutch. I'm a huge guy. I wear bright colors. I am easily identifiable. The word would surely spread through the poker room and might even anger the poker gods who have been pissed off enough with me. How many 2-7 and 10-3 offsuits could one person endure. The last time I saw a pair of Kings was during the Eisenhower Administration. So the answer wasn't easy. I had to open the stall door, face my opponent, look him in the eye and convince him he really doesn't have to go to the bathroom at this particular time. There are only a few stalls in the Caesar's Palace Poker Room and Race and Sports Book bathroom. And like I said before, only one fuckin' handicap stall. And the nightclub "Pure" is a stone's throw away. They must have figured that the degenerates who play poker and bet on horses and go to nightclubs and drink a lot don't go to the bathroom much. They never figured on poker tournaments that have 300 people playing in them and they all get the same 10-minute break every 2 hours. They never figured on the 150 people playing cash games at the same time the tournaments were being played. They never figured on the popular nightclub adjacent to the poker room, with a huge crowd of people drinking, using the same bathroom. They never figured. Another knock- more pronounced, more desperate, "What are you doing in there?" the guy said. "I'm almost done," I said. I held my breath and said a small prayer to all of my gods that I worship including Catholic Gods, Mormon Gods (there's a lot of Mormons and they might be right) and of course Poker Gods. I pushed the flusher and the fuckin' bowl filled with water and it got right to the tippy tippy top of the bowl and nothing fuckin' happened. Nothing. The 20-foot fuckin' python embedded in a cornfield was still staring at me. Another knock- and I didn't have to look, but I just knew this guy knocking had to be a crippled fuck, more crippled than me, and probably in a wheelchair or one of those fuckin' scooters that has "I'm fat and old and need to drive a scooter" written all over it. I looked around for a window and I really didn't give a fuck if it was one that faced the patio or the picnic area, but there are no windows in bathroom Hell. I only had one move. I had to revert to the David Sedaris book of "What to do when confronted with enormous turds". There was no plunger handle to bail me out. I had to make due with the equipment I had available. I had keys and money in one pocket and I knew they were out of the question. I had my favorite pen in my shirt pocket. This had to be it. I took my trusty pen with the Colorado Belle logo from Laughlin, Nevada. My buddy Curtis Jacks has been down in Laughlin for many years as the Belle's General Manager and he gave me a really nice pen when he ordered them as a promotion. I took out the pen and repeatedly stabbed at this mass of human leftovers to break it up. The guy who did this must have lost 30 pounds when he left this load behind. I kept flushing until everything was gone but the pen. I said my tearful goodbyes to my pen that had served me so well for so long and flushed it down the toilet like a father flushes his son's beloved goldfish when it dies. It was an emotional farewell that was loudly interrupted by another banging on the door and a desperate plea for entrance. It was time for my exit and I swung the door open and I came face to face with a really pissed off guy in a wheelchair. I said, "I'm sorry it took so long," and he said, "Fuck you!" I said, "Have a nice day," as he rolled past me, my large boot cast I wear, and my crutch. As I left the men's room after scrubbing like I was going into surgery, I thought I could faintly hear someone in a stall munching on corn.....

Random Thought

When in doubt, do the right thing. All the rest of the time do whatever the fuck you want.

An Evening With The "Stars"

On October 7th The Venetian hosted it's first Super Bounty Tournament in their open, spacious, smoke-free poker room. There were about 300 participants and 25-30 people from the Professional Poker Players Organization. They all wore Professional Poker Player shirts, and for some of them, it was the first time in weeks they had a clean shirt on. Most of them were accessible, cordial, friendly, fun and smelled pretty good. The format was a standard tournament format with a $200 buy-in that gave you $3,500 in chips. Every table had one or two pros or "recognizable" names on it. Daniel Negreanu's table had the most attention by the crowd. He was his usual "chatty" self and was clocked at 155 words a minute with gusts up to 170. I was at a table with Hoyt Corkins sitting on one side of me and Mike Caro, The Mad Genius, two seats to my right. I kept putting my hand on Hoyt's knee and he seemed to enjoy it. John Juanda, Phil Laak and Mike Caro all begrudgingly took pictures with me. Phil Laak said "God bless you" to me 27 times. And he kept calling me "bro". The "God bless you" made me wonder if he had access to my medical charts. I called my mom when I got home to check on the "bro" part. She assured me that I was her only begotten son and that the $50 I send her monthly is both appreciated and due. She lives with my sister Trudy in Sacramento and is well taken care of. I told her the $50 will be sent as soon as she accounts for the last $50 I sent her. Trudy does accounting and forgot to send me the spreadsheet. I was sorry to hear that Phil was not really my "bro" and he was probably just using it as an endearing term to a guy that looks like he's on his last leg. He didn't have on his "Unabomber" outfit so most people just thought he was another degenerate poker fuck with dirty jeans. He was very nice and did not get provoked easily. I like that in a person. He was very clean cut. No earphones, no sunglasses, no sweatshirt, no visible wires, no detonator device- just Phil Laak the humanoid.

Doyle Brunson came in on his little scooter. Doyle is about 75 years old, but parts of him look a lot younger. He has really great teeth. I mean really really straight, shiny, perfect fuckin' teeth. If I had Doyle's teeth, I would post a security guard next to the glass I kept them in at night. They are very very expensive looking. They would make a fantastic card cover. I talk a lot about him in this book because he is the Godfather of Poker. And I saw the movie The Godfather, and believe me, everything I write about Doyle will be respectful and kind. Well, almost everything. You know me. Sometimes I can't help myself. I introduced myself and told him I really enjoyed his first book. The Book of Genesis. I especially liked the line "Let there be light". Thank God Jamie Gold didn't say that. He might have changed his mind and we'd all be living in the dark. Mike Sexton, The Ambassador of Poker, was also at the Venetian tournament. He had his sleeves rolled up and he looked like he was looking for an arm wrestling match. He was very kind, very nice and said, "Hi, I'm Mike Sexton- The Ambassador of Poker," 627 times. If I was going to pick an Ambassador of Poker, I would pick Mike Sexton. It was obvious to all he doesn't go anywhere without his makeup and hair person.

Scotty Nguyen sat down at my table about 10 minutes before I moved all-in with A-J suited. It always feels so much more comforting to be suited when you go all-in. Until, of course, the flop comes. Anyway, Scotty was having a really, really great time. He likes to have fun, drink, talk to everyone, drink, show off his jewelry, and did I mention- drink? I asked him to let me know when he was leaving so I could call the wife and get the kids off the sidewalk. Scotty wears a lot of jewelry. He had 2 or 3 gold chains on. I called it his Mr. T Starter Kit. He laughed and called me "baby". The sports book had the over-under on him saying "baby" during the tournament at 794. The over won, easily. That's about how many times he told us his watch cost $73,000. Plus tax and tip. Scotty seemed very nice. He was having fun and everyone around him was having a good time. You can't ask for any more than that. Todd Brunson was walking around and it was obvious this kid hasn't missed too many buffets. They say that a camera puts on about 20 pounds when you're on television. Not in Todd's case. People kept tripping on his ponytail. He looked like he could brew incredible farts if encouraged. This was a great event and the Venetian scored a homerun sponsoring it. They have a very conscientious, friendly staff. And excellent cocktail waitresses. Everyone that attended the event had a happy ending. I know I did.

Random Thought

One thing really stands out about the nice guys, the respected guys, the classy guys of poker. When they win a really big, important hand, they don't get hysterical, they don't pound their chest, they don't high five the crowd. They may fart- but that's acceptable.

His Name Was Jacop

How rampant is Hold 'em? How far reaching is it? Take the case of Jacop Weisman. His name has been changed to protect his parents. And his grandmother. His actual name is Jacob Weisman. But you didn't read that here. Jacop plays poker at family gatherings and wins. He plays at home games and wins. He plays at Internet sites and wins. He loves to play Hold 'em. His parents limit his play so as not to interfere with his schoolwork. Jacop is very bright. He's very smart. He's very cute. Jacop is 8. Eight. Ocho. As in right before 9. I can just picture the little guy sitting in front of his computer with his cup of coffee, three sugars, two creams. How rampant is Hold 'em? How far reaching is it? You figure it out, pal. Jacob's grandpa was my favorite Jewish friend. I have one favorite friend in each of the 4,350 religions. And one favorite friend in each of the 712 races. And creeds? I don't know how many favorite friends I have in creeds because I don't know what a creed is. Anyway, my favorite Jewish friend was Jacob's grandpa Bernie. I use to call him Uncle Bernie. If Uncle Bernie was in the living room and called his wife, Myra, while she was in the kitchen, Myras from as far as 5 miles away would turn their collective heads. Uncle Bernie had a very powerful New York voice. Many New Yorkers have that "booming" type penetrating voice. It's probably from all those years of living in New York and yelling for help. And for taxis. And for hot dogs in Yankee Stadium. I love hot dogs in baseball stadiums. Especially the last game of the season when they've been in the steamer for the whole year. Now that is tender eatin' my friend.

Anyway, Bernie and his family owned and operated the world's largest newsstand called "World Book and News" in Hollywood, California near Hollywood and Vine. Myra and the kids still operate it and that's where I'm going to start my book tour. In memory of Bernie. And, of course, it's the greatest location in the world. There's got to be 75 million people an hour that walk by the store. I'm only looking for 1 million to stop and buy the book. That's not asking too much. I'll set up a nice table with a lot of schmaltz. That's a Jewish word. It means something Jewish. Anyway, it sounds Jewish. Like my name. I was only 2 letters away from being Jewish.

Kaufman would have made me Jewish. I asked my mom when I was younger, "Mom, you sure we're not Jewish?" She said, "You're not Jewish. You don't want to be Jewish. The food is terrible." So I grew up eating Italian food. My mom is 100% Italian. My dad was German. Once in a while we had German pancakes, but the other 99.9% of the time- Italian. And the traditions between the Jewish and Italian people are quite different. When Italians die, they take forever to bury their dead. Sometimes weeks. They have the wakes. And the mass. And the parades. And the celebrations at the Irish pub. And they're not even Irish. It goes on and on. The Jewish people, on the other hand, bury their dead very quickly. I mean really really quickly. I use to tell Uncle Bernie as he grew older, "Don't take any long naps." Twice he woke up with a guy standing in his living room holding a shovel. Three times he woke up to the reading of his will. Uncle Bernie left his mark on everyone he came in contact with. He would have been very proud of his grandson's poker playing skills. (Jacop's house was being surrounded by Child Protective Services as this was being written. I had nothing to do with that. Absolutely nothing. Well, almost nothing. I hate getting beat by 8 year olds).

Random Thought

My evaluation of people is pretty simple. Are you white, black, Muslim, Jewish, fat, bald, crippled? I really don't give a fuck. My measuring stick is not very long. My criteria is simple. Are you kind? Are you caring? Are you fun? Are you nice? That's about it. I'll even take 3 out of the 4. Like a wrestling match.

Embarrassing Social Gas

Once in a while you sit next to someone who emits embarrassing social gas. Yes, they fart. It's a nice way of saying it. I had a dog once that could clear out a room. He was great when the "relatives that would never leave" would come over uninvited and sit on your couch for hours. We would feed Milow, our giant French poodle, my wife's meatloaf and boy the fun would start. It would take about 20 minutes for the eruptions to begin. Twenty great minutes of anticipation. You see, my wife's meatloaf, and I say this in the kindest sense, is a weapon of mass destruction. F.D.R. said it best in his famous speech that was actually edited. He said, "The only thing we have to fear is fear itself." The rest of that sentence, which was edited, was, "...and Linda Korfman's Meatloaf." When I married my wife, I loved meatloaf. She would make it 4 times a week. The other 3 days we had leftovers. But every meatloaf was different. I love my meat well done. Some chefs won't cook a steak well done. They insist you will spoil the meat by having it cooked so much. It won't be juicy. It won't be tender. I ordered a steak once and I could tell the chef was one of those kinds of people who thought **he** knew what was best for me and cooked the steak the way he thought it should be cooked. Not the way I wanted it cooked. Anyway, this fuckin' steak was absolutely fuckin' raw. I swear if we had called a vet we could have saved it. It wasn't rare. It was raw. It winked at me. Then it ate my vegetables. My wife has never winked at me. And she's never eaten my vegetables. She was my official meatloaf maker. I say "was" because she doesn't cook much anymore. She's paid her dues and for the past few years since the kids have all grown up, we eat out a lot. What amazed me about her meatloaf was her ability to make every single one different. I was sure that her meatloafs would someday make the cover of Scientific Journal. Or Mechanic Illustrated. One thing I know for sure, her meatloaf glowed in the dark. She had the uncanny ability to mix beef, lamb, pork, breadcrumbs and eggs and get electricity. Sometimes it would just sit there like an incredibly large burrito and pulsate. We had scientists, scientologists and clergymen knock on our door (we had no doorbell- we were poor) and want to talk to her. NASA called. NASCAR called. The NBA, NBC, NRA, NSA and the CIA called. And the nasty guy who lived next door called. His calls had nothing to do with her meatloaf. He was a heavy breather. But it broke up the day. Dog trainers called when they heard that we had a very high success rate of her meatloaf breaking our dog's habit of begging for food at the table. Except for Milow.

We gave Milow the nickname "Meatloaf" because of his iron stomach and ability to eat and digest large quantities of my wife's recipe. Every time she turned around, Meatloaf would get another large portion of my wife's creation from one of our plates. We owe him a deep debt of gratitude. And probably our lives. The thing that amazed me most about my wife's meatloaf, or any dinner she cooked, was once it got in you, it immediately wanted to get out. To this day I thank our giant Standard Poodle for his life long service to our family. We actually had him cremated and he sits on our mantle, still faintly emitting some of the gasses he was so famous for. He reminds me a lot of a guy I used to play poker with when I was in college. I always hung around with older guys and every Saturday night we would gather at a buddy of mine's house- Dan Young. Dan was a worker at the same grocery store I worked at and through him I met Louie who was a mailman. Louie had 6 or 8 kids (he was never sure) and would actually bring home magazines he was supposed to deliver on his route. He would read them and then deliver them a few days later. Who was the wiser? The only problem was when Louie had the magazines at home they were sometimes used by the kids for placemats. It's hard to explain to the subscribers why your magazine gets delivered with marinara sauce or mustard on it. But Louie would just shrug his shoulders and wipe off the stain as best he could. Louie was a champion when it came to shrugging his shoulders. And farting. He was incredible. When you have 7 guys in a smoke filled room all laughing and drinking and smoking and playing poker, and you have the ability to clear out the room by farting, you, my friend, are a fuckin' champion. Forget Muhammad Ali, forget Babe Ruth, forget Mickey Mantle. You are the champion of the world. Louie's farts would linger. And linger. Dan's wife Joy would go into the kitchen for days after we finished playing poker, looking for rotten meat. Cleaning out the fridge. Scrubbing the stove. Looking for the source of the smell. I think Dan's kitchen was painted more times than the Golden Gate Bridge. Louie left his mark. On all of us. His spirit is still with us and so is his smell. I think it's still in my pores.

Meatloaf, our poodle, had a lot of Louie in him. Louie had never eaten my wife's meatloaf, but if he had I'm sure the C.I.A. would have kidnapped him and used him in any part of the world where we had a problem. Sometimes people would come over to play poker who hadn't played with us before, and their reaction was astonishing. Their eyes would burn, their throat would close up and sometimes they would sob uncontrollably. And Louie hadn't even switched gears yet. He was in his warm-up mode. He hadn't even gotten to half time or the seventh inning stretch, and the fuckin' paint was peeling off the kitchen walls. Louie was in a poker room one time and his gas was so bad the oxygen masks deployed from the poker room ceiling and he set off the sprinklers. If I was unlucky enough to sit next to him at the weekly home game, I would carry a canary. If the canary keeled over, I knew it was time to run. The guys adored and admired Louie. He was the greatest. Louie never made the cover of any magazines. But he delivered a lot of them. Stains and all. I miss Louie......

Random Thought

I've always had the feeling my mom and dad didn't like me. One time they dropped me off at a cockfight with a note attached to my lapel. My sister was in the back seat of the car laughing her ass off. It was obvious to me my family didn't want me. I was very upset, sobbing uncontrollably and very confused. I felt a very real sense of abandonment. Fortunately, I was 24 and took a cab home. But family dinners were never the same.

Who the Fuck Am I?

George Carlin is a funny fuck. He writes his own shit and his delivery is fuckin' funny. I saw him do a standup routine that had a segment that started out with: I'm a modern man- a man for the new millennium. Smoke free, drug free, fat free. And it goes on for 10 minutes. It's great. He got me thinking. What kind of guy am I? So since he inspired me to write this, I guess I owe him. Thanks George. You're a funny fuck.

I'm Tony Korfman- I eat, sleep, breathe and bathe on a daily basis. I don't upload, download or freeload. I like sports, have had warts and change my shorts, at least weekly. I don't swim, gym and am definitely not slim. I don't smoke, I'm not broke and I don't choke when the pressure's on. I like cars, candy bars and to look at the stars. Don't fuck with my space, in my place, get in my face or talk race. I don't jog, blog, eat frog, clog or keep a log. I play poker, with or without a joker, won't sit next to a smoker and enjoy watching Al Roker. I don't like jerks, quirks and my hot dog always has the works. I get mad, sad, glad, never get caught up in a fad and once helped a kid named Chad. And I miss my dad. I like rentals, yentils, lentils and carry credentials. I love my mom, never bought a CD ROM and grew up worrying about the atomic bomb. I don't fly, lie or spy, but I did have a sty in my eye, once. I diet, don't like to fry it and I like my peace and quiet. I love my kids, their kids, and my wife, my life. I'm a leader, a greeter, never a cheater and not a bleeder. I like sunflower seeds, good deeds, moral creeds, my wife's steeds and I make good reads. I surround myself with people who are caring, sharing, sometimes daring, always smart and sometimes fart. I scrutinize, don't generalize, sometimes fantasize and try not to plagiarize (I said "try" not to). I'm not political, analytical, cynical or critical. I don't like junk food, junk cars, junk bonds, junk collectors or junk mail. I enjoy feeding fish, feeding ducks and feeding quail. I also enjoy them barbequed. But I don't hunt. I like oil wells, water wells and Wells Fargo. I'm a good neighbor, a good friend, a good leader, a good spouse and good for the economy. I pay well, don't smell and never tell. I take power naps, I don't read maps, when I play poker I set traps, I get sad when I hear "TAPS". I give, I forgive, I've been forgiven. I love, I trust, I believe, I grieve. My attitude is always gratitude. I'm always grateful, never hateful. I am privileged and thankful. I try and avoid fast food, fast lanes and fast crowds. I'm among the big tippers, I wear slippers and I've never worn flippers. I'm the real deal, I like a good meal, I never steal, my word is my seal. I'm solid, I'm steady, I'm ready, I'm true down to the core. When the end is near, I'll have no fear, I won't talk to a seer, I won't drink a beer. I won't scream and yell, I don't believe in Hell. Our Hell is on earth, we've all struggled since birth, we try to shake and jive, we all strive, but no one leaves this third rock from the Sun alive. I don't do drugs, don't like bugs and once knew a girl named Scruggs. Friends influence your thoughts, your deeds, your actions, your life. Mine have. Yours will too. I'm funny, I'm sunny, I give away money, my friends say I'm a dummy. They say there will always be the needy, the greedy, the seedy and I can't make a difference. I think I can. I think I have. I know one thing for sure as I listen to the radio and sing along in my rattling jar that is my old convertible car. I did it my way. And most of the time I think I got it right. I'm Tony Korfman. And not only did I approve this message- I wrote it.

We Miss You Benny

The day the music died. The lyrics to an old song that talked about the deaths of three rock and roll stars who died in a plane crash many years ago. The day the music died in the poker world was in 2004 when the last World Series of Poker was held at Binion's Horseshoe in downtown Las Vegas. Enter Harrah's Corporation who bought the World Series of Poker and turned it into the giant cash cow we see and will continue to experience and see from now on. Hopefully Harrah's, in it's infinite "accountant mentality" wisdom, will try and improve the bad experiences so many dealers and customers experienced in the last World Series of Poker held at the Rio. At least I think it was the Rio. It was held in a huge convention / cavern / tent type room that had so many disgruntled people in it there was actually a storm cloud forming over tables 101 through 125. I understand that a type of player's union is forming to try and negotiate with Harrah's for some rule changes that would or could benefit both players and stockholders. Because, my dear friends, that is what it's all about. Stockholders. Money. And, of course, did I mention, Money? Come to think of it, that's what everything is about. Money. Everything else is conversation. Actually, there are a lot of things in life that aren't about money. In fact there are hundreds of things. I just can't think of any right now. But I will. I promise…

P.S. I didn't write this book for the money. Even though your money is not refundable, I didn't write it for the money. I wrote it for… fun. Yeah, that's it. I wrote it for fun. I spent 700 hours of my lonely fuckin' life writing this for fun. And, of course, for the money. You knew that anyway. But I'll spend it wisely. I promise.

NakedPoker.com- You Got to be Fuckin' Kidding

NakedPoker.com is a new online poker site launched on July 7th, 2006. What next? RetiredHookers.com? Over300pounds.com? We already have DoylesRoom.com (for those of us in the decomposing stage). Pamela's Room, named after Pamela Anderson, should have been called Youwon'tbelievethesizeofmyfuckin'tits.com. NakedPoker.com is not all about tits and ass according to its founder Ron (I'm all about tits and ass) Jeremy. I say, beware of anyone that has two first names for their first and last name. Especially if they're from Ohio. I don't know if Ron's from Ohio, but I'm really dubious of anyone that is from a state that has 3 vowels out of its 4 letters. But at the end of the day, NakedPoker.com meshes sex and poker together. The site features topless women in high heels instead of the normal topless middle-aged men in high heels (my high heels kill me every time I wear them. I don't know how you girls do it. Day after day. Night after night. Trick after trick.). A new version of the software will give you an option to change the size of the dealer's breasts. But again, the marketing director does not want you to think that the site is all about T and A. Or breasts. It's a poker site first. A poker site where players can enjoy beautiful women while playing with themselves. Excuse me. Playing poker. I'm sure every wife of every poker playing husband will put the software under her husband's Christmas tree. Or possibly up his ass if he buys it for himself. But women will just have to understand that their boyfriends and husbands have needs that go beyond poker. At some point in time it's not Doyle Brunson that their men will look up to, and enjoy watching move "all-in" in a tournament hand where millions are at stake. It will be a stunning blond beauty with huge tits and- you got the idea. I'm sure the wives and girlfriends in America will embrace this one. Big time. NakedPoker.com. Coming to a computer near you.

Random Thought

The problem with tournaments is that you might be trapped next to a player for many many hours. At times it can seem like an eternity. I'm sitting next to a guy at a tournament at the Bellagio and this mother fucker just wouldn't shut up. Somewhere in his ongoing bullshit about him telling me how great he is, how great he plays and how much money he has, I lost consciousness. I can hang in there with the best of them, but listening to this guy drone on and on- fuckin' painful. I'm thinking, this guy probably hasn't had a blowjob in so long, he's forgotten how it tastes. Resistance was futile. Until the kid in the 4 seat busted him. God bless every kid in every 4 seat in the world.

Egg On My Face

Last night I played in a $540 buy-in tournament at the
Mandalay Bay. The crew from the Bellagio goes over to the Mandalay
Bay to conduct their tournaments, so it was run very professionally. I
played with a kid named Steve P., a tournament addict. There's a lot of
them. Their life is tournaments. Early in the tournament, a player
called him with 4-6 suited and there were 3 people in the pot. After the
flop, 2 of the players were all-in and Steve P. called and had some
chips left over. When the hands were shown and the river card came,
Steve P. didn't improve on his pocket pair of Queens, the guy with the
4-6 had 2 pairs- 4's and 6's and the other guy made a flush. Steve P.
went nuts. Not because the guy made a flush on him, but because the
other guy called with 4-6. Even though 4-6 lost the pot along with
Steve P., Steve talked about that hand and how bad that guy played for
the next 6 hours. He wouldn't stop. Of course, I didn't help the
situation as I egged him on and on. I love chaos. He finally lost it and
said he was going to "crack me like a fuckin' egg". Me. Nice guy me.
He was showing a complete lack of respect. So it was with tremendous
respect that about one hour later I put him out of his misery when he
went all-in on a short stack. But, I didn't say a word. I have too much
class. Not really. I just didn't want him going to his car and coming
back with a loaf of Jewish rye and banging me over the head with it
and cracking my head open like a fuckin' egg. Even though I love
Jewish rye.

Random Thought

If you can't be kind, at least have the common decency to be
vague.

What Would You Rather Have?

What would you rather have? A great looking SUV that has a lot of space, plenty of headroom, comfortable seats, a powerful engine and 30 coats of lacquer paint that makes your neighbors wring their hands with envy; Or a car called a Hybrid that you need to take yoga lessons to get into- a death trap if you or your family are ever in it during an accident, that your neighbors point and giggle at, that you have to make 3 trips back and forth to the grocery store because there's no room in the fuckin' thing? Oh, the Hybrid gets better mileage. And it doesn't cause so much damage to the ozone layer. So if all of us drove a Hybrid, the ozone layer won't disappear in 3 or 4 million years. Of course the price tag may be out of reach for some. If the ozone layer was so important, why doesn't the government give us a coupon worth $25,000 to buy a Hybrid? I guess it's not that big a deal. I think the really big question here is: how will it affect your ability to breathe and, of course, get to the final table? It won't. Fuck Hybrids.

What would you rather have? A desert area crawling with rattle snakes, spiders and, of course, the most feared creature in existence to the American builder, the American way and the American family- the Desert Tortoise; Or own a lovely home in a lovely subdivision on a lovely street with a lovely kitchen and a lovely pot of Desert Tortoise stew on the lovely stove? What would you rather have?

What would you rather have? A delicious, thick steak marinated in teriyaki sauce and grilled to perfection on the BBQ grill, smothered in onions and mushrooms with a slab of butter or a chunk of bleu cheese on top of it and 4 crispy onion rings riding sidesaddle; Or an organic carrot? What would you rather have? If you picked the carrot, and I know someone has, please, I'm begging you, please seek help immediately, keep away from sharp objects and get rid of all the ammo you have in the house. Keep the guns. If someone breaks in, they won't know if the gun has bullets in it or not. When you encounter an intruder, just say to him or her (her? Yeah, sure), "I have a gun and I'm going to give you 1 minute to run away before I start shooting. I swear. And when you're running, just because you don't hear bullets whizzing by your ear doesn't mean I'm not pulling the trigger. I will be pulling the trigger. I don't have bullets, but I will still pull the trigger." If the intruder asks why you don't have bullets, tell him, "Because I answered 'carrots'."

This ends "What Would You Rather Have?" I have to go to church.

Card Covers, Voodoo Mary and Stackers

I'm going to make this really simple. A very simple rule. Don't fuck with anyone that has voodoo-like material in front of them. Especially if they have a lot of stuff that at first glance looks like an innocent card cover, just sitting there waiting to be gently placed on top of a pocket pair of Aces, but on second glance is the shrunken skull of a gnome-like creature that you could swear just fuckin' winked at you (I'm going to use "gnome-like creature" a lot of times in this book. I like the sound of it. It's 3 words long, so it takes a lot of space, and I think it's humorous. You have my permission to use it in your everyday vocabulary if you wish. We may be able to start a national trend. Of course I realize we will be pissing off the gnome population of the world, but what can I say? I'm sorry? I apologize? I really feel for you that you were born a gnome? Everyone has disabilities. No matter how great they look. You just can't see many of the disabilities of most people. They might be depressed, mentally unbalanced, lactose intolerant or bedwetters. You, my dear gnomes, at least have your disability right out there in the open. And you are able to climb on the Disability Act bandwagon and demand lower toilets, lower sinks and smaller portions at Denny's. Besides that, I'm trying to give you national recognition with a "saying" that will become part of the American language. "Gnome-like creatures" will then be used by men, women, children, clergymen, educators and, of course, gnomes. So you can see, my heart, my soul, my liver and my pancreas are all in the right place. So if there are still some gnome-like creatures that still have a problem with the phrase, go fuck yourselves. I think this is the longest parenthesis ever used in a literary work. Records are being made here, my friend). (Actually, Korfman did not research his final sentence in his last parenthesis adequately. The actual record for a parenthesis comment was in 1951 in a school in the Bronx. P.S. 67 became famous when a 9th grader went on a tangent rampage and actually wrote a parenthesis with 37,462 words in it. The student was rushed to New York Medical Center where he was sedated, medicated and berated. He was enrolled at the Betty Ford Clinic for "parenthesis abusers" and now, many years later, runs the Parenthesis Abuser Hotline. He doesn't want his name published even though he holds this prestigious record. He has been described as pleasant, friendly, outgoing and gnome-like.) So I get busted out of a tournament at the Venetian and I'm watching my buddy play on another table, and I've told him a million times, there are certain people you don't fuck with at the table. You leave them the fuck alone. You don't agitate, aggravate or even "kid" with them. One of those people is Voodoo Mary. And who is Ken (not his real name. His real name is Kenny) fuckin' with? Voodoo Mary. Mary is one-of-a-kind. You can't miss her. She's a large woman with large breasts. She dresses like she's going straight from the tournament to go trick or treating. She has more artifacts, skulls, bat wings and bags of sand (at least I think it's sand) in front of her than any player I've ever seen. Why would anyone want to fuck with her? It's insane. She has this one male voodoo doll that she plays with that is anatomically correct. When she sticks her knitting needle into this doll's testicles, every man within 50 feet groans and grabs his balls. Why would you fuck with someone like that? You got to be fuckin' nuts. In my opinion, though, I think the Medicine Man Mask she wears and the candles circling her hole cards are over the top. I know the Venetian stopped her from building a bonfire in the card room even though she had a permit from the county. Anyway, Kenny goes all-in on her and you can tell her irritation level rose to 9.4 (10 is when the building starts shaking). She pondered, stared at him, pondered some more and then started to shake various objects around her cards and moan some god awful Steven Spielberg sounds. I said 2 Our Fathers and 3 Hail Marys. But nothing was going to stand in her way. She called the bet and I mumbled, "Oh Fuck." Kenny looked at me and said, "I got the best of it." Those were the last intelligible words I understood before he grabbed his balls. Mary had her voodoo doll under the table and I know she was doing the "testicle stomp" on it. Kenny revealed his A-K with one hand while holding his nuts with the other. Mary turned over A-Q and smiled as crooked a smile as I've ever seen a human do and she fuckin' winked at me. The dreaded wink. The room was silent. There wasn't a cloud in the sky, a sunny, bright afternoon in Las Vegas. The Venetian card room had only been open for a few months, yet it was raining on game 66 in the poker room. The flop came 7-9-J. Mary looked constipated. She was straining. It was obvious the cheese Danish she had for lunch had her bowels pretty bound up. The turn card was a 2. Kenny was almost home. Then a Queen came on the river and Kenny *went* home. Sore nuts and all. I told him again, "Kenny, you don't fuck with Voodoo Mary."

There are certain types you leave alone. Certain people have "tells" that are screaming at you not to fuck with them. Let someone else get lucky and bust them. Let someone else endure extreme testicular pain. Maybe someone with testicular numbness. Or "numb nuts" as they were referred to in high school. Another type of player that is just screaming out to you not to fuck with him is the guy that stacks his chips perfectly. Every design is perfectly aligned with the design of the chip under it. And if he has 500 chips they are all perfect. His shirt is wrinkled, his teeth are crooked, his shorts are dirty, his breath smells, but his chips are fuckin' perfect. These people only play pocket Aces before the flop. After the flop they only play quads. And their chips are always perfect. And perfect chips mean trouble. Trouble, my friends. Right here in poker city. With a capital T and it rhymes with P and it stands for perfect. Let someone else fuck with the perfect chip stacker. Yes, folks. Someone like Voodoo Mary. And what I like to do is kind of encourage confrontations. Let me give you an example that I know will stimulate your thought process. You see, it's not necessary for you to eliminate or beat everyone in a tournament. Let other people do the work. Sometimes they need just a little nudge to get involved with mediocre hands. Also, you want to be friendly with people who play at the table. They are more apt to call you if they like you, unless you ask them not to, and then they will throw their hand away. Many times they won't fuck with your big blind if they're sitting next to you. Why would you want to steal a blind from a nice friendly guy who has his hand on your knee? No fuckin' reason in the world. Encouraging involvement doesn't really take a lot of doing. A typical conversation might go like this:

Me: Those are the most perfectly stacked chips I've ever seen. I love the architecture. Are you an architect?

Perfect Chip Stacker: Why, no. I'm not. But thank you for the compliment.

Me: It's a shame that everyone at the table doesn't feel the same way.

Perfect Chip Stacker: What do you mean?

Me: Someone just mentioned on the last break that they thought you had an obsessive compulsive disorder and that your stacks are distasteful, disgusting and repugnant. No big deal. Oh, and your underwear probably has "skidmarks".

Perfect Chip Stacker: WHAT? Who the fuck said that about my beautiful chip stacks? Who?

Me: Calm down, pal. She might hear you.

Perfect Chip Stacker: SHE? SHE? We only have one "she" at the table. The cunt in the 4 seat with the voodoo doll hanging around her fuckin' neck!

Me: I rest my case.

Perfect Chip Stacker: Next time she's in a pot, I'm going to ram my perfectly stacked chips right up her ass!

Me: I would too. She needs to be disciplined.

Within 5 to ten minutes tops, you should be shaking hands with the perfect chip stacker and wishing him well. Tournaments are won by carefully plotting a strategy as the evening wears on with only one goal in mind: to cause as much animosity between your fellow opponents as possible so they keep eliminating each other. Of course, the final table is a tougher issue. The tournament has been narrowed down to the final 10. No matter how big the tournament is, no matter how big or small the buy-ins, no matter what country you're playing in, you eventually get to the final table. The final 10. These are the people that have been through the "tournament journey" with you. The tired, the weak, the beat, the spent, the pooped, the sleepy, the exhausted 10 that have endured 12-15 hours of Hold 'em and have "made it" to the final table. The final table is always comprised of people in all shapes, sizes and odors. And the most important thing that I look for at every final table- card covers. Card covers are like people. They come in all shapes and sizes. Many players believe their card covers are lucky. People have their parish priests bless their precious card covers. I've never had any of mine blessed. Probably because I have so many favorites. I really like my July 4th chip from the old Gold Strike Inn. And my Edgewater die from a craps table. And of course the gold coin my grandpa gave me. When I die, I want to die just like my grandpa- peacefully in my sleep. Not screaming like the passengers in his car. One of my favorite people was his wife who I called "Grandma". Grandma always made me feel warm and fuzzy. She would make me these big cups of black coffee with 6 or 7 teaspoons of sugar and we would sit in the kitchen and drink coffee and eat cookies. I was only 6 years old, but the memories are precious. Looking back, I wonder if her meals and "treats" had anything to do with me weighing 350 pounds in the 3rd grade. Oh well, there was nothing better than drinking a cup of syrup with Grandma. She always said nice things to me. So when she died we had her cremated and put in an urn. A big urn. A huge urn. She was an enormous woman. Think sumo wrestler. Think King Kong. Think all 15 Baldwin brothers together. You can imagine the size of the urn. Anyway, I brought the urn with me to a tournament to use as a card cover. It was my "good luck" charm. It really pissed off the other players at the table. They finally asked me to take it off the table. It was too tall. Planes were having trouble seeing the control tower. There was no sympathy at the table. In fact, my approval rating dropped below 10%. And I'm not even Republican. I'm Catholic. Some of the time. I've been known to be Jewish if the need arises. But I've never been very popular. Even when I was a little kid my imaginary friend use to play with the kid across the street. My mom and dad took me to the carnival one time and I got lost. I was really upset and asked a policeman to help me find them. I found out at an early age that cute, blond-haired kids get treated much nicer than us fat Italian kids. I asked the nice policeman, "Do you think we'll ever find them?" The cop said, "I don't know kid. There are so many places they can hide." What a prick. We always had a dog while I was growing up. They are so friendly. They never judged me. They were always there to lick me whenever I came home. My favorite dog was Old Shep. He was $^{1}/2$ German Shepherd. That's all. He was in a wheelchair. I don't have a German Shepherd card cover- or even half of one. But I do have an enormous piggy bank that is one of my top favorites. It's pretty big. It's cumbersome. It's heavy. I keep it full of change. In case my bankroll runs low. You never know when you'll need $540 in quarters for a tournament buy-in. I am very respected in the card rooms I play in mainly because I show respect to the people in the room. Well, most of the people. The people that are nice, polite, well-mannered, well dressed and smell good. OK, so I'm respectful to about 10% of the room. My piggy bank usually doesn't bother too many people. I know it covers a big area. I know if I don't position it just right, it's hard to see the flop. I know that sometimes it covers the guy's cards next to me making his card cover useless, ineffective and, if it's a picture, my card cover leaves a big pig foot imprint on the photo. I know these things. And I feel bad about the guy having foot imprints on his family photos. I try and handle these situations with the utmost of tact, diplomacy and respect. The destruction or denting of family photos borders on the sacrilegious. So I am gentle with these people. I am respectful. I am kind. A typical conversation goes like this:

> **Opponent Sitting Next to Me:** Sir, your enormous pig card cover is also covering my hand.
>
> **Me:** And?
>
> **Opponent Sitting Next to Me:** Your card cover is covering my cards. I can't lift it up to look at my hand. Your pig is huge. And heavy.
>
> **Me:** (looking at a picture of him and his wife under the pig's left rear hoof) Looks like your pig is pretty huge also. And heavy.
>
> **Opponent Sitting Next to Me:** Sir, that's uncalled for.
>
> **Me:** You started it. If you don't make fun of my pig, I won't make fun of yours.
>
> **Opponent Sitting Next to Me:** I've only been here a few minutes and you've already insulted me, my wife and my heritage.

Me: Can I have your rack? The way you play, you won't need it.

Opponent Sitting Next to Me: I'm all-in.

Me: Call- I have the nut flush.

Opponent Sitting Next to Me: Fuck you and your pig!

Me: (yelling loudly) Seat open!

New Opponent Sitting Next to Me: Sir, your pig card cover is covering my cards.

Me: And?

As you can see, sometimes big and unusual card covers can help bust an opponent. Tournaments and cash games are getting tougher and tougher to win. And that trend will continue. People are getting more educated on the way to play. The "soft" players, the "fish", the mediocre, are becoming a rare breed. Mainly because they either learn to play better and tougher or they run out of fuckin' money. Plain and simple.

Random Thought

They say that the brain sometimes confuses fear with passion. So the next time someone bets all their chips at you, and it will cost you all your chips to call, and you already have a ton of your chips in the pot, and your tournament life is on the line if you call the bet, it's possible that you don't fear your opponent- you may just want to fuck him.

Diaries, Dairies and Uncle Sam

If you are reading this book, you probably play Hold 'em. And
if you play Hold 'em, you probably play tournaments. And if you play
tournaments, you need to buy a diary. I didn't say dairy. I'm not trying
to turn you into a dairy farmer. I hate early mornings. It's a diary you
need. A small one. A notebook will do. It doesn't have to be a leather-
bound book that looks like it should be on a bookshelf next to Chaucer
or Shakespeare with a big, heavy fuckin' lock on it. Just a small
notebook, or better yet one of those pocket size planners with the day
and date on each page. And whenever you buy into a tournament, put
down the place your playing, the time, the total buy-in and if you do a
re-buy or add-on, write that down also. This is invaluable information
in case you win a big tournament. Even if it's not real big- maybe just
a few thousand, you will still get a tax form when you get your cash.
The form they give you has more than one part. There are numerous
copies. You get one, one goes to the accounting department of the
casino, and the most important one goes to the I.R.S. If you don't
declare the income on your tax return, you are going to get a letter
from Uncle Sam. The form you give your tax guy is filed with your
return and it better match up with the forms that are being sent in by
the casinos. If you do not pay tax on your winnings, you are looking at
huge penalties, fines, interest and worst of all, possibly jail time. And
I'm not making this shit up. You are allowed to deduct your gambling
losses from your winnings. Hence the diary. You can't just say you
lost money. You have to prove it. A diary usually will be enough
documentation to show how many tournaments you have played in.
Also, save the receipts from when you enter a tournament. Put them in
a Manila envelope. Or an Italian envelope. I think Poland has
envelopes too, but they haven't perfected them. But I know they'll get
it right someday. I love their sausage. They got that right. Manila
envelopes have always been my envelope of choice. And you'll be
surprised how it begins to fill up when you put every tournament
receipt in one of them. The important thing about keeping a diary all
year long is that just in case you win a big tournament in November or
December, you'll have accurate documentation of the amount of
money you've spent for the year. You will get to write off your entry
fees and re-buys and add-ons against your winnings. For example, if

you won a tournament and were paid $100,000, you can deduct tournament entry fees for the tax year. If you spent $25,000 on tournaments, you would only pay taxes on $75,000. Check with your tax advisor in any case, but you cannot go wrong with buying a diary. Come to think of it, you probably can't go wrong if you buy a dairy either. Everyone drinks milk. I love the milk mustache commercials. Got Milk? Got Poker? Got Diary?

Random Thought

A poll amongst poker dealers was taken about who would be a better parent among professional poker players (I used "amongst" and "among" because I wasn't sure which one was correct, so I knew I'd get one right). The choices were Sam Farha, Scott Fischman, Phil Hellmuth Jr. and Mike "The Mouth" Matusow. Farha got 3% of the votes, Hellmuth 2%, Fischman 1% and we needed a Richter scale to record those who voted for Matusow. 93.7% of the dealers polled said that the kids would be better off taking their chances on the streets.

A Chip and a Chair- I Lived It

What a fuckin' day yesterday was. It was the start of the Bellagio Cup (whatever the fuck that means) and they have a tournament starting at 2 P.M. and another one at 7 P.M., and satellites before and after. I played in two tournaments and three satellites. If Betty Ford opens a clinic for tournament and satellite players, I will be the first to join. I started at 10 A.M. and got home at 4 A.M. the next morning. And I'm an old fuck. I'm beginning to realize that this is a young man's game. Earphones, sunglasses, smoky breath, bad breath, no breath- I was subjected to it all. By the way, it makes sense to wear your sunglasses upside down like Marcel Luce. There's a method to his madness. You can still see your cards clearly without the possibility of misreading your hand and still accomplish the reason you wear sunglasses to start with- to hide your eyes from telling everyone at the table you just smoked a joint. So anyways, a really really weird thing happened at the 7 P.M. tournament. I'm playing really good and having fun and harassing the most irritating players (someone has to do it), when I run into a pair of nines with my (drum roll please) Ace King suited. This was my monster hand after over 2 hours of shit. Ace King is so pretty. Especially suited. I have a new name for A-K suited. It's called a real fuckin' pretty no-pair. So I raise and pocket nines goes all-in. I go all-in and you know the rest of the story. Real fuckin' pretty no-pair gets beat. So believe it or not, I have two $25 chips left. Two fuckin' chips. I stand up ready to go. The antes are $75 and the blinds are $400 and $800. I'm done. I'm toast. I'm ready for the drive home. Valet is warming up my car. The button is to my left, then the $400 blind in the 3 seat and the $800 blind in the 4 seat. The 5 seat mucks his hand (throws it away), 6 seat mucks, 7 seat makes it $7,000, 8 seat mucks, 9 seat mucks and I look down at a 6-2 offsuit. The button mucks, the small blind doesn't want to call the raise and neither does the big blind. They both muck and the dealer pushes the big pot to the raiser. He mucks. I'm standing there ready to go home with my 6-2 on the table with my card cover "coin" on them. It was then that the table realized that everyone mucked but me. I had my $50 ante X 9 players coming to me. The raiser mucked his hand, so his hand was automatically dead. And he had fuckin' Kings. I was dead meat if he hadn't forgotten I was in the pot for part of the antes.

So now I had $450. The players were absolutely livid against the 7 seat. Especially after I went all-in again. And won. And again. And again. Three hours later I had $42,000. Forty two thousand fuckin' dollars. Everyone at the table had been knocked out and I wish I could say I won the $40,950 first place prize money, but I didn't. I did win $4,400. I did tell everyone at the table this fiasco started at that if I won first place I would give everyone their $1,080 entry fee back. And I meant it. But I went stone cold for almost 2 hours at the end. And you need to get some cards at the end of a tournament. I didn't. So with the blinds at $1,500 and $3,000 and the antes at $500, I bet my last $8,000 on King-3 suited. The guy across from me had pocket Jacks and I didn't improve. Oh well. What a fuckin' ride. A chip and a chair. You've heard it. I've heard it. I lived it. It was fun. Really fun.

Random Thought

There is no doubt that luck plays a huge part of today's tournaments. It has to. There are too many people in the tournaments playing too many combinations of hands. If you go all-in with pocket Aces and some drunk fuck in seat 4 calls you with 2-7 offsuit, he will win 11 times out of 100. I know how disgusting that sounds, but it's true. And it's probably not going to be 2-7. It might be J-10 or 6-9 or any one of a hundred combinations that you dominate. And then it won't make you an 89% favorite. You may only be a 60% favorite or a 70% favorite, but you know what? When he beats you and you make your cell phone call to your buddy and give him all the gory details of how you got knocked out of the tournament and he sympathizes with you and tells you all about his latest bad beat, you will still feel like shit. The thing is, no one died, and if you choose to, you can still eat a huge steak for dinner the next day. Life is good. And poker is fun. And luck plays a huge part. Make no mistake about it.

Eat, Play and Be Merry

As we all know but few admit, life is short. It's fleeting. That's probably where the word "fleet" came from in "Fleet enema" (the word enema in itself is a bad beat). Anyway, as I was saying, no one leaves this fuckin' rock alive. No one. Howard Hughes couldn't do it. Elvis couldn't do it. And we won't be able to do it. So we should have some pleasure while we are here. Legal pleasure. So here are my most pleasurable substances that I spoil myself with periodically. These are in no particular order as they are all equally great. If Viagra doesn't work for you, I'm sure one of these things will. The first thing that comes to mind is Imus Ranch Black Bean Salsa. As a lot of you that are philanthropic know, Imus Ranch is a working cattle ranch for kids with cancer. Don Imus' wife Deirdre is probably the one behind the food products because they are fresh, healthy and delicious. A far cry from the decomposing state of her husband. Imus needs to open a ranch for those of us who aren't kids. Maybe the Don Imus Ranch for Old Fucks With Drool Cups and Shawls. There are a lot of us. The Betty Ford Clinic refuses to accept my suggestions or phone calls. But Don Imus- he's so accessible. And loving- and caring. Maybe I'm confusing him with Don Knotts. Or Don Rickles. Or Don Johnson. Anyway, his black bean salsa is fuckin' delicious. It's very low calorie, nutritious and filling. I eat it right from the jar. I keep at least 12 jars in my cupboard and have given it to everybody from my paperboy to my papergirl to my local priest. I'll never forget good old Father What's His Name. Many a priest will forever remember my confessions from the days of old. Bless me father for I have sinned- but haven't we all? Not a good opening line for a Sunday morning confession. Many of the earthquakes in San Francisco were attributed to my Sunday morning confessions. Father Vito didn't have much of a sense of humor. He wasn't a very kind person. I know I was an ugly kid, but you'd think he could have made at least one pass at me to give me a little self-esteem. A little self confidence. But nooooooo. All his attention had to be on my 14-year-old buddy Jeffrey with the blond hair and the penetrating blue eyes with the 6-pack abs and the muscular arms. We use to wrestle a lot and I would fantasize about his perfect mouth and soft lips enveloping- HOLY FUCK BATMAN! Bless me Father, for I have sinned... As I was saying, Imus Ranch

Black Bean Salsa can be purchased online at www.Imusranchfoods.com. I mention this online stuff because I know most of you poker fucks never leave the house unless it's on fire. You can have this delivered right to your door and keep it next to your computer with a plastic spoon for instant nutrition. Then the only reason you'll have to leave the poker site will be to go to the bathroom. The next item up for bid- Actually, the next great, and I mean fuckin' great, item that you must have in your house is Enstrom Milk Chocolate Toffee. This is unlike any toffee I have ever known. The almonds in each piece are the size of Buicks. It is made from the finest butter, the finest chocolate, then dipped in powdered sugar. I'm telling you people- it's a slice of fuckin' Heaven. I send it to a lot of people for Christmas and I have had friends threaten to maim me if I send them anymore because they can't stop eating it once they start. Enstrom is based out of Colorado and they are the Toffee Kings of the World. Enstrom can be located at www.enstrom.com or 1-800-367-8766. Enstrom's Almond Toffee is the fuckin' greatest. I swear. Now, if you like bleu cheese dressing, you have got to try Cindy's Kitchen Bleu Cheese Dressing and Dipping Sauce. I get it at Whole Foods Market in Las Vegas. I'm sure there's a Whole Foods Market near you. I always go there hungry. They have samples of everything. Crusty pulled pork, tender as young love brisquet, various pizzas, cheeses, crackers, fruits. What a fuckin' place. My challenge every time I go to Whole Foods is to try and leave without spending a "C Note" ($100). I haven't attained that goal yet. Their selection of cheeses and wines is unreal. They actually categorize their cheese by country. But their Cindy's Kitchen Bleu Cheese salad dressing is why I go there. Chunks of bleu cheese the size of Jeffrey's testicles. Oh man, bless me Father for I have sinned...

So if you have Imus Ranch Black Bean Salsa, Enstrom Toffee and Cindy's Kitchen Dressing, believe me Bucco, you can die a happy poker fuck. Along with quad Aces of course...

Wake Up and Smell the Aces

We all love pocket Aces. When we do get them we sometimes misplay them. When we get them "cracked", we replay that hand numerous times in our minds. Chances are we got them cracked because we slow-played them and too many people limped into the pot with a whole bunch of shit and someone hits two pair or better. Pocket Aces are rare. About once out of 220 hands. If a dealer is an average dealer and deals 25-30 hands an hour, we can expect pocket Aces about once every 8 hours. Pocket Aces usually win very small pots or lose very big pots. If you are "under the gun" (the first to act after the big blind), you have to raise **something** with pocket Aces. Even if it's 2x the big blind. At least some of the field will be eliminated. The ideal situation with pocket Aces is to get all of your money in the middle before the flop and for sure you would have the best hand before the flop. The worst hand in Hold 'em is a 2-7 offsuit. Before the flop, pocket Aces are an 89% favorite against the worst hand of 2-7 offsuit, which means that 2-7 offsuit will win 11% of the time. That is fuckin' scary. But that's Hold 'em. 11 Times out of 100 times, 2-7 off is going to beat pocket Aces. I get constipated just writing that. I remember a tournament at Binion's Horseshoe in Downtown Las Vegas where we had pocket Aces 8 times in one hour at the table. Nine handed, pocket Aces 8 times by various players- in one fuckin' hour. Unbelievable. Ironically, they held up every time and it was only once it didn't get good action. So obviously the 1-220 hands is based on millions if not billions of hands. We had 8 pairs of pocket Aces in one hour, which goes to show you that if you play enough poker, you will eventually see everything. But the long-term fact is that 1 of every 220 hands, you will be dealt pocket Aces. So, carrying out my scenario further, if you play 20 hours a week, you should get pocket Aces 2-3 times. If you play every week, the probability of getting pocket Aces is then about 10 times a month. When you do the math, there are 4.3 weeks in a month- not 4 as most people think. If there were 4 weeks in a month, there would only be 48 weeks in a year. Most of us know we work our fingers to the bone trying to make a living 52 weeks a year. So 4.3 weeks X 500 hands per week = 2150 hands of poker a month. Divided by 220 = 9.77 times you'll get pocket Aces each month. Call it 10 times per month. That's 120 times a year if you play at least 20 hours a week. So if you're reading this and you are 30 years old, and you die at 60, you can only expect pocket Aces 3600 times in your entire life. But if you're as unlucky as I am with "card averages", you can expect them 2 or 3 times. Maybe 4. Tops.

So unlucky fucks like us cannot depend on pocket Aces to bust the prick across from us. They're not all pricks. That's a generalization. And I hate generalizations. I do like percentages though. I do believe about 10% of the people playing poker are uncaring, cheap, low, sordid, smelly individuals that are wearing dirty underwear with skid marks. That means 1 out of 10. So when you're at a tournament table or a cash game, one of them is a prick. If it's not you, you've narrowed down the field. Do you have skidmarks in your underwear? I rest my case. And the worst part of it all is that the pricks seem to get more than their share of pocket Aces. But the nice thing is that someday they're going to die. But then so will you. Oh well. You think pocket Aces are rare? Try flopping a flush. Or a full house. Or quads. These are very rare occurrences, but if your opponent happens to flop one of these monster hands, you need to pick up that information as soon as possible. That's why watching players' faces precisely when the flop comes is sometimes priceless information. Especially when you watch the very old. They can't contain themselves. They just hit the fuckin' lottery on the flop for Christ's sake. They're ecstatic. They're excited. They're peeing. Literally. The younger players are harder to decipher. But sometimes they tremble when making their bet. They are so fuckin' excited by the monster flop that they cannot control their brain and trembling occurs. It is critically important to observe the hands being played even if you are not in the pot. And if the hand doesn't go to the river and one of the participants is sitting next to you, try and find out what he had. This is information that you didn't have to pay for and you store it in your memory bank for future reference. If you play at a local game at someone's house every week, you get to know how everyone plays. Who plays tight, who plays loose, who bluffs a lot, who the tough players are. You need to have that assessment of your opponent's play in the first hour of play when you play in tournaments and casino cash games. By paying attention, you can quickly figure out who the good players are and play them appropriately. Tournament players must make a quick assessment, and if it's not accurate, they will be out of the tournament quickly. They will be taking the long walk out of the tournament room pondering their last decision, between sobs, and how it could have been different.

Random Thought

Pocket Aces are good for two things: winning a small pot or losing a big one.

Fine Tune Your Game

Some of the smaller colleges in the Las Vegas area are trying to jump on the "Hold 'em bandwagon" and offer courses that apply to playing the game for fun or for a living. I was instrumental in helping to create courses I thought would be very beneficial to the people who want to embrace this career. Among the courses offered are:

Course #	Course Title
L- 11000	Creative Suffering After a Bad Beat
L- 11001	Distracting Opponents With Your Birthmark
L- 11002	Hold 'em Without Sex
L- 11003	Bad Beat Gratification Through Violence
L- 11004	Dealing With Post-Flop Depression
L- 11005	Whine Your Way to the Final Table
L- 11006	Poker Opportunities in El Salvador
L- 11007	Using Your Body for Tournament Buy-Ins
L- 11008	Accumulating a Bankroll Through Arson
L- 11009	Memorizing Your "Hole Cards" for the Senile
L- 11010	Throwing Your Opponent Off His Game By Staring at His Genitalia
L- 11011	Converting Your Card Cover Into an Automatic Rifle
L- 11012	1001 Uses for Your Card Cover

L- 11013   Using Your "Miracle Ear" to Your Tournament Advantage

L- 11014   Final Tables and Tooth Decay- Is There a Correlation

L- 11015   Exorcism, Acne and Pocket Aces

L- 11016   Suicide and Bad Beats

L- 11017   Tap Dance Your Way to Final Table Ridicule

L- 11018   Popping Bubble Wrap Before and After the Flop

Many of these courses are filling up fast, so I would suggest you move all-in at your earliest convenience.

Don't Leave the House Until You Check Your Chart

I love looking at the stars. There are billions of them. And one day, thousands of years ago, someone was looking at the sky and said, "I bet I can section off the sky and convince people that their life revolves around the stars and the planets. And if I craft this bullshit just right, I can sell it to every newspaper in the country when newspapers are invented. Anyway, it's something I can do in my spare time since I'm here in prison for the next 20 years just because I ran over some soldier's foot in my chariot. I'll change the predictions every day so people will be forced to revolve their lives around what I say. And if enough people read it, some of it will come true and they will tell their friends. Man, this could be fuckin' huge." And so my dear readers, Astrology was born. The origin of the word is from Greece and broken down it means "Never drop the soap in the shower of a Greek prison". I'm sure everyone reading this has knowledge of their favorite players including their birthday. It's amazing how accurate some of these are.

Aquarius- Jan. 20-Feb. 18: You have an inventive mind and are inclined to be progressive. On the other hand, you are inclined to be careless and impractical because you are stupid. You play 2-7 offsuit every time you get it. Everyone thinks you are a fuckin' jerk.

Pisces- Feb. 19-March 20: You have a vivid imagination and often think you're being followed. People resent you for flaunting your power. You lack confidence and are generally a coward. You piss off everyone you come in contact with. You only raise with the nuts. Pisces people like to screw small animals.

Aries- March 21-April 19: You are the pioneer type and hold most people in contempt. You are quick tempered, impatient and scornful of advice. You show up late for all tournaments. You are a prick.

Taurus- April 20-May 20: You are practical and persistent. You work like hell. Most people think you are stubborn and bullheaded. You have never been bluffed out of a pot. People have a tendency to fart when they are near you.

Gemini- May 21-June 20: You are a quick intelligent thinker. People like you because you are bisexual. However, you expect too much for too little. This means you are fuckin' cheap and never tip even when you win a huge pot. Geminis are notorious for thriving on incest.

Cancer- June 21-July 22: You are sympathetic and understanding to other people's bad beat stories. Everyone thinks you're a fuckin' sucker. You are always putting things off and that is why you will always be on welfare or close to it. You're never going to be worth a shit. Most people in prison are Cancers.

Leo- July 23-August 22: You consider yourself a born leader while most people think you're a fuckin' pussy. Most Leos are bullies. They raise every pot with nothing. Their arrogance is disgusting. So is their breath. Leo people are always thieving bastards and enjoy masturbating to pictures of farm animals.

Virgo- August 23-Sept. 22: You are the logical type and hate disorder. Your nit-picking drives your friends fuckin' nuts. You arrange all of your chips in perfect order with every chip design aligned with the chip below it. You are cold and unemotional and often fall asleep while making love. Virgos make excellent bus drivers and pimps.

Libra- Sept. 23-Oct. 22: You are the artistic type and have a difficult time dealing with reality. If you are a male, you are probably queer. You have a very elaborate card cover that you usually take to bed with you. It may even be a blow-up card cover. Most Libra women make excellent whores. All Libras die of venereal disease.

Scorpio- Oct. 23-Nov. 21: You are the worst of the lot. You are a shrewd business type and cannot be trusted. You always achieve success because you have no ethics. You attack the weak, the old and the sickly at your table. You are a no good son-of-a-bitch. Most Scorpios are murdered.

Sagittarius- Nov 22-Dec 21: You are optimistic and enthusiastic. You have a reckless tendency to rely on luck since you lack talent. You consistently pay raises to draw two cards to a flush. The majority of Sagittarians are drunks. People laugh at you and you are always getting fucked.

Capricorn- Dec 22-Jan 19: You are very conservative and afraid of taking risks. You have never made a final table and probably never will. There has never been a Capricorn of any importance. You are a bedwetter and probably should consider suicide.

The Ultimate Father and Son "Chat"

Son: Dad, I've got some really good news for you and mom. I've finally decided what I want to do with my life.

Dad: I thought you had already decided, son. You've been in college for almost 6 years now and I thought you were going to be a CPA.

Son: Fuck accounting. Dad, you have to love what you do. And I don't love accounting. I just like it.

Dad: Wow, your mom is probably going to be very upset. She hasn't bought a dress or painted the house and we haven't even gone on a trip making sure we paid for your college education. This means many more years of college if you're going to switch majors. But that's OK, son. Somehow we'll make it. What career is it that you seem to have totally embraced?

Son: I'm going to play sports.

Dad: Sports?

Son: Well, actually a sport. Now you can brag to all of your friends and people you think are your friends that your son is playing professional sports.

Dad: I'm very confused. The closest you ever got to sports was when you were caught blowing the quarterback in high school.

Son: You always bring that up. Whenever I try and have a talk with you about anything, I can always sense that you are thinking about that one isolated incident in my life that was caught on school cameras and distributed over the Internet by my own mother thinking that the embarrassment would teach me a lesson I would never forget. It was so wrong of her to do that. And she was wrong in her assumption.

Dad: Your mother and I have always done what we thought

was best for you.

Son: So you were a part of that also?

Dad: Fuck no, son. The bitch did it on her own.

Son: I thought so. Now she'll really be pissed when she finds out I want to make my living in professional sports.

Dad: I'm still confused about that, son. Which sport are you going to play?

Son: Poker.

Dad: Poker?

Son: Yes, dad. Poker is a sport now.

Dad: What? What the fuck are you talking about?

Son: Poker is a sport, dad. It was on all the television stations that televise poker tournaments. Isn't that exciting?

Dad: What the fuck is this world coming to? Poker is a sport, Pluto isn't a planet anymore. Is global warming affecting peoples' brains?

Son: Anyway, dad, I'm going to be playing poker professionally. I'm going to be a sports pro.

Dad: The closest you will be to a pro, son, is being a prophylactic. You remember when you went trick or treating when you were 14 dressed as a Trojan condom? That's as close to a pro as you'll ever be. You're not blowing my fuckin' money playing poker.

Son: There you go again with that "blowing" episode.

Dad: (calling his wife) Mary! Mary! Come talk to your fuckin' son. He wants to blow some poker guy he met. He thinks poker is a fuckin' sport.

Son: It is, dad. Why else would it be named the "World Series of Poker" if it wasn't a sport.

Mom: Calm down, you two. I overheard everything. If our son wants to pursue a life of bad beats and be miserable to the bone, we should let him.

Dad: But...

Mom: No buts, honey. Now Son, what do your father and I have to do to make your dream of becoming a sports figure come true?

Son: Mom, I know I can do this. I know how to play small pocket pairs and I never fall into traps. I just set them for other people. I win all the time, mom. I'm just going through a little rough period right now. But I'll bounce back, I promise.

Mom: OK, son. I believe you. Your father and I are glad that after so many years of college and us supporting you and paying your tuition and room and board, that we can finally have some rest and start paying off the huge debt we've accumulated making your CPA dream come true.

Son: Believe me, mom. As soon as I win a big tournament, I'll help you pay off the house. All four mortgages. I know it's been rough.

Mom: Yes it has, son.

Son: And mom... I need a bankroll to start my new career. My new sport. Let's just call it gear. With any sport you need gear.

Mom: How much gear, son?

Son: Just $10,000, mom.

Mom: Go fuck yourself, son.

This is a typical conversation happening in many households from sea to shining sea.

Random Thought

My grandson Torin is more into science than he is sports. I gave him a microscope one Christmas and when I took him to a ballgame, he spent most of the game looking for rodent hairs in his hot dog. He found 3. I won the bet though. I bet the under 6.

Don't Bug Me

Bed bugs have been reported in hotel beds in 48 states. Is there something you should be asking the next hotel clerk at the next hotel you decide to stay in? Ask for the bedbug discount, which sometimes is as good as many of the other discounts hotels offer. There are so many now a days. If you're a senior citizen, there's the AARP discount. Kids? We discount kids under 10. Pets? We love pets and have discounts for our urine infested pet rooms. Are you disabled? Dyslexic? Disinfected? Distended? Discouraged? All are eligible for discounts. Las Vegas hotels always have discounts. Ask for them. You'll have more money to play poker.

This message brought to you by the National Council of Religions, Churches and Delicatessens.

A Short Poker Fairy Tale

Once upon a time, a guy asked a girl to marry him. The girl said "No". The guy went home. He drank beer, watched TV, controlled the remote at all times, played poker, came home late whenever he wanted, farted at will and always left the toilet seat up. He lived happily ever after.

The End

WSOP (World Series of Poker)

The first day of the WSOP was a combination of a casino employees $500 buy-in tournament, a ton of satellite tournaments, a half a ton of live cash games and the most important thing- lots of toilets. I like using the word "toilet" because it sounds offensive and this is an offensive book and the real world of poker has a lot of offensive people in it trying to make people sob uncontrollably with "bad beats". Anyway, (and I never know if it's anyway or anyways. So I usually use anyway in the hopes that it's anyways and I'm offending some purist English major who has made it his life's ambition to find typos and incorrect English usage in books and graffiti. Especially graffiti on bathroom walls. We need these purist English fucks to keep the rest of us in line and they will spend most of their boring, lonely lives finding errors in the writings of people who write because they have boring and lonely lives- more boring and lonely than theirs. But we will deal with those issues and other issues in the chapter "Dr. Phil Was Bored and Lonely Too Until He Became Incredibly Lucky and Married Oprah". Or was it Stedman he married? I get confused. I'm old). Anyway, as I was saying a few hundred words ago, the first day of the WSOP was organized chaos. The employee event had 660 casino employees play in it last year with a $500 buy-in. This year it had 1400 players. You started with $1,000 in chips and the event lasts two days. It pays about 100 places and the winner gets enough to pay his rent and maybe take a small vacation to a nearby town with less than three 7-11's. I came in 395th out of 1400. Barely out of the money. The story of my life. When I first got my seat assignment, I was on table 208 seat 9. After hobbling around on my crutch for 6 or 7 minutes looking at all the numbered tables, I realized that table 208 didn't exist. So I figured I was either on Candid Camera or in the Twilight Zone. Neither was true. Table 208 really didn't exist. So I asked a few of the employees that were roaming around if they would help and we all agreed that table 208 didn't exist. There was a 205, a 206, a 207, but no 208. So I asked a passerby in a suit with a nametag that said Gary Thompson. I sat at an empty table and he went on a quest to find table 208. I love when people quest for me. I've been thinking about hiring a quester. And when I'm in a hand, I sometimes ponder. So I would need a quester that was also good at pondering. I said pondering. Not pandering. But pandering could work too. Also, I really need a drummer on wheels that could do rim shots for me when I say something humorous. This would be a part time position. Finding a person that could do all three would be like striking the mother lode- or getting pocket Aces. The employment ad would read: "Needed: A quester, ponderer, rim-shotter. Call for appointment." I should call a head-hunting employment agency. Maybe tomorrow. Remind me.

Anyway, Gary Thompson, I found out, was one of the execs of the WSOP. But he went out of his way to help me. I appreciated that. The event was actually won by a kid who deals poker at Caesar's Palace named Chris Gros. He won $130,000 and I was really surprised how pleased and excited all of the dealers at Caesar's were about his good fortune. He's a really nice kid and very well liked. He had just bought a home that month, and after taxes he should have enough for a George Foreman Grill and a mortgage payment.

Random Thought

Winning tournaments, especially the gigantic, huge immense, gargantuan ones like the World Series of Poker, means you have to have the ability to scratch and claw and rip and tear your opponents apart. The intensity, the gouging, the gashing is non-stop. And this is just while you're in line to pay your entry fee. Then the situation gets a lot more serious. It's not for the weak, the timid, the tired. That's why I never made it past the line. I did last about 20 minutes though. And I stand taller because of it. But I'll be back next year. I know I can make it to the window. I know I can.

Trains, Planes, Automobiles

And, of Course, Phil Hellmuth Jr.

I don't travel well. I just don't. I don't like trains. They go too fast, and you just never know when some little prick is going to put a penny on the track and derail the train. Sure, the penny is very small, and it really flattens out when the huge, heavy locomotive goes over it. But it can also cause a huge derailment. I know this for a fact. When I was 10 years old I derailed a train with a penny. Actually it was a bag of pennies. A big bag. 5,000 pennies. And I had a rather large rock in the bag. I didn't want the bag to blow away. It was a windy day. Actually, the rock could be classified as a boulder. I was going to take the flattened pennies and sell them at school for five cents. The train derailment really fucked everything up. It cost me a lot. Plus pennies were everywhere. What a fuckin' mess. The train engineer was really pissed. I think everything would have been fine if he hadn't slammed on his fuckin' brakes. So as you can see, my fear of trains is not unfounded. And my message is clear. If you're on a train and see some little kid near the tracks staring at the wheels of the train, hold on. Chances are he's got at least one penny on the track.

Planes and I have never gotten along either. I don't like to fly. I don't even like to drive people to the airport. Friends of mine have private jets. They are tiny projectiles that land and take off at millions of miles per hour. They are really tiny. They are so fuckin' small that Houdini couldn't get out of the bathroom even **without** chains on. It's like climbing into a 45 caliber bullet with 3 or 4 other people and everyone holds their breath that 1) The takeoff goes smooth; 2) The landing goes smooth; and 3) Nobody farts. But of course, owning your own jet is a status symbol. Or a phallus symbol. Depending on your point of view. Of course there are different size private jets. A normal conversation between private jet owners goes something like this:

Jet Owner #1: My jet seats 7.

Jet Owner #2: I use to have a small one like that. My jet seats 12.

Jet Owner #1: I have a customized sound system.

Jet Owner #2: I use to have one of those too. Now I have a
live band.

Jet Owner #1: My penis is 8 inches long.

Jet Owner #2: I use to have one like that. Now I have a live
band.

As you can see, the competition among jet owners is fierce. It's
not any better with RV owners or bus owners. Humans by their very
nature are extremely competitive. And we have so many choices. No
matter what we are buying, the choices are incredible. I haven't had a
hot dog in a long time and stopped by Albertson's to get a package of
them. There were a mind-boggling amount of choices just to buy a
fuckin' package of hot dogs. One of the packages had hot dogs in it so
big I was looking to see if they took batteries. It could have been billed
as a "hot dog for lunch, a pleasuring device for nighttime". I'm
thinking, "No bun could house this fuckin' monster." And when you
cook it, it says it will "plump up". Plump up? The fuckin' thing was 6
inches in diameter in a relaxed state. And pulsating. My God. And
they allow kids in this section. Then of course they have the hot dog
eating competition. I don't know if you have ever witnessed one of
these fiascos, but they are sponsored by hot dog makers and what these
contests have to do with the increase in hot dog sales is beyond me.
Watching people consume extremely large quantities of a product and
sometimes vomiting it into a bucket and then stuffing their mouth with
more of the product does not entice me to jump into my car and rush to
my local grocery store and fill my cart with said hot dogs. Maybe if it
was chocolate cake my feelings would be different. I love chocolate
cake. Whenever my wife and I travel I order chocolate cake in each
restaurant. Each one is different. If it's really really good, I get a piece
"to go' and eat it in my car. Speaking of cars, I really enjoy my cars.
Much better than I enjoy trains and planes. I like just driving around
our little town of Boulder City, Nevada and waving at people with the
top down. I love the top being down. I don't like highway driving.
Some people drive crazy. They think that their car is a thrill ride. An E
ticket ride at Disneyland. I always use my cruise control. 65 or 70 is as

fast as I go. Kick back, radio on, tunes playing, singing along, going 65 and some fuckin' guy passes me going 250. Unreal. Risking lives. But I guess he's in a hurry. I guess the tournament is about to start. It's sure as shit not Phil Hellmuth Jr. He's never been on time for a tournament and probably never will be. That's his trademark. Along with 10 others that separate him from most other assholes. And maybe that's a strategy he hasn't revealed yet. When he shows up about an hour or two late, about 20% to 30% of the field is either on the short stack or have been eliminated. Has anyone done a study on late entries? Maybe there is something to people being "fashionably late". Research needs to be done.

Random Thought

I'm playing a big buy-in tournament at the Bellagio and there's a camera crew from some European country that hates us at one of the tables. They are filming some guy that they are doing a reality show about. The lights were a little bright and some kid at our table commented about the bright lights. That made me remember many years ago when my dad became the proud owner of an 8mm movie camera. And of course, the companion to every 8mm camera was the 5,000 megawatt flood lights. Every birthday, he'd plug them in and all the lights in the neighborhood would dim like there was an electrocution. Our party hats would explode in flames. The cake would catch on fire. The pets would scramble to safety. God, those were fun times. And this fuckin' kid is complaining about bright lights. If he only knew.....

The Square Circle

Whenever I get beat and have to leave the tournament area, I think the same thought- would I have done better if I used performance-enhancing drugs? I know one guy that says he's done a lot better since he started taking steroids. He said he's made the final table more often and he seems to put the opposing players in a trance like state when he starts popping his pimples. I have been tempted to put Viagra powder in my opponents' water bottles during a break. Now **that** could be a humorous sight. Some of those guys around the table haven't had a hard on in years and the puzzled looks on their collective faces would surely have them betting with mediocre hands. Their lower body would be on tilt and their concentration level would diminish, which would result in bad play. Then, when they lose their chips, the fun really begins. They have to stand up and leave the room. If there's one thing a guy has trouble hiding, it's a hard on. If there is one common denominator among poker players, it's to pretend to be normal, which lends itself to the question: Do poker players have erectile dysfunction more than say, chess players? Chess players might be a bad analogy. People aren't proud they play chess. They never say loudly, "I PLAY CHESS!" It's a very quiet, very subdued response if you ask them. Not like poker. You ask a poker player if he plays poker and he bellows, "FUCK YES!" Then he proceeds to tell you 10 bad beat stories. Like the magician who asks you if you want to see a card trick and you say "No", so he shows you 10 of them. But chess is a very quiet, very subdued game. Chess players don't need anger management classes. There are no bad beats. In chess you can see the bad beat coming 6 moves from Friday. It would be like knowing you are going to lose the hand before the flop. Or even before the deal. Like Kreskin would. If you haven't seen Kreskin, you're not missing a fuckin' thing. He's a self-proclaimed psychic. Whatever that means. Hold 'em tournaments have been around a long time and have become fairly standardized except for the loud assholes that play them. There are a few in every card room. We all know who they are. I think it would be great to get every irritating player in every card room and have a special tournament just for them. Card rooms all over the country would vote who they are going to send to this event to represent them. This could be huge. The final table would then be the angriest, most aggravating, most obnoxious, most belligerent, players that have ever been assembled on one table. We are talking a Pay Per View event. And just like Outback Steakhouse- No Rules. The final table would be in a cage just like Ultimate Fighting. The dealer will wear a hockey goalkeeper's outfit to protect himself from flying water bottles. Penalties would be almost non-existent. Sharp objects would not be allowed. Even if you say it's your card cover. Gun play forbidden. We need to draw the line somewhere. I'm telling you- this is the next stage for an evolving sport. I love this fuckin' country.

Random Thought

This one fuck sits down with a bag of stuff for when he gets hungry. An obvious poker degenerate. So about 20 minutes later, out comes a small container of milk and a bowl and a box of Cap'n Crunch Cereal. You know, the cereal with the wholesome goodness and delightful crunch of corn and nut clusters sweetened with a touch of brown sugar in a hermetically sealed package that is almost impossible to open without causing a big fuckin' mess. I was surprised that this retarded fuck didn't have the Cap'n Crunch hat in his fuckin' pack. Some people do things just to aggravate me. I'm sure of it.

Another Fuckin' Quiz?

I like quick quizzes. I've said that before. I like this one because it is quick and it has a great message. Not massage. Message. But this message has a "happy ending". Like some massages.

1) Name the five wealthiest people in the world.

2) Name the last five Heisman Trophy winners.

3) Name the last five winners of the Miss America contest.

4) Name ten people who have won the Nobel or Pulitzer Prize.

5) Name the last five people who have won the Academy Award for Best Actor and Actress.

6) Name the World Series winners for the last ten years.

How did you do? Chances are you sucked. The point is, of course, none of us remember the headlines of yesterday. The applause dies. The awards tarnish. Achievements are forgotten. Certificates and plaques are buried with their owners. The people that make a difference in your life are not the ones with the most credentials, the most money or the most awards. The people that make a difference in your life are the ones that care about you. I'll bet you do a lot better on this next quiz than you did on the last one.

1) List a few teachers who aided in your journey through school.

2) Name three friends who have been there for you during a rough time in your life.

3) Name five people who have taught you something worthwhile.

4) Name two people who have made you feel appreciated or special.

5) Name five people you enjoy spending time with.

6) List some of your heroes whose stories have inspired you.

What has this got to do with fuckin' poker? Fuck, I don't know. But when I read it I liked it- so I wanted to share it with you. If you don't like it, tear the fuckin' page out. There are no refunds so you can tear out pages with no consequences.

Random Thought

Don't like the book? Keep it in the car to use as an ice scraper or wheel block when parking on a steep hill.

Way Beyond Books On Tape

A copy of this book is available on CD, DVD, VD, Beta, VHS, Sega, Atari, XBOX, 45, 78 and 33 1/3 phonograph records, Morse Code, hieroglyphics, smoke signals, 1-800 numbers, 1-900 numbers, sign language, graffiti and Braille. We are working to get it on the head of a pin for specialty gift shops. I know. I'm trying to please everyone. It's a compulsion I live with. These items can be purchased in poker rooms, bookstores, Mr. Roger's neighborhood, Pee Wee's Playhouse, Neverland Ranch, Sherry's Ranch, farm houses, crack houses, whore houses, pancake houses, finer restaurants with and without serious health code violations, health food stores, religious bookstores, psycho, psychotic and psychic bookstores and college campuses near large supermarkets everywhere. The book itself is beginning to show up at swap meets, garage sales, and homeless shelters at deep discount prices. I had 50,000 copies printed, so you might want to check the dumpster by my house for additional copies. I think I need a better distribution network. I'm really sorry I pissed off Barnes and Noble. Actually, I get along good with Barnes. It's Noble who I got in the "beef" with. I tried to make amends by sending him the latest Turbo Nose Hair Trimmer from the Sharper Image catalogue, and that **really** pissed him off. He said I was inferring he had excessive nose hair. I said to him, "Man, you ever look in the fuckin' mirror? It's not fuckin' normal to have nose hair getting tangled up in your fork while you're eating. You need two fuckin' Turbo Nose Hair Trimmers- not one. After that he was always nasty to me. But I like Barnes. Fuck Noble. But I might have to make peace with him. I need his distribution network. And he knows it.

Random Thought

Hold 'em poker can be described in two words- Astounding growth. Or three words- Astounding fuckin' growth. I watched the same thing happen in the late 70's and early 80's with Video Poker.

Decisions, Decisions, Decisions

Hold 'em poker is fraught with decisions. I think it's been years since I used the word "fraught". I will probably never use it again. Unless I write another poker book. But I'll have to change the sentence. Like, "Hold 'em poker is fraught with indecisive players. And it's fraught with assholes. And incredibly smelly individuals." But aside from that, I love the game. And it's fraught with decisions. When I was younger, I use to do card magic and I invented a simple trick called "Decisions". It involved a lot of decisions that the person would have to make. As I shuffled the deck, you would have to decide when to tell me to stop shuffling. They were all legitimate shuffles. Then I would spread the deck on the table and you would have to decide which card to pick. Then you would decide where to insert the card in the deck. Then I would start shuffling again and you would decide when to tell me to stop. Then I would deal the cards on the table one at a time, holding the deck in one hand and placing each card face down on the table with the other hand. You would then tell me when to stop and your final decision was whether you wanted the card on the table or the next one off the deck. You would then announce the name of your card and I would turn over the card you chose. It was a neat trick. It was a fuckin' miracle. Well, not really. But it did look like one. Until I let you examine the cards. All the cards were the same. I only did this for other magicians because it was fun to do and we would all laugh. You see, I knew what they were looking for when I shuffled, and there were no bad moves in the whole trick. And if they even suspected a one-way deck, their suspicion was completely gone for one fleeting second. For one second I had them by the balls. They were blown away by the trick because they knew if it was a trick deck, I wouldn't let them examine it. And when I offered the deck of cards to them, for those few seconds I owned them. Hold 'em reminds me a lot of that trick. A lot. There are tons of decisions every time you play a hand. Every hand. Do you play or muck the hand? Raise or call? The flop comes. Raise, call or muck? The turn- raise, call or muck? And of course, the River. Decisions, decisions, decisions. And if you have the nuts, you own your opponent. If you are playing a tournament, your tournament life is at constant risk every time you play a hand. Every time. Your involvement in a hand begins with the decision to play the hand initially. And with each card it gets tougher and tougher to get away from the hand and throw it into the muck. Poker is not for the faint of heart. It's not for the squeamish. It's not for pussies. Poker is a tough fuckin' game. Don't ever forget that.

Random Thought

Every situation in poker is different. Every single one. Folding Kings or Queens pre-flop takes balls. Folding a flush takes balls. You won't always make the right call, but after a careful assessment, if your gut tells you you're beat, and your mind agrees, you have got to fold the hand. Especially to survive. And tournaments are all about survival.

Clown Phobia

At this point in my life I'm still trying to figure out why I'm fearful of things. I think I'm fearful of heights because my uncle hung me upside down off the roof of the old apartment building we lived in when I was young. It was in New York and we lived on the fifth floor and we played on the roof. My uncle thought it was funny to do abusive things to kids. He use to think a lot of things were funny after he drank 8 or 10 beers. My fear of clowns has been tougher for me to figure out. I think it may have something to do with my dad taking me to the circus when I was 6 and a clown killed him. It was either that or the time a clown came to my birthday party and made me a really really bad balloon animal that I couldn't tell what the fuck it was. I was really embarrassed. It gave me diarrhea. I hate clowns. They scare the shit out of me. Literally.

Petri Dish Revisit

The guy next to me is picking his nose, the guy across from me is licking his fingers while eating greasy French fries and then I go to the bathroom and one of the players comes out of the stall and doesn't wash his hands. I'm thinking, "The fuckin' cards are actually Petri dishes." Bacteria city. Fuck the sunglasses and headphones. We should be wearing surgical gloves and masks. We all touch the cards in the same spots when we are peeking at them so we are receiving billions and I mean billions of fuckin' bacteria on our fingers that will probably be transferred to our mouths at some point. And we're worried about getting rivered? We should be worried about getting lockjaw. I think about that every time I'm at a game and I put a French fry in my mouth. You should too.

Thank God! The Rocky Statue Was Saved!

It Was Almost Replaced With Todd Brunson

It was recently reported that the bronze statue of Sylvester Stallone portraying the boxer in the film "Rocky" will be a permanent fixture at the bottom of the steps of the Philadelphia Museum of Art in where else- Philadelphia. Stallone donated the statue to the city after he used it in a scene of Rocky 650. The statue has been moved around numerous times before finally settling at it's present site. The city has finally made it's final decision to keep and display this bronze statue that has left a huge imprint on Philadelphia as the city of the underdog. The art commission voted 6-2 to put it in front of the museum on a street level pedestal. The other two commissioners voted for a bronze statue of Todd Brunson standing in line at a buffet. The Rocky statue is 9 feet 11 inches tall and weighs about 1300 pounds. Todd, who is no stranger to those dimensions, was saddened to hear the final choice of the commissioners. Both statues are very impressive with the "Rocky" statue holding his arms in the air and Todd's statue holding a plate of crab legs up high. Like Rocky, Todd has no plans of giving up. Ongoing discussions are leaning towards changing the plate of crab legs to a huge Philly cheesesteak sandwich, which will definitely make Todd a "contender" in the city of Philadelphia.

Random Thought

Andrew, a dealer at Binion's, once told me he likes to deliver bone-crushing, bankroll-crushing, soul-crushing river cards. He said he enjoys slamming people's nutsacks in car doors. Andrew enjoys his job.

Thanks Kenny

I was playing No Limit Hold 'em at the Venetian one night and met a nice older guy named Kenny. Kenny's been playing Hold 'em for his whole life. I knew his knowledge could launch my newfound love- Hold 'em poker. Kenny tutored me, he mentored me- thank God he never fondled me. Kenny is about 80. I'm old, but he's really really fuckin' old. Well, maybe not 80. I have a tendency to exaggerate. But if you put him and Doyle Brunson at the same game, and Daniel Negreanu between them, they would look like Gargoyle bookends. Anyway, Kenny has played in thousands of tournaments and won money in hundreds and hundreds of them. I learned and learned and learned from Kenny. Before our tutoring sessions, I use to come in the money once in a while in tournaments. Very seldom. Usually, though, I would come close to the top 10 even if I didn't "cash". All that has changed since Kenny came into my life. I haven't come into the money in ages. Not a fuckin' penny. Thanks Kenny. Thanks a fuckin' lot.

Random Thought

The youngest guy at the final table was in his fifties. It smelled like a Ben Gay convention. Everyone seemed to be in a friendly mood. Our meds were kicking in nicely. We were all looking forward to the break when the wheelchair wrestling challenge was going to take place between the guy in seat 3 and the guy in seat 6. Betting already had taken on a furious pace with most of the money being bet on the guy in seat 3. Wheelchair wrestling is popular in parts of Europe. It's just beginning to find its way here. Good things take time.

Stacking Chips

I like to keep my chips in racks, but they don't allow that in most card rooms. Green Valley Ranch allows it and I like to play there except for the fact that as of this writing, they don't have tournaments-yet. They said they were expanding and would have them at some point in time. The Fertitta kids that run the Station Casinos do a first class job. I've been in the casino business for a long long fuckin' time and these kids hire the right people and have the right philosophy. They take care of the customer and their buffet is the greatest. I'll talk about food and buffets elsewhere, but right now we're chatting about stacking chips. Some guys stack their chips like a phallic symbol. Like mini Trump high rises. Others have the diamond shape approach, and still others build a wall around their little area with their chips. I watched one kid buy in for $500, a rack of $5 chips in a 2-5 No Limit cash game, then proceed to arrange every fuckin' chip in a perfectly symmetrical order in 5 stacks, whereby the design on each chip was aligned with the chip beneath it. I was thinking, "Welcome to the Night of the Living Dead." This fuckin' kid needed Dr. Phil. STAT! Then he took out his headphones and put on sunglasses. I left about an hour later and he hadn't played a hand yet. I asked about him later and a guy told me he finally played a hand and lost all his chips. He was dealt pocket Aces and the guy he was playing against was dealt pocket Kings. He made Aces full and the other guy made 4 Kings. The kid went to the bathroom and there was a loud noise that sounded like a gunshot. As far as I know, to this day, no one has checked on him. Oh well, some players just aren't well liked.

Random Thought

Whenever you encounter a streak of bad luck or a series of bad beats and you think you have bad luck, REMEMBER- and I capitalize remember- when it really counted, when it really really counted- you hit the Good Luck Jackpot. You were born in the United States of America. Only one out of twenty people in the world get to call this country home. One out of twenty. A 5% chance. I got fuckin' lucky. So did you...

Moments of Truth

There are what I call "moments of truth" in any tournament. I have never been in a tournament that I haven't identified a moment of truth. Yesterday was an example at the Bellagio. I've got about $12,000 in tournament chips at level 5. The blinds are climbing. They're at 300-600. I'm not in bad shape, but a lot of people have a lot more chips. I get an A-Q suited and I'm on the button. The guy to my left goes all in with about $6,000 and mumbles fuck it- I'm tired. I caught a glimpse of a 5, so I knew he either had A-5, K-5 or a pair of 5's at the very best. Everyone folds except the guy to my right. He calls. We both have about the same amount of chips. So I move all-in. What the fuck. A-Q suited. I'm due. Right? Fuck no. I'm not right. This guy calls and we all flip our cards over. Guy to my left has pocket 5's. Guy to my right has pocket Kings. I figured- well, here's my moment of truth. If I catch an Ace or three spades, I will probably go onto the final table. There's only 60 people left and first place is $65,000- real money. I went on alright. I went on home. No one got any help. I'm thinking, "I think the guy who had the Kings came in a car, which means he has to cross a dark parking lot alone. Do I wait? Then what? I walk with a crutch since I broke my foot in 5 places. It couldn't be 2 or 3 places, it had to be 5 fuckin' places. And when they find this guy with a crutch up his ass, I'm pretty sure it's not going to take a detective like Colombo or Monk to figure out who put it there. So I did the gentlemanly thing. I told him he was a fuckin' asshole and I hoped that huge warts grew in his children's ears. Actually I just smiled and said, "Have a nice day, and each of you can suck me off." Actually, I am always nice at the table. Not real nice. But nice. I say funny things that 40% of the people think are humorous. The other 60% haven't had sex in over a year and are very tense. They wouldn't laugh at anything no matter how humorous.....

Random Thought

So this kid sitting next to me kept putting his hand on my knee. Usually I'm the knee-holder at the table. I didn't think that much of it, but after the game he told me he wanted to take me home with him and introduce me to his parents. He's 34 years old and still lives with his parents. And they live with **their** parents. Where does it end?

Why Not Many Women Play Poker Professionally

1) There's always an overbearing mother figure at the table.

2) Can't get a manicure while playing.

3) Mike Matusow aroma.

4) Makes them feel slimy and slutty (wait a minute… that's why not many women are hookers professionally).

5) Breaks are too short to do any serious shopping.

6) McDonald's pays more than tournaments.

7) They don't enjoy winning tuition money from the young players as much as guys do.

8) It makes them feel cheap with the terminology used in the game- Flopped, Turned and Rivered.

9) Bright lights melt their makeup.

10) They're too fuckin' smart.

Random Thought

"If a woman has to choose between catching a fly ball and saving an infant's life, she will choose to save the infant's life every time, without even considering if there is a man on base".

- Dave Barry

Book Tour

I am planning a book signing tour. Nationwide. Worldwide. But I hate to travel. I don't fly. I don't bus well. Since no one knows what I look like, I shouldn't have any problem finding a Tony Korfman impersonator. There are a lot of big fat ugly guys out there I could hire. They could be in multiple cities at once. Each city would think that I was in their city only. I would "yield up" like hotel management does. Or ticket sellers do when there is a popular event. If you book a hotel room early, your rate might be $129. The guy next door to you- same room- paid $279. Why? As the rooms were sold, the price kept going up. Supply and demand. The basis of the entire economic system. I could start a trend in book tours. Selling books in 10 different cities at the same time with 10 different people impersonating me. The only problem that I have is that I am on the cover. But it's not a good picture. Actually it's a great picture. I love airbrushing. For just a hundred dollar bill the airbrush guy made me look like Doyle Brunson and John Madden had a kid. It was me. Look for me at a book signing at a Barnes and Noble near you. Or a Krispy Kreme store. I love them both. But it might not be me. You never know.

Random Thought

It was about 4 PM at a cash game. 2-5 No Limit Hold 'em. The guy in the 4 seat raised. I called. After the flop, he checked- I checked. After the turn, he checked- I checked. On the river he checked- I checked. I showed him A-K, he showed me A-K. We tied. We split the pot. The hand was over. The hand wasn't very exciting or interesting, but I didn't say it would be.

You May Be Depressed but We Are Not In a Depression

We are not in a depression. It may seem like we are because you're out of work and they told you they were cutting back when they laid you off from your crummy $8 an hour job, which really didn't matter since you weren't able to pay your bills anyway. Unemployment is paying you $7.50 an hour to stay home. The big difference is you can watch TV all day and not miss any Ellen or Oprah shows, which is well worth the 50 cents an hour you're losing. It doesn't matter anyway because you couldn't pay your bills when you worked and you can't pay your bills now. But I want to assure you that we are not in a depression. How do I know this for certain? I was at the World Series of Poker. People were in lines. Long lines. They weren't lining up to get bread in a bread line. They weren't lining up to get a block or two of government cheese. They were lining up to hand fistfuls of $100 bills to a girl behind a counter. Or a guy. They weren't fussy. They didn't care. As long as someone took their money. Lots of it. All of it. They were in a state of mass hysteria. Hysteria I tell you. With a capital H and it rhymes with P and it stands for Poker. Oh we got trouble, right here in River City. I love that song. From The Music Man. I know. I wander. I'm a wandering soul. But a kind one. But don't mistake kindness for weakness. So I'm telling you people- I was at the World Series of Poker. And at the Bellagio during the WSOP events. And at Caesar's for their nighttime tournament. There is no shortage of money in this country. We are not in a depression. No matter what you think. No matter how many car payments you are behind. You just need to improve on your poker playing skills. Right here in River City...

Random Thought

At the WSOP, security was very tight. I was questioned, patted down, searched, probed and groped. I thoroughly enjoyed the event. I can't wait to go back next year. If I can get the same security guard, I think I can have a happy ending.

Another Solution to Wars and Strife

I have no fuckin' idea what strife is, but I have a solution to it anyway. It's really very simple. Imus Ranch Black Bean Salsa and Enstrom's Chocolate Almond Toffee. We bomb the Middle East with cases of both. 24 Hours a day. 7 days a week. Once they start eating those two items, peace will prevail. The Muslims will stop hating the Jews, the Jews will stop hating the Christians, the Christians will stop hating the Yankees and the Yankees will stop hating the Red Sox. A peace will come over this Earth like no other peace we've ever known. I can hear the chorus of Glory Glory Hallelujah now. In the background getting louder. People will be hugging in the streets. And Black Bean Salsa and Enstrom's Candy will abound. And the best part is yet to come. Steven Spielberg will be there to film it all. And Mel Gibson will be filming Spielberg filming it. I'm telling you this is really good fuckin' stuff.

Random Thought

I am not mechanically inclined. I have never been. I have only one thing in my toolbox at home. It's a hundred piece socket set. Maybe it's 200 pieces. It's sealed in a thick plastic container I have never figured out how to open. No need to. I don't have anything I need to use sockets on. My wife bought me the set one Father's Day. She has a sense of humor too. There use to be a screwdriver and a hammer in our toolbox. Now there's a hammer, a screwdriver and a socket set. Talk about tool heaven. Call me the Tool Doctor. Call me the Ultimate Tool Man. But the screwdriver disappeared about 3 years ago and was never heard from again, and then about a year later the hammer ran off with someone else. Now it's just the socket set. All alone. One of these days I expect that will also be gone. It's just a matter of time...

David Sedaris and Dave Barry-

I Wish My Name Was Dave

I think most people like to laugh. At least smile. Or chuckle. People don't chuckle much anymore. You hardly ever see the word "chuckle" in an article. Or a book. But I think people still chuckle. But maybe they don't admit it. Most people smile quite a bit during the day. That's why teeth whitener is such a huge product. And don't forget implants. So that you can have crowns and your teeth can be perfectly straight when you smile. Or chuckle. Or laugh. I don't read a lot, but I usually get a book "going" when I'm on vacation or just sitting in my chair, lazy like. I'm liable to pick up one of the 5 or 6 books that I have "in waiting". They are sitting there just waiting for me to read them. Here's my problem with reading a book. I started reading Stephen King's "The Stand" about 5 years ago. I lost interest about half way through and then when the TV movie came out there was no reason to finish the book. But I still feel guilty about not finishing it. You see, I left the old lady on the porch and I think she's waiting for me to finish the book so she can get on with her life. I know it's a fictional character, but I still feel I let her down. I know. I need help. I'm a sick fuck. That's why I like to read David Sedaris. He's humorous and he writes a bunch of short essays in his books. And he doesn't have any old ladies in rocking chairs on porches. I like humorous. I like funny. I like to smile and chuckle and laugh. And if you want to smile, you need to read David Sedaris. If you want to laugh out loud and have everyone on the train or bus stare at you while you're holding your crotch and trying not to pee, you need to read Dave Barry. This guy is one funny fuck. He writes incredibly funny shit. He always gives me ideas when I read his books. He use to have a column in the newspaper, but he retired recently. And he moved to Florida. It's in our constitution. It's the law. When you get old you have to move to Florida. It's like a "must move" poker game. I'm now reading Dave Barry's "Bad Habits". It's a 100% fact free book. My kind of reading. The book is a must read in trains, planes, streetcars, churches, synagogues and temples. Very solemn, crowded areas are the best areas to read his "works". I call his books "works" because they rate up there with Shakespeare and Kathy Lee. Whatever happened to Kathy Lee? And that cute little kid actor that played her son Coby. Or was it Cory? I forget. I'm old. Dave Barry. He guarantees you will love his books or you can move in with him. I'm not making this up. Or am I? I forget. I'm old.

Random Thought

As I'm writing, I'm eating sunflower seeds. In the shell. There are certain things that should be done in the privacy of your own home. Or apartment. Or room. One of them is eating sunflower seeds. My favorite are SPITZ. They are fuckin' great. I have tried every seed known to man. These are the best. Big, plump and pulsating. Wow. Sounds like an ad on a porn channel. Other private acts that should be done in your home are chewing tobacco, smoking and eating pomegranates. A friend of mine really gets turned on by pomegranates. He ate two of them one evening and his wife said he made the most incredible passionate love to her she had ever experienced. But she said the rest of the people in the restaurant weren't too crazy about it. I'll stick to sunflower seeds, thank you.

Nevada- The Land of Milk, Honey, Escalades and Turtles

I live in Nevada. Great state. I've been here forever and it's growth has been huge. We have no state income tax. Not to be confused with Federal Income Tax, which is like a huge shark taking multiple bites out of your tender, soft flesh. But of course, we are free. Well, sort of free. There is no such thing as a free lunch. It has to be taxed. We have to pay for our highways and byways and freeways and levees. Don't forget the levees. New Orleans won't. Anyway, we use to have a very inexpensive cost of living in Nevada. We use to point at California and smile and chuckle and sometimes even laugh out loud at their expensive restaurants, their high rents, their high cost of insurance and their shiny white teeth. Nevada is catching up. Except in the teeth department. We still have some work to do there. But I think we have passed and surpassed California in auto registration fees, charges and other costs related to owning or thinking about owning a car, bus or horse drawn carriage. I am a driver of American cars. Many people I know have Mercedes and BMWs, but I choose to drive and support Ford, General Motors and Chrysler. My recent truck was an Escalade pickup. It was expensive, but I buy my autos wholesale and I usually buy them when they're 6 or 8 months old, and someone else has taken the huge depreciation hit you have experienced if you bought new.

Salesman: I'm sure you'll enjoy your new Cadillac. Its ride is smooth, its look dynamic and its payment book comes in a really nice converted toilet paper carton that measures 3 feet by 4 feet.

You: Well thank you for being so nice. And kind. And I really appreciate how you were able to qualify me for a $50,000 car loan with a $950 a month payment. Especially when my Social Security check is only $1,100 a month. You truly are a miracle worker. God bless you.

Salesman: I'm here to help. And satisfy. And get a huge commission check. Not necessarily in that order.

You: I can't wait to pick up the girls at the Senior Center and take us all to Bingo in my new Cad.

Salesman: Well, don't overdue it. Remember, your first payment is due in 4 hours. And Bingo is an expensive hobby.

You: Well God bless you for reminding me. I almost forgot about the payment. I'll skip Bingo and eating this week.

Salesman: We can all afford to lose a few pounds. Well, take care. I have to go sell someone else a car they can't afford.

Five weeks later you return to the dealership.

Salesman: Back already?

You: I need to trade in my car for something more economical.

Salesman: Economical sounds cheap. We now use the term Hybrid.

You: Call it what the fuck you want. I haven't eaten in 5 weeks.

Salesman: You're a testy old fart aren't you.

You: Listen Sonny, I'm hungry from not eating. I'm tired from lugging around the payment book for this fuckin' thing. And I'm depressed from having to choose between gas and meals.

Salesman: Well, woe is you. Let's see, how about a nice used 1985 Cadillac Sedan De' Ville 4 door?

You: How much?

Salesman: Well, first we have to see what your car is worth. You've had it for quite a while.

You: I've had it for 5 fuckin' weeks!

Salesman: Wow, you paid $50,000 for this? Where did you buy this thing? I hate to tell you, but you got fucked!

You: But I bought it here! From you!

Salesman: Oh. Well let me talk to my manager. We'll try and get you $9,000 for it.

You: But I paid $50,000!

Salesman: You are a victim of depreciation.

That's why I buy cars that are 6 or 8 months old. I'm never a victim of depreciation until the new cars come out. So I have 4 months of enjoyable driving. Until, of course, I go to register my "new" vehicle. Here are my latest Nevada registration fees for my Escalade:

Basic Registration	$67.00
Charge for calculating Basic Registration	64.00
Highway Charge	94.00
Freeway Charge	72.00
Charge for calculating Highway & Freeway Charges	37.00
Privilege Tax	96.00
Special Privilege Tax	87.00
You're a lucky fuck to be able to afford to drive an Escalade Tax	2,750.00

Tax to Save the Desert Tortoise	350.00

Burial Charges to bury Desert Tortoises
you will probably kill because we've
saved too many of them and they're all
over the fuckin' highway   535.00

Charge to calculate Burial Charges   120.00

Tip   45.00

TOTAL   **$4,317.00**

When I called the Department of Motor Vehicles I was informed by a recording that if I was calling to question my registration fees, I would incur a small additional tax based on the retail cost of my vehicle. California, here I come. Actually, I'm almost eligible to live in Florida. I'm sure that registration on electric carts can't be much.....

When Boms Collide

If you had just one day to spend with someone you wish was **gone**, who would it be? What would you say? Would every sentence start with the words "Listen, asshole"? A story, not by the great Mitch Albom, but by his evil twin Tony Korfman-bom. No kin to Badda-Bing, Badda Boom, Badda-Bom. P.S, this work was not endorsed by Al Einstein, Al Franken, Al Jolsen, Aloe Vera or any other body lotion (there were some hand lotions that thought it was cute though). Speaking of boms, Mitch Albom is far from being a bom or a bomb. His works have tripled my investment in Kleenex stock over the years. Hankys are out. Kleenex is in. Hankys promote germs. The average hanky has 27 billion germs on it. That's before you use it. Then it gets filled with stuff you can't describe. You wouldn't **want** to describe it. It is so despicable, so disgusting that humans have come up with a very short word for it. An unmistakable word. A simple, short, right to the heart of the matter word. Snot. There, I said it, so let's move on. Mitch Albom writes tearjerkers. Gut wrenching, hold your stomach, sobbing tearjerkers. And that's after just reading the titles. Tears start welling up. You don't need to buy the book. Just read the title, think about it for a few minutes, breakdown and sob uncontrollably, ask the Barnes and Noble girl for some Kleenex and get on with your life. I personally have bought every one of his books and have never gotten past the table of contents. So when I read the cover of "Parade", an insert in my local Sunday paper, I knew I wasn't going to read the article. The entire cover of Parade said, "If you had one day to spend with someone who's gone… who would it be? What would you do? A story by Mitch Albom." That was enough to finish me. After sobbing uncontrollably for 15 minutes, I regained my composure. Much to the delight of the trucker sitting next to me at the counter of Denny's.

Then I knew I had to react. With fierce abandonment. Whatever the fuck that means. I started writing immediately. To the manager of the restaurant about the incredibly bad breakfast I just had. Eggs, perfectly done, bacon just right, toast- delicious. I wasn't use to that kind of breakfast. I knew every breakfast I would have from then on would never live up to that breakfast experience, which would be a very depressing scenario. That's how I think. I know. I'm a sick fuck.

Anyway, after looking at the cover of "Parade" with the title of Mitch's article on a background of blue sky, white clouds, the ocean and two people walking on the beach, I knew a response was forthcoming. It was brewing. It was churning. But that might have been the 7 eggs I just ate. And the triple order of bacon. And let's not forget the loaf of toast. But I had to react. I just had to. I figured I could always blame it on the toast. So I got to thinking about all the assholes in poker. And if you could spend one whole day with them from early morning til the next morning- what would you say? What would you do? Can you imagine? At 6 A.M. knocking on Phil Hellmuth or Mike Matusow's door and showering with them? Then having breakfast and doing morning prayers. And the laundry. And sorting out their undergarments. And watching them pop blackheads. And dress. And accessorize. What tremendous insight you would have into their hearts- their souls- their underwear drawer. Then of course the evening conversation before you both retire to bed. The day in retrospect. A re-enactment of every event, every conversation, every pimple popped. Man, what fun. What a day! I'm getting excited just thinking about it. If I only had one day to spend with someone I wish was gone. Just one…

A Side Note:
(whatever the fuck that is)

Mitch Albom has sold over 3 billion copies of "Tuesdays With Morrie". I know this is hard to believe because the population of this country is 300 million, which means that every man, woman, child and man-child bought 10 books. And they wouldn't have bought them for their friends, family and co-workers because everyone already had 10 copies. "Tuesdays With Morrie" is a riveting, sad story about a guy who visits a guy named "Morrie" every Tuesday and has sex with him. Wait a minute, that "Tuesdays with Laurie". About a guy who meets with a hooker every Tuesday. "Tuesdays With Morrie" is really really sad. Morrie is dying and every Tuesday his new friend visits him and gains insight to Morrie's incredible wisdom. This person (whose name totally escapes me) takes notes and recordings documenting Morrie's last Tuesdays on Earth so that he can share Morrie's inspiring story, his wisdom, knowledge, experience, erudition, sagacity, intelligence, smarts, acumen, savvy and foresight with the world and, of course, make a few million bucks in the process. And to quote Seinfeld, "There's nothing wrong with that." But we all know going in that Morrie is going to die. Every Tuesday brings him closer to death. The next book I plan to write is a follow-up to "Tuesdays With Morrie". It's called "Tuesday Isn't Good Morrie, Can We Shoot For Thursday?" This may not be the tearjerker that "Tuesdays With Morrie" was, but I figure most people don't want to sob uncontrollably when they're reading a book on a bus or train or in church or on a motorcycle sidecar. "Tuesdays With Morrie" is a must read- in the privacy of your own home. Or apartment. Or shelter.

End of Side Note

Random Thought

It is with regret that I have to inform you that Johnny Chan has been deluged with lawsuits because of his shirt collection. It seems the outrageously bright colors and designs have caused headaches, anxiety, suicide, blindness and insanity to those who stare at them. His shirts have been mistaken for welcome mats by many shoppers. 3 out of 5 attorneys polled agree that a class action suit may have some merit. Field tests are incomplete and inconclusive but 4 out of 5 dentists do agree that Chan's teeth need a cleaning. The other dentist is part of the class action suit.

Updating Live Tournaments

I think live tournament play would be much more interesting and fun if there were a few rules implemented:

1) If you get a pocket pair, you have to do a shot.

2) A showgirl would escort any player that got busted out of the room. This would turn an embarrassing situation into an enviable one. Especially if instead of saying, "I hope you had fun at the tournament", she would stick her tongue down your throat. The women players would have a Chippendale dancer as an escort.

3) Anyone who screamed, yelled or high fived someone when they won a pot on the river would have to relinquish the pot. It would be split by the remaining players at the table. Entourages would still be allowed to high five each other in the stands.

4) The loser of any large pot would have to do a double shot. And remove an article of clothing.

5) If you're one of those pesky, annoying fucks that know it all, you will have to give a lap dance to the first person eliminated from the tournament. Voting on each table would determine who the pesky, annoying fucks are.

6) At the final table- blindfolds.

7) Illegal holds during confrontations will be encouraged.

8) Performance-enhancing drugs like Viagra and steroids will be given to everyone before the first hand at the final table is dealt. This will make everyone irritable, cranky and combative. It should be fun to watch.

9) Every player will have a scantily dressed, very hot babe

to stack his chips and brush the crumbs off his lap when he eats.

10) Lobster buffet served tableside.

11) Casey Kasem would do the top 10 countdown at the final table with Dick Clark as a backup.

12) Small caliber weapons will be issued before the tournament started. Usage would be encouraged and possibly mandated.

My Favorite Card Covers

My Favorite Card Covers Continued

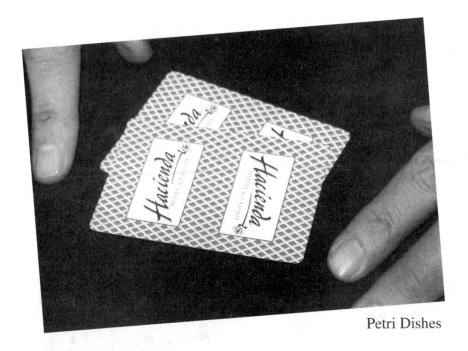

Petri Dishes

This sometimes results in a 20 minute penalty, depending where you play. Some places it's only 10.

My favorite kind of dog - soft - cuddly - always there and doesn't shit.

A Pair

Quads

The Marie Antoinette card cover with the "bad beat ejector head" feature is a must for every Hold 'em player. The gift that keeps on giving, and ejecting. It gives "reloading" a whole new meaning. Some comments from poker degenerates are:

"I love the way the head comes off cleanly with no mess"

"Just push the button and the head goes flying. No more having to carry around a heavy, cumbersome guillotine.

The Marie Antoinette Action Figure Doll with the ejector head. Look for it at your local delicatessen. A must have for your next bad beat.

Marie Antoinette Doll before bad beat.

After bad beat

Reloaded

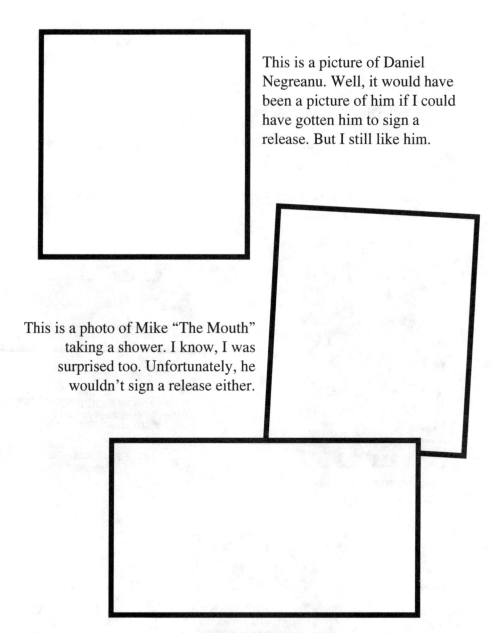

This is a picture of Daniel Negreanu. Well, it would have been a picture of him if I could have gotten him to sign a release. But I still like him.

This is a photo of Mike "The Mouth" taking a shower. I know, I was surprised too. Unfortunately, he wouldn't sign a release either.

This was going to be a picture of Phil Hellmuth, but we all know what the prick looks like. Actually, he is probably a nice guy. But the word "prick" is funnier.

A Chip and a Chair. Releases were signed by both the chip and the chair. Thanks guys.

A Phil Hellmuth Aftershock

I saw this cartoon by F. Andrew Taylor in our local paper. I liked it. After they ate they sat down to a game of Texas Hold'em.

The Few- The Proud- The Marines
Being All That They Can Be- And More- Much More

The warrior is fighting a war through no fault of his own. He would rather be home with his family. He would rather be home with his friends. He would rather be home with his poker playing buddies. Hate the war. Never the warrior. He'd rather be home. Like you are. Just like you are. You lucky fuck.

I think it was **Will Rogers** who said, **"I never met an Elvis I didn't like."** Or something like that. Anyway, **neither have I.**

Hold 'em players come in all ages, shapes and sizes. Just like Elvises.

"Krispy Kreme- The Power of Donuts.

Elvis before he was "The King". Before him and I worked at the
Las Vegas Hilton. Way before.

Twas the night before Christmas,
and all through the house, not a
creature was stirring- not even
Santa. He was "stuck" $2,500 at
Binion's Horseshoe and not too
fuckin' happy about it. Sorry
kids- there's alway next year.

I included this picture of really
old guys playing poker because
I wanted to show two things:
1) How you "young guns" who
never shave are going to look
in a few years; and 2), the
all-important number two. Fuck,
I forgot what number two was.
I'm old- I forget.

My family- the people in my life that count- a lot.

I make the living- She makes the living worthwhile.

They say behind every successful man is a woman- rolling her eyes.
This is her. My love- my life- my wife. For almost 40 years. How
wonderful life is with her in my world. I love you baby.

A donkey all of the time

A donkey some of
the time

A big part of my life- The future of America

Great Balls of Fire!

Balls the Size of Buicks

This was the Bellagio Christmas tree in the main entrance in December of 2006. Most guys just stopped and stared at it, including me, because we have never seen balls that fuckin' big. Talk about ball envy. I love the Bellagio. It's a very classy joint. I even enjoy walking into their bathrooms. There's nothing like the smell of raspberry pine scented urine to complete my day. I love raspberry, especially with pine. I want to thank the young couple from Oklahoma who took the picture for me with their camera and then emailed it to me. I don't know their names, but I remember they had 2 different last names and his shirt was all wrinkled and she looked exhausted. I'm sure their parents thought they were at college studying. But they were taking a picture of me at the Bellegio instead. Even if I knew their names, I wouldn't tell you. They were too nice. I think her name was Christian. Or Kristian. What goes on in Vegas stays in Vegas. I'm sworn to abide by that (I think his name was Dwayne).

Gambling Times

In February of 1977 the first issue of a magazine called *Gambling Times* was published. It had really good articles about- what else? Gambling. The publisher was Stanley Sludikoff and its first issue had an eight-page interview with Doyle Brunson. He had just won the 1976 Championship (Texas) Hold 'em Poker Tournament at the Horseshoe in Las Vegas and collected $220,000. A few days before that he had won $90,000 in the Deuce-to-Seven (Kansas City) Lowball Championship Tournament. Even then Uncle Doyle was called one of the best in the world in ALL forms of poker. If you get a chance, try and get a copy of the interview. It's a really in depth discussion with Doyle that is personal, riveting, revealing and stops just a little short of discussing penis length. In case you've ever wondered or pondered where the famous, or infamous (I've never figured out the difference so I use them both), Doyle Brunson 10-2 hand came from, this was the tournament. In the 76' Championship Hold 'em game, the final hand Brunson was dealt was the 10-2 of Spades. He was against A-J suited in Hearts. Doyle's opponent was Jesse Alto. The flop came As-Jd-2h. Alto had flopped top two pair, Brunson had a pair of twos. Alto bet $8,500- Brunson called. The turn card was a 10-d. Alto moved all-in. Brunson called. He had two pair now. Tens and deuces against Alto's top two pair of Aces and Jacks. The river- the almighty river- a ten of clubs, which gave Doyle tens full. **And** immortality. The Doyle Brunson 10-2 was born. When later asked about playing the 10-2 Brunson said, "I thought he was bluffin." Not "bluffing"- but "bluffin". That's what he said. I listened to the tapes. No one knew it, but I was secretly recording the whole event. I didn't discover these very valuable tapes until I was going through my "secretly taped" tape collection, which is comprised mostly of moans and groans my wife makes when I come home from a poker game with no money. Any other moans and groans on the tapes are purely fabricated. The Brunson tapes were mixed up between those and the Nixon tapes. My Nixon tapes didn't have any erasures because my secretary wasn't as clumsy as Nixon's. Chances are no one knows what the fuck I'm talking about, so I just had a very humorous concept go right down the toilet. Just like Nixon did. Oh well. Anyway, the 1976 Hold 'em Championship, which morphed into the World Series of Poker, lasted three days. The final day's session on Sunday May 16, 1976 began at 2:15 P.M. and ended at 3:50 A.M. on Monday morning. There were 2 thirty-minute breaks, 1 fifteen-minute break, 2 ten-minute breaks and 1 five-minute break. Then at 3:50 A.M., they broke until the following May. The pictures of the players revealed some fascinating facts. No one wore headphones, there were no iPods, XBOXes or cell phones in front of anyone. Maybe they weren't allowed at the table. No one wore sunglasses. Everyone had on nice clothes. Some sport coats, some ties, some silk shirts and an occasional leisure suit. And one spectator had an Elvis jumpsuit on. And all the players smelled good. They were required to put on men's cologne every break. A cologne break. Now it's called a pee break. I love making shit up. But the following is fact. When play started at the beginning of the tournament on May 14, 1976 at 7:45 P.M., there were 22 players. The first one out was Jay Heimowitz less than an hour after the tournament started. I can still feel his pain. When interviewed after the game, Heimowitz, who is no relation to the Heimlich maneuver, said that he didn't believe in luck at the poker table or same sex marriage. He was from New York and also said his luggage had never been stolen. He came in last- 22nd place- and when asked if he would have done anything different, he said, "I should have adopted Phil Hellmuth's philosophy and came to the tournament late. Half the field would have been eliminated and I would have gotten a lot more attention from the television cameras when I entered the room." The following list shows how everyone finished in the 1976 Hold 'em Championship. There are 4 reasons why I'm sharing this valuable information:

1) I need to fill up some space.

2) I thought you'd like to know.

3) I am guaranteed to sell at least 22 books to family members of the 22 players.

4) I forgot the 4th reason.

-The Winner- Of course, Doyle "Texas Dolly" Brunson from Fort Worth Texas.

-2nd Place- Jesse Alto from Houston, Texas. He came so close. So fuckin' close. If he wins the hand, the A-J would have been known as the Jesse Alto. The world would have been different. The sky bluer. Food would have tasted better. I'm sick about it.

-3rd Place- Tommy Hufnagle from Schwenksville, Pennsylvania. Schwenksville- that's fuckin' funny. I can't even keep my pen steady while I'm writing this shit, I'm laughing so hard. Hufnagle from Schwenksville. Everyone knows that a guy's penis is called his Johnson. Why the fuck didn't we name it a Schwenksville? Or a Schwenk for short. Or a Schwenk **if** it's short. Let's do it, guys. Especially the guys named Johnson. I know they would vote for the new name.

-4th Place- Crandall Addington from San Antonio, Texas. This guy was the best dressed player at the table. Suit, tie, hat, big cigar. He exuded class. And cigar smoke. A lot of it. I'm an exuder also. I exude incredible farts. Maybe I'm not classy. But I do exude.

-5th Place- Bryan "Sailor" Roberts from San Angelo, Texas. Sailor was probably the best liked by his peers. Very soft spoken, very modest and generous to a fault. Never said "no" to someone in need. A gentle soul. It sounds like Mike "The Mouth" Matusow has a fuckin' twin! In 1975, Sailor won the event and $220,000 because of his good Karma.

-6th Place (tie)- Bert Rice from Houston, Texas. His actual business was selling valves to major gas transmission companies. I have no fuckin' idea what that means. It just means he made a lot of money to be able to afford the $10,000 buy-in.

-6th Place (tie)- "Puggy" Pearson from Nashville, Tennessee. He was called extremely aggressive and a terror at the table. This sounds like dealer terminology for "prick". In 1972 he came in second and in 1973 he won the event and $130,000. Must have been because of the good Karma he exuded. So much for fuckin' Karma.

-8th Place- Bobby Baldwin from Dallas, Texas. His star was rising fast in 1976. They said in poker he was already a Prince. A little more seasoning and they said he would become a King. Well, he did better than that. He became Steve Wynn's buddy and now he's helping Kirk Kerkorian run his empire. He still plays in the World Series of Poker and as far as I know smells really good and expensive. He exudes wealth.

9th Place- Gary "Bones" Berland from Los Angeles, California. Bones was known as a superior mathematician who could compute the price on a particular Hold 'em hand instantaneously. I just wanted to mention that so I could use the word "instantaneously", which is the longest word I've used or will ever use in my life. I can't fuckin' believe I've spelled it correctly twice.

-10th Place- Aubrey Day from Tuscaloosa, Alabama. Now, I know what you're thinking. Who the fuck would name their kid Aubrey? At first that's what I thought. Then I did like a Jack Handy Deep Thought. It could have been worse. They could have named him "Rainy". Then every day in class he would dread role call. Rainy Day- are you here Rainy Day? Or "Foggy". Or "Dark Dreary". Dark Dreary Day- are you here? And the class would laugh hysterically and point at him giving him anal leakage. Every time he would make a reservation, people would snicker. So Aubry isn't so bad. It has three vowels and three consonants. A nice balance. Parents always narrow down their choices of names for kids to two or three before the wife makes the final decision. I'm really curious what the other two choices could have been. I wonder if "Doyle" could have been one of them.

-11th Place- "Cadillac" Jack Grimm from Abilene, Texas. Now here is a great fuckin' name- Cadillac Jack. Of course with a name like that, the pressure would always be on you. You could never drive a Chevy or a Ford.

-12th Place- "Amarillo Slim" Preston from Amarillo Texas. Thank God he was born in Amarillo. It made it so much easier to explain his name. He was known as poker's goodwill ambassador, tirelessly giving up his time to talk shows, interviews and anyone else who wanted to hear a bad beat poker story. He was Mike Sexton with a cowboy hat.

-13th Place- Howard "Tahoe" Andrew from Pleasanton, California. "Tahoe" was an industrial engineer. I haven't got a fuckin' clue as to what an industrial engineer does. Maybe he drove an industrial train. Anyway, they say he had a sore arm in this tournament from pushing his chips to the center of the pot so often. In fact, the soreness of his shoulder almost became known as "Tahoe" Tunnel Syndrome, but a kid came along whose dad had a ton of fuckin' money and wanted to name something after himself to make his college roommate in med school really jealous. This kid's name was Freddy Carpal and the rest is history. Carpal tunnel syndrome still affects many poker players today, especially the ones that look at their hole cards incorrectly. As a side note- Freddy Carpal is no relation to Freddy Deeb- even though their names are spelled the same.

-14th Place- Dick Carson from Dallas, Texas. I don't know how I would cope going through life with a name like "Dick". They called Carson "Dickie". I'm not going to elaborate on Dick's name. First of all, I like the name "Carson". I have a grandkid named Carson and I liked Kit Carson. And second of all, I'm going to have enough lawsuits over this fuckin' book without adding another one from Dickie's family.

-15th Place- Bob Hooks from Edgewood, Texas. Bob was known as a money manager, which is what I've tried to instill in my wife. I try to tell her it's OK to go through a full day and not shop. God will not be pissed. Bob was known to have held on to most of his winnings. Fully translated this probably means he was tighter than two coats of paint. And that's OK. Some people are generous in other ways than with their money. The accumulation of tremendous amounts of money is a critical part of some people's lives. And I'm sure they will have some of the prettiest tombstones in the cemetery. And we are all aware of tombstone envy. Which is way past penis envy. Way past.

-16th Place- Al Ethier from Bristol, Rhode Island. I didn't even realize Rhode Island was in the United States. He played mostly in card clubs in Gardena, California before he moved to Las Vegas. He was a consistent, solid player. Which of course meant that he played tight. And to play tight you have to have patience. And so this tight, patient player came in 16th in a field of 22. Sounds like he needs to develop a new strategy.

-17th Place- Ed "Junior" Whited from Austin, Texas. "Junior" said he'll gamble on anything. "Horses, fish, license plates, cracks in cement, you name it." He's a steady winner and can adjust his play to accommodate any game. And I love his "Elvis" hairdo.

-18th Place- Jack "Tree Top" Strauss from Houston, Texas. I see two patterns developing here. Almost everyone has a nickname and almost everyone is from Texas. But not everyone is 6'5'' tall. "Tree Top" was called a different breed. Aggressive, highly analytical and well dressed. Of course, the one compelling question never asked when he was interviewed- boxers or briefs? Maybe next time.

-19th Place- "Jolly" Roger Van Arsdale from Caruthersville, Missouri. Described as a gentleman that took his losses in stride and never lost his temper. An obvious Phil Hellmuth clone.

-20th Place- Johnny Moss from Odessa, Texas. "Texas Johnny", the Grand Old Man of Poker. He won the championship in 1970, its first year. His gambling exploits are legendary. He always dressed nice and no one ever called him a prick. If you can play poker for a living and leave that legacy, you are a success story.

-21st Place- Jack "Rabbit" Wright from Fort Wayne, Indiana. Poker was his hobby and his lack of experience was obvious at the table when he tried to rebuy chips. And when the dealer put the "dealer button" in front of him he said "thank you" and put it in his pocket. Other than that he was fine.

-22nd Place- Jay Heimowitz from Monticello, New York. Jay said, "Wait til next year." I'm still waiting Jay.

Tournament poker has come a long ways, baby. This past year over 8700 players paid $10,000 each to play in the World Series of Poker. From 22 players to over 8700. Fuckin' amazing. And I'm not bluffin about those numbers.

Bad News - Good News - Great News

After an all night poker session, Mr. Smith was so excited about winning a tournament he couldn't sleep, so he went fishing to relax. After not returning by evening time, Mrs. Smith called the police. Three days later, a somber policeman came to her door. "Mrs. Smith, we have some information about your husband", he said. "Did you find him?", Mrs. Smith yelled. The officer shuffled his feet and said, "Well, we have some bad news, some good news and some great news." "Give me the bad news first", a pale Mrs. Smith said. The officer said, "I'm sorry to tell you but we found your husband's body this morning." "Oh my God!" exclaimed Mrs Smith. "What's the good news?" The officer continued, "When we pulled him up he had 15 twenty pound King Crabs and five good size lobsters clinging to him." Stunned, Mrs. Smith said, "If that's the good news, what's the great news?" The officer said, "We're going to pull him up again tomorrow."

A Morality Issue

This is a test. It's a simple test. It only has one question, but it's an important one. It's about morals. We all talk about being moral- our word is our bond- blah blah blah. But this cuts to the chase. You will know how moral you are when no one is watching. And that's when morality shows the most. Pour yourself a stiff drink because we don't always want to know the truth about ourselves. You will be given a situation and you will need to make a decision. An important one. Your answer needs to be honest and spontaneous. Read each line carefully. Very carefully.

The Situation:

You are in Florida. Miami to be specific. There is chaos all around you caused by a hurricane. There is severe flooding. A huge fuckin' flood. You're a photojournalist working for a major newspaper. And here you are caught in this disaster. The situation all around you is nearly hopeless. You're trying to shoot career-making photos. Houses and people are swirling all around you and some are disappearing under the water. Chaos. Mother Nature is unleashing a tremendous amount of destructive fury.

The Test:

Suddenly you see a man in the water. He is literally fighting for his life. He's trying not to be taken down under with the debris around him. You move closer. Somehow the man looks familiar. You suddenly realize who it is. It's Phil Hellmuth Jr.! At the same time you notice that the raging waters are about to take him under forever. You have two options: you can save the life of Phil Hellmuth Jr. or shoot a dramatic Pulitzer Prize winning photo documenting the death of one of the world's most parasitic poker players.

The Question:

Here's the question and please give an honest answer. Would you select high contrast color film or go with the classic simplicity of black and white?

He Died Peacefully In His Sleep

I hate those words. Who the fuck in this whole wide, complicated, crowded, greedy world wants to die peacefully in their sleep? If you raised your hand, you're a fuckin' liar. Everyone wants to go to Heaven, but nobody wants to die to get there. Die? Who the fuck wants to die and find out there is no Heaven. Or Anything! And to die peacefully in my sleep? Fuck You! I want the obituary to read, "He died screaming and yelling. He was throwing bedpans and mother fucking the doctors. His final act was to down a shot of Crown Royal and chase it with a glass of Holy Water the priest was using to give him Final Absolution. And he doesn't even drink!" He died peacefully in his sleep? Give me a break. Give me a fucking break.

Aladdin's Lamp

If I had just one wish- one incredible wish- it would be for Peace on Earth and for the children of the world to never feel hunger while choirs of Angels sang "Glory, Glory Hallelujah" in the background. If I had just two wishes- two incredible wishes- the first would be for Peace on Earth and for the children of the world to never feel hunger while choirs of Angels sang "Glory, Glory Hallelujah" in the background; and the second wish would be to get $100 million dollars a year tax free with annual cost of living increases. If I had just three wishes- three incredible wishes- the first would be for Peace on Earth and for the children of the world to never feel hunger while choirs of Angels sang "Glory, Glory Hallelujah" in the background; the second wish would be to get 100 million dollars a year tax free with annual cost of living increases; and my third wish would be for total world domination. If I had just four wishes- four incredible wishes- my first would be that crap about world peace and hungry kids, my second wish would be for 100 million dollars a year tax free with annual cost of living increases, my third wish would be for total world domination and my fourth wish would be to see everyone's hole cards whenever I play in any Hold 'em game. Hold on just a fuckin' minute. Let's be realistic. It would be impossible to have Peace on Earth. Maybe we could attain Peace on Your Street or even Peace in Your Neighborhood. But Peace on Earth? It can't fuckin' happen. There are too many pissed off people out there. And kids never being hungry? Give me a fuckin' break. Some kid somewhere is going to wake up at 2 A.M. and want something to eat. So we need to make some changes on our list. Just minor ones. The first wish would be the money with annual cost of living increases, the second wish would be the world domination thing, the third wish would be to know everyone's hand when I play cards and the fourth wish would be for Peace on Earth and for the children of the world to never feel hunger while choirs of Angels sing "Glory, Glory Hallelujah" in the background.

Merry Christmas Everyone

Random Thought

It was Christmas Eve when they entered the card room and it was obvious they were in need. He was a carpenter with a tool belt and she was very pregnant. All they needed was an exhausted looking mule that looked like it hadn't eaten in 2 weeks to complete the picture. I'm thinking, "Man, I use to just **think** everyone plays poker and now I know it for certain." When he was seated next to me, I couldn't help it. I said, "Joseph?" He said, "No, Clyde." I said, "I'm sorry, you reminded me of someone." His pregnant wife sat behind him. He said, "This is my wife, Mary." I said, "Perfect." When they both ordered double vodkas with cranberry juice, I knew I had them mixed up with someone else.

Signs That Mike "The Mouth" Matusow

Has Gone Over the Edge

Mike "The Mouth" Matusow is one of the most colorful, most irritating, most vocal players the game of poker has ever seen. Sometimes he walks right up to the very edge of the cliff and we all hold our breath waiting for him to take one more step. Here are some signs that he has taken that step:

1) Whenever he gets rivered he bites off the head of a chicken.

2) When a photographer shoots him from a bad angle he throws hot coffee in his eyes.

3) He crushes opponents' ball sacks with his teeth.

4) He gets upset when his family isn't at tournaments to heckle him.

5) He gets so pissed he asks for the launch codes.

6) He names each of his facial warts.

7) He carries a loaded salad shooter with him at all times and uses it as a card cover.

8) He forces people at the final table to form a naked pyramid.

9) He tries to sell people at his table thigh cream.

10) He says it's not bestiality if it's consensual.

11) He wants to be referred to as "The Dark Prince of Poker".

No Limit- The Pain Game

I'm playing in a cash game at Caesar's Palace. I've got about $3,000 in front of me. 5-10 No Limit. Older guy next to me has about the same amount of money in front of him. I look down at pocket Aces. Raise, re-raise, All-in. It happens quick. I turn over my Aces, he turns over his Kings. He had a Diamond King. I didn't have a diamond. Can you see this one coming down the track like the fuckin' Super Chief locomotive? Flop is 3 Diamonds. Next card- Ace of Clubs. He has 4 Diamonds. I have 3 Aces. The fuckin' River? What else? A Diamond that doesn't pair the fuckin' board. Game, Set, Match. He picks up my cash, my chips, and does a fuckin' dance. At that point, I'm hoping, actually praying, for his heart to give out. And also that the defibrillator in the security room has a dead battery. But, alas- He lived- I grieved. But I rebounded nicely thinking about him choking on a chicken bone. Oh well. There's no animosity in me. None whatsoever.

Random Thought

I think it was Gandhi that said, "I object to violence after you've been rivered." Or maybe it was Phil Hellmuth. I get the two mixed up.

Are You A Poker Degenerate?

Answer these questions honestly with a "Yes" or "No". There are no other answers. No other outs. Be truthful. Be honest. Be forthright. Score $6^{1}/_{2}$ points for each "No" answer. Score $9^{1}/_{2}$ points for each "Yes". Multiply the total by 2.7 and divide that total by 12.954. Then call David Sklansky and see what it all means. He has the score chart.

Y / N -You gamble money earmarked for other things like little Jimmy's operation.

Y / N -You hate little Jimmy because he's fuckin' with your poker money.

Y / N -You play bad cards, get bad beats and have bad breath.

Y / N -You have no life except poker.

Y / N -You eat at the poker table.

Y / N -Your kids learned to count 1,2,3,4,5,6,7,8,9,10,J,Q,K.

Y / N -You named your last kid "Suited Connectors".

Y / N -The ATM machine at your local casino vibrates violently when you approach it because it knows you have cold hands.

Y / N -Has gambling caused a decrease in your sperm count?

Y / N -After losing a big pot to an asshole, have you found yourself in a dark parking lot waiting for him with your goalie mask on?

Y / N -Do you usually carry a goalie mask?

Y / N -When you win, do you want to win more and more until you have all the money in the universe and then yell "I am the King of the Universe" and order a double cheeseburger with extra onions?

Y / N   -With extra secret sauce?

-Deduct 3 points if you answered yes to the "With extra secret sauce" question. There is no secret sauce. It was a trick question.

Y / N   -Have you ever gambled until your last dollar was gone?

Y / N   -Until your last pair of underwear was gone?

Y / N   -Have you ever borrowed money to gamble?

Y / N   -Have you ever borrowed underwear to gamble?

Y / N   -Boxers or briefs?

Y / N   -Have you ever used your gambling money for something insignificant like your kids' braces, which is, as we all know, a real waste of fuckin' money.

Y / N   -Have you ever gambled for long periods of time and missed 1st period?

Y / N   -If you are a woman, have you ever missed your period because you were too busy gambling?

Y / N   -Have you ever committed an illegal act, more than the acceptable three times, to gamble?

Y / N   -Has gambling ever caused you a sleeping problem?

Y / N   -Has sleeping ever caused you a gambling problem?

Y / N   -If given a choice, would you play Hold 'em rather than be with a gorgeous girl with a trick pelvis?

Y / N   -If you have an argument, do you get the urge to

gamble?

Y / N   -If you have an argument, do you get the urge to have sex?

Y / N   -If you have an argument, do you get the urge to eat a cheeseburger while you're having sex?

Y / N   -Have you ever considered suicide because of your gambling?

Y / N   -Have you ever considered suicide because the game broke up while you were a loser and McDonald's was closed?

Y / N   -Have you ever considered suicide because you **are** a loser, period?

Y / N   -Have you ever considered buying a McDonald's franchise and having a poker game in the back room?

Y / N   -Do you feel that if you quit the game the growth of poker would be impeded?

Y / N   -Do you know what impeded means?

Y / N   -Do you have a small penis?

Sklansky awaits your call.

Random Thought

9 *Out of 10 poker players agree that they have no life. Or life insurance.*

The 43 Second Rule

I would rather be the aggressor and put you in the position to ponder calling me rather than me having to ponder whether or not I should call you. I hate fuckin' pondering. It makes my head ache, my stomach growl and my asshole twitch. I'd rather someone else pondered. When you are calling someone on the river, you will win one-third of the time. One time out of three. How do I know that? I could tell you I have been charting hands since puberty and I majored in statistics in college. Actually, I think I read it somewhere. Or I made it up. I forget. I'm old. Anyway, my point is, and I do have a point, that if you have to ponder more than 43 seconds, throw the fuckin' hand away. Another one is just a minute away.

The Good Old USA

We live in a country where people from other countries risk their lives to get into. They risk their fuckin' lives. They come from Mexico and walk across the hot desert. They get crammed in the back of enclosed trucks and can barely breathe. They come from Cuba and cross the ocean in small boats, rafts and crates. They risk their lives for a better life. They risk their lives to make a living. They risk their lives to feed their families and put a roof over their heads. Things we take for granted every day. Every single day. The Brooks and Dunn song says it best, "We all get a chance. Everybody gets to dance. Only in America. Only in America." And once in a while we get very lucky- we get very fuckin' lucky. One of them can throw a split-fingered fastball.

The Role Models of Hold 'em

(Give or Take One or Two)

Chris Moneymaker- This is the guy that helped to jumpstart this mania that is sweeping the country. He qualified in a $40 satellite on PokerStars.com and wound up winning the 2003 Main Event. Last year, out of 8,700 players, over 4,000 qualified online. Unfuckinbelievable. You can't make this shit up. All of the popular poker sites were giving away seats to the Main Event. Everyone made a fuckin' fortune. The Harrah's executives had to be jerking off to the financial statements generated from last year's tournament. And all the participants walked away with smiles on their faces. We all got a $10 voucher to get a burger or a piece of pizza at the Crisco tent that was set up to feed us at the Rio. The lobster buffet was cancelled. The burger tent made more sense to Harrah's. God I love this country. And its burgers. Especially the Double Fatburger with double cheese. My cholesterol count goes up as I'm ordering it. But it's worth it. Is there a Fatburger near you? Their goal is to get your cholesterol count as high as your SAT score. Then you get a free burger. I've gotten a lot of free ones. It looks like Moneymaker has also.

Antonio Esfandiari- It's a tough time for Antonio. Oil for his hair is over $60 a barrel. He's known as "The Magician". I guess he use to do magic. He licks his lips a lot. And I thought I saw him lick his forehead once. That's fuckin' magic in anybody's book. Look for him in Antonio and Tina's Wedding coming to a Playboy Club near you. I hope he does his slinky dance.

TJ Cloutier- Everyone who likes him still lives with their parents. He's suppose to star in an upcoming movie about a poker site that signs him to be a spokesman called "Death of a Franchise". He once asked his wife how many great poker players there are. She said, "One less than you think." TJ has been playing poker for over 2 years past his expiration date. He usually brings his wife to the tournaments he plays. Probably so he doesn't have to kiss her goodbye.

Barry Greenstein- Barry is not very tall. Actually, he is very short. He could have modeled as a hood ornament. But he is a giant in stature. He donates his tournament winnings to charity. All of it. That's pretty strong. He's a very quiet, very conservative person. Never screams and yells after a really bad beat. Never gives the dealer the finger. Never whines. He's never abusive. There's nothing wrong with being short. I'm a big huge guy and from my perspective there are a lot of good things about being a short guy:

1) No one ever calls you "a big fat fuck".

2) You can save money at your wedding by standing on your own wedding cake, eliminating the need for that costly little statue of the groom.

3) No harassment in gym class. You're expected to not do well in sports. You're expected to have a small penis.

I like Barry Greenstein. If I ever play on the same table with him, I'm going to go all-in with nothing so that he can win all my chips.

Chris "Jesus" Ferguson- Ferguson seems like a nice, quiet guy. Never loses his temper- he's polite. Even if I didn't like him I wouldn't say anything bad about him. His name is "Jesus" for Christ's sake. One day he ordered an order of onion rings from the food server at the game and passed it around and fed the entire room. With one order of onion rings. I was impressed. I thought, "Just like his namesake." Some people wear a bracelet that says "WWJD" (What Would Jesus Do?). Ferguson wears a bracelet that says "WWID" (What Would I Do?). Whenever he asks, no matter how crowded the hotel is, they never tell him there is no room at the Inn. Why take a fuckin' chance? His name is Jesus for Christ's sake.

Phil Hellmuth Jr.- This fuckin' guy is going to be late for his own funeral. He was two hours late at the WSOP. He's famous for that. And usually when he exits he sings a show tune that can be heard from near and far. His exit came after only two and a half hours of play and he didn't mother fuck or sing to anyone. He did pee in the guy's coffee cup that beat him, but that's a mild exit for Phil. I really wanted a show tune. Phil has been accused on three different occasions of head butting an opponent. Speaking of heads, returning astronauts have claimed they can see Phil's head from space.

Mike Sexton- It would be impossible for me to say anything bad or negative about Mike Sexton. How could I? He's the Ambassador of Poker for Christ's sake. The Ambassador! He's mellow, courteous, congenial, rich, plays good poker, never loses his temper, wins graciously and speaks softly. He's my exact polar opposite. When he won the Tournament of Champions he donated half of his prize money, $500,000, to various charities. He gave $100,000 each to the Special Olympics, the Buoniconti Fund (to help find a cure for paralysis), the Paralyzed Veterans of America, the Wounded Warrior Project (helps families of service men and women wounded or killed in battle) and Children Incorporated (helps provide food, school supplies etc. for underprivileged kids around the world). Children Incorporated is also where Barry Greenstein donates most of his tournament winnings. Finally, a really genuine, nice guy. How fuckin' depressing. There's got to be something wrong with him. There just has to be.

Howard Lederer- Here's another nice guy. What the fuck is the poker world coming to? The only thing I find suspicious about Howard is his last name. Confucius says, "Beware of man who has last name with 3 vowels all the same." I had to search through 350,000 Confucius sayings to find that one. It took me 12 hours. Actually, it wasn't really there. I had to make it up. Thank you, Howard, for being nice. My other favorite Howard is Howard Doody. Or maybe it was Howdy. Well, it's close enough.

Vince Van Patten- On TV he's Mike Sexton's sidekick. Sexton needs him like he needs crotch itch. Or menstrual cramps. I guess these kids of celebrities have to work. They should thank God they're a member of the Lucky Sperm Club.

David Einhorn- This kid won $659,000 in the WSOP Main Event and donated all of it to Parkinson's Disease Research. All of it. Not 10%. Not half. All of it. How can I say anything nasty about this kid. He has a huge heart. An incredible heart. And according to my sources, incredible farts. That's how he made it so far in the tournament. And what's wrong with that? There's nothing like a good fart in a full game to liven up the action. Nice going David. Have you thought about donating a few bucks towards Fart Research? Just an "outside the box" thought.

Chip Reese- Graduated from Dartmouth. I can barely spell Dartmouth. Chip has been called underrated. He's probably the best all around poker player in the game. He says he doesn't play that many tournaments because of all the time they take. And he probably would have trouble listening to Mike "The Mouth" for 10 hours. Who wouldn't? Who the fuck wouldn't?

Scott Fischman- I played against this kid for about 6 hours one tournament at the Bellagio. He sees a lot of flops. A lot. He's not a raiser. He calls a lot. If he calls you after the flop, you're probably in deep shit. I was disappointed a few days later to find out his attitude on tipping dealers. He's an ex-dealer, which makes his stand on anti-tipping even more disappointing to me. Granted, I over tip everyone. The cocktail waitress always gets $5 from me. Even the fat ones. Valet gets $10 when I get there and $10 when I leave. Of course there is always spot for me. No matter how busy. No matter if there's barricades saying "Valet Full". No matter. But that's Vegas. That's what I love about this town. And if I can afford to play poker, if I can afford to go to the restaurants, if I can afford to go the shows, I can afford to take care of the people that make our great town go round. Apparently Scott Fish-head and I don't see eye to eye on that. Fuck Scott Fishman.

Todd Brunson- When you ask dealers about Todd, they all say the same thing. He's a cheap bastard. Maybe Scott and Todd were joined at the hip. For everyone that says his dad is a class act there are 3 that say Todd isn't. But what can you do? Different strokes for different folks. Todd doesn't like to care and share. Well maybe he cares. About someone. About something. Todd is obviously a far cry from Barry Greenstein or David Einhorn, but I'm sure he cares about something. Or someone. Maybe. (Since I wrote this, I have played many hours with Todd. I was prepared not to like him. I was prepared to call him a cheap bastard and harass him. I was prepared for him to get obnoxious and abusive to the dealers so I could come to their defense and put Todd in his place. None of those things happened. The information I got from the dealers was not correct in my viewpoint. Todd took some really bad beats and lost big pots. He was a gentleman. He tipped generously. He was fun to be around. I like the kid. I didn't delete what I had already written just to show how sometimes, when information is relayed, it can be distorted. So don't believe everything you read. I'm glad I met and played with Todd. We played a total of about 20 hours on two separate occasions. There's no way he could have hidden bad behavior for that long a period of time. Thanks Todd. You taught me something- Much more important than poker).

Annie Duke- Annie wrote an article I recently read in Card Player. She writes very well and talked about the psychological profile of a poker player. She said she would talk to her husband about her wins and losses and sometimes that would cause problems in their marriage. I have been married for a very long time and my words of advice to all married couples are the following: In marriage, honesty is very important. It must be completely avoided. One of the really nice things about being married is you can let yourself go. The race is over. I like Annie Duke. She's a beacon of loveliness. She hasn't let herself go.

Joe Hachem- I played at the same table with him at the Venetian a while back. He was very nice, cooperative, kind to people and only gave me the finger twice. That's well below the average with the people that play at my table. I seem to bring out the worst in everyone. Joe is one of those really really good-looking guys that other guys love to hate. But girls love the guy. They're on him like a half price carnival ride. They say he's good-looking, personable and hung like a mule.

Daniel Negreanu- Dealers really like this kid. There wasn't one that I talked to that didn't rate him as one of their top 5 favorites. Daniel is always perky, always smiling. If he worked at a Starbucks he would be the Café Latte Manager of the Year. I know I would vote for him. He looks just like a kid I saw in a high school hygiene film. The clean, wholesome look. I played with him at a Venetian tournament. Not the hygiene film kid. I played with Daniel. Nice kid. He only gave me the finger once.

Phil Ivey- I played with him at a tournament at the Bellagio. He had a huge bet on a football game so he was pretty preoccupied watching the game. He is very quiet when he plays. Even when he speaks he's quiet. An inspiration to those of us with big mouths.

Eric Drake- Everyone likes this guy. Well maybe not everyone. I didn't talk to everyone. But no one I talked to had anything bad to say about him. So I might be forced to make some shit up. No one escapes me.

Freddy Deeb- I loved Freddy in "March of the Penguins". What a great movie. About fuckin' penguins. Like anyone gives a shit. But they are cute. That's why penguin BBQ's have never caught on. Freddy could be up for an Academy Award as the lead penguin. Isn't he married to Carla from Cheers? Or is that his twin brother Danny Devito? I get them confused. I'm old. Freddy likes to spend time with his family, which is great. He just got back from Disneyland. Unfortunately he wasn't tall enough to ride the rides. Next time, Freddy. Next time.

Sam Farha- This guy has to be loved by someone. We don't know who, but it's sure as shit not by poker dealers. Or anyone that wants to be a poker dealer. Or anyone that knows a poker dealer. But I know somewhere, someone loves this guy. Or at least likes him. Or doesn't hate him. Quotes I got from poker dealers when I was doing research for this book had a big range for Farha. Everything from "I hate the mother fucker" to "I hope they didn't allow him to mate". One kid told me he thought they would have to subpoena pall bearers when Sammy dies. When he farts he actually leaks Radon Gas.

Gavin Smith- What's with Gavin Smith? Was he on Star Trek? He looks like he's boldly let himself go. He's like the Will Rogers of today. Will use to say he never met a man he didn't like. Gavin looks like he's never seen a buffet he didn't like. So now he's a spokesman for PartyPoker.com. What happened? They couldn't get the lizard from Geico? We all want the same things in life- to live long, have lots of money and watch Gavin Smith on top of Phil Hellmuth humping him. God help us.

Mike "The Mouth" Matusow- It's so hard to believe he beat out 10 million other sperm. This guy is so unpopular that even Uncle John on MySpace won't be his friend. Some people are alive simply because it's against the law to kill them. This guy definitely turned down lucky street. I wonder how long he would last in a prison yard. Mike's parents are now pro choice. I think he must have suffered a massive head wound at some time in his life. Or he wants one. Or needs one. Or deserves one. Or maybe all of the above. I use to hate that choice on tests. All of the above. That means you can't guess at the answer. It throws a whole new dimension to the question. What kind of sick fuck came up with "All of the above"? Speaking of tests, when I think of high school, I think of a loud piercing voice that belonged to a kid named Speck. Speck's voice would penetrate even a very noisy stadium. I was at the table next to where Mike "The Mouth" was playing and I'm thinking, "Holy fuck, it's Speck." But it wasn't. It was Mike. Being around him for long periods of time can cause blindness and anal leakage. You have to wonder what color the fuckin' sky is in his world. Mike "The Mouth" might be the reason the terrorists hate us. But alas, he wants to be known for so much more than being a village idiot. The problem he has is that the village won't stop calling him to come home.

Kathy Liebert- Think Attorney General Janet Reno. No one fucked with Janet Reno. She didn't believe in knocking on a door. She went through it. It was like, "Don't get up. I'll let myself in." When I watch

Kathy Liebert I get that same feeling. She's a tough, no-nonsense kind of player. I love her impersonation of a mean woman prison guard when she's staring down her opponent. I would love to watch her wrestle Phil Hellmuth Jr. A definite Pay Per View event. I know I would pony up $39.95.

Steve Dannenman- This guy plays to have a good time. And it shows. I watched him in a big pot one time where he got rivered and he had a look on his face like his diaper just burst. But he rebounded nicely. And let's face it, we've all had that look.

Dimitri Nobles- Who the fuck is Dimitri Nobles? He was a chip leader for a while at the WSOP. I think 27 seconds. Give or take. I just like saying Dimitri Nobles. I wonder if that's his stage name.

Phil Laak- The Unabomber. Everyone seems to like this kid. It's hard to say anything nasty about him. But give me a minute. Something will come up.

Allen Cunningham- You want quiet? This guy would be a star at a mime convention. He's intelligent, smart, rich, cute- oh- and did I mention- quiet?

Carlos Mortenson- Carlos always plays a steady game and has a nice demeanor about him. His hygiene is above reproach. Or below reproach, depending on the time of day or night, whatever the case may be. Also, above or below reproach depends on where you define his reproach.

Scotty Nguyen- When I first saw Scotty's last name I was going to call Vanna White to buy some more vowels. Scotty is a lot like the other professionals in the game of poker. He plays other games. I guess that goes with the lifestyle. He usually only plays evenings because it takes most of the morning to put on all his jewelry. He has a ton of it.

John Juanda- John is one of those quiet, kind souls that never seems to get upset at anything. I like his style. I doubt he would ever own a pit bull. He once played 15 hours without blinking.

Michael "The Grinder" Mizrachi- I see this kid at a lot of tournaments and he always has his little "entourage" around him- following him, listening to his wisdom, hoping for some crumbs when he cuts the loaf of bread. You see that a lot in card rooms. It's really quite humorous.

Johnny Chan- When I asked numerous dealers about Johnny Chan, they all had one thing in common. They didn't like him. Usually, if you're not liked by the working man or woman, you're not a nice person. I always thought Chan would look good in a chauffeur's cap. Whenever I see him, I ask the obvious question- is he wearing clothing or upholstery? But I think he likes me. When he came back from Hawaii he brought me a beautiful 10 piece Hawaiian Punch Bowl set made out of porpoise shit.

Greg Raymer- Known, of course, as "Fossilman" because of his fossil card cover. A few years ago, Raymer won the WSOP and a tidy sum of 5 million bucks. He had multiple backers to sponsor his entry fee of $10,000 and wound up paying them back about $2.4 million. His word was gold. A man of honor. A man of integrity. He did a lot for the game. So did the previous winner Chris Moneymaker. And then there was Jamie Gold. Excuse me, I have to go to the bathroom and throw up.

Gus Hanson- He use to flex his arms when he won, but I haven't noticed him doing that anymore. Maybe his Thighmaster broke and he doesn't exercise anymore. Gus is delightfully quirky. He's been described as a missile with no guidance system. He's a nice kid, well mannered and I worry about him. He needs me. He just doesn't know it.

Jennifer Tilly- Jennifer Tilly is married to Phil Laak. She always wears very low-cut dresses that I'm sure have a very distracting effect on her opponents. Even gay guys have to wonder whether or not one of her 45's is going to fall out of its holster. Someone told me she chews gum all the time while she's playing. Next time I watch her play, I'm going to look at her face to confirm that. Jennifer seems like she is a very nice, caring girl. She looks like she could cook 30-minute brownies in 20 minutes. I have no idea what that means, but I only write this shit. I'm not here to understand it.

Cyndy Violette- Born in Queens and moved to Las Vegas as a kid. Her first career was as a dealer in Reno. It was obvious to everyone she was way too cute to be making minimum wage. She's ranked in the top ten on the Women's All-Time Money List. She's a believer in physical and spiritual health. She's a vegetarian. Vegetarian is an old Indian word that means "Doesn't hunt well". For a while I was a vegetarian. But not a real strict one. I ate beef, pork and some chicken. And once in a while veal chops- real thick. I just couldn't give those up.

Satellites and The King

A satellite gives you the opportunity to win a seat in a bigger tournament by winning a smaller tournament called a satellite. Usually, a satellite is only one table. It's like a one-table mini-tournament. If the main tournament seat is a $1,000 buy-in, then the satellite for that tournament would be $100 plus a $10 or $20 charge, which goes to the casino. The winner of the satellite would then get a seat in the $1,000 event. Some satellites award two seats for, of course, twice the buy-in. Instead of $100, the buy-in would be $200 plus the service charge. There are no re-buys in satellites. Satellites usually last about 1-1$\frac{1}{2}$ hours. The blind levels usually go up every 15 minutes. And as we all know, blinds drive the action. The King of Satellite Bosses is a guy at the Bellagio named Alan Feiner. Kirk Kerkorian, who owns the MGM Mirage Corporation of which the Bellagio in Las Vegas is a part, should have a picture of Alan on his nightstand. Satellite profitability is huge for the casino. A simple satellite of $120 generates $1,200 ($120 X 10 players), of which the player that wins gets $1,000 and the casino gets $200. From that, they pay the dealer $6 an hour. If the satellite is for a bigger event, the pot gets bigger. For a $10,000 event, satellites are usually $1,040 or $1,060. If the casino charges $1,040 and gives a seat to the winner, they made $400 for tying up a table for about an hour and a half. At $1,060, they made about $600. Minus the $6 an hour that the dealer gets, and of course, let's not forget the bottle of water that everyone probably ordered so that would be 10 X $0.20 per bottle- another $2.00 off the top. As you can see, satellites are very profitable. And Alan squeezes every ounce of profit from his satellites.

I watched Alan at his finest hour one evening. The main tournament was about to start in 40 minutes. Alan got on the microphone and announced, "One last satellite guys." Ten guys clamored over to give him their money. Like sharks during a feeding frenzy. "We haven't got much time, guys," he said, "Blinds will be going up every 10 minutes." The "normal" 15-minute increase in blinds is bad enough, but 10 minutes- Holy fuck Batman. That's OK, Robin, I know you can do it. Well, as it turned out, the cards were not cooperating for Alan. There was only 25 minutes left until the tournament and only 2 players out of the original 10 had busted out of the satellite. Alan was pacing nervously like Michael Jackson at a Little League game. You could see the wheels turning. More people needed to be eliminated- quickly. The main tournament was about to begin and all the tables were needed. "OK, guys," he said, "5-minute levels." In the next 10 minutes, 6 more players busted out. The final 2 players were taking forever to decide the match. The chips were pretty even. The blinds were ridiculous and there was only about 6 minutes left. "2-Minute levels," Alan announced. That was the end of it. The blinds had gotten so big that it was a complete crapshoot. Two hands later, the satellite was over. Many times when you get down to 2 players in a satellite, the players make a deal. Deals are common. If the prize is a $1,000 entry, I might offer you $300 and I'll take the seat if I'm the dominant chip leader. Or vice versa. At that point, it's usually anybody's game. Something is better than nothing. You try and make the best deal you can. There was one satellite that Alan had that was the "topper". The satellite of all satellites. The Main Event- a $10,000 buy-in was going to start in 10 minutes. Alan knew he could extract a little more blood from the turnip. A little more water from the rock. So he announced, "Anyone interested in a final satellite- come to the podium." When about 15 guys showed up he said, "One last satellite for a seat in the Main Event. $1,060 buy-in. One hand." One fuckin' hand. 10 Guys jumped on it. It was their last chance to get into the $10,000 event for only a thousand bucks (plus, of course, the small entry fee). One fuckin' hand. And Alan made the joint $600 it never would have had if he wasn't there. He is truly the fuckin' King. Maybe not the King of Rock N Roll, but the fuckin' King of Satellites.

Random Thought

I like Andre Agassi. He just retired. It was sad. I think. I didn't see it. I'm not much of a sports person. I am not even sure what a sport is anymore. Ping pong, tennis, football, badminton, luge, jacks, hopscotch, now poker? Sports? All of them? Any of them? Sports is just a word with anything involving the slightest hint of competition. Hot dog eating is competitive. Modeling? Yep. Dog shows? Yep. Watermelon eating contests? Very competitive. Circle jerks? Maybe. Anyway, Andre retired. Not from circle jerks but from tennis. He served the "sport" well. And it served him well. And he has given back to his community in numerous ways. He has a very large charitable foundation that does a lot of good work. Maybe that's why I like him. And his smile. And his perfect teeth. I wonder if there is a perfect teeth competition, or tooth if you happen to live in_____ (fill in the blank with a city of your choice. I'm not going to fuck with that one. I get enough hate mail).

Timmy, Fluffy and Obesity

A kid I know who is in a wheelchair through no fault of his own likes to write letters to poker players that he says are "his heroes". When he told me that, it was obvious to me how sick this kid really was. He's in a wheelchair because I accidentally backed over him with my car, and when he told me that he writes letters to poker players I began to wonder if I backed over his fuckin' head in addition to his legs. Anyway, I'm not going to use his real name because of ongoing litigation from the "accident". I know what you're thinking, "What is this world coming to? Does every little accident that results in paralysis have to wind up in a lawsuit? Have we become that litigious?" I know. But I figure suing the little fucker will stop him from putting his legs under people's tires again. He recently wrote to one of his favorite obese poker players asking him for a wide-angle photo and received the following curt, rude, snappy, gruff, impolite reply that had little Timmy sobbing. It was either that or he had just learned that I "accidentally" backed over his dog "Fluffy" (I can't wait for this fuckin' family to move). I'm going to "white out" the identification of this poker player "star" so as to not embarrass him or his boyfriend or his family.

Dear Little Timmy,

Thank you for the nice letter. What a nice fuckin' letter. I'll bet you're a nice fuckin' kid. Well listen up, kid- I don't send free autographed pictures to anyone. Even crippled kids. It's not my fuckin' fault you're in a wheelchair. Or is it? Are you the idiot kid who got in my way at the Las Vegas Hilton buffet last month? Man, those fuckin' crab legs were as big as Buicks. I've still got a "memory stain" on one of my shirts from that meal. Anyway, I'm glad to see that 12 year olds are becoming addicted to Hold 'em so that I can continue to make a fortune from their poor play online. Let me know when you want to visit a real casino so I can send you a genuine fake ID. They are only $14.95 and come with a coupon for a Philly Cheesesteak sandwich with extra cheese. I have to go now as

*the $6.95 special at the Crisco Café is about to start. I am
sending you a copy of my new book and will bill your parents'
credit card. It's a self-help book called "Masturbation
Techniques I Use After 8-Course Meals". The sub title is "Why
I Really Wear My Hat Backwards". My public relations people
are trying to get it into public schools as a textbook. Anything
is possible when you're a celebrity- no matter how fat and ugly
you are. Remember that in your quest to be popular. Even
though you are laughed at in school because you are crippled
and kids are constantly loosening your lug nuts, you can be
popular like me. Kids are cruel, Timmy, but remember that
someday, and maybe someday soon, you will be dead and it
won't matter. And keep in mind, Timmy, as you wheel through
life, there are no wheelchairs in Heaven. Why? Because there's
no fuckin' Heaven. Keep in touch.*

*Yours in Christ,
Your Favorite Obese Poker Player*

I usually love fan mail. But it's as clear as that thing on
Michael Jackson's face where everyone else has a nose, that this poker
player doesn't like kids. But it's like the great W.C. Fields said,
"Anybody that hates kids and dogs can't be all bad." And W.C. was a
poker player. So am I. So are you. So are 3 out of 5 dentists. And let's
face reality. Most of us hate kids and dogs.

Mystery Solved:

Why There Has Been No Contact

An intergalactic memo was intercepted by my paperboy who gave it to my poolboy who gave it to me. It solves a question that has plagued me for many years. There are billions and billions of stars that have billions and billions of planets orbiting them. Why haven't we been contacted? Why haven't the aliens landed? What is Martinizing and why does it only take 1 hour? Is wrestling fixed? These are questions that I demand answers to. And I'm hoping now that the Democrats have control of the House and the Senate we can get answers. I need answers. I demand answers. I can handle the truth. I know I can. This memo has provided some answers.

Stardate: 7394

Time: 8:30 Planet "X" time

After observing the planet Earth for the past 2,000 years, we have come to some very disturbing conclusions. There are many Earthlings who consume their valuable time (they only have 70 or 80 years as a life form) playing a game called Hold 'em in what they call "tournaments". They sit around a table and play this game and some of them do boring tricks with small cylindrical objects they call "chips". Sometimes they sit for 9 or 10 hours and don't "cash". That's fuckin' nuts! One of these players actually says he's from our planet- Planet "X". He even knows our secret code words to annihilate any enemy we encounter- "Quack Quack". He licks his lips incessantly like we do and seems to have taken a human life form. Please have Security Chief Matusow check all of our villages to see if anyone is missing. His Earth name is Paul Madrigal, which when unscrambled is GLMDALPUARIA, a very common family name on our planet. His interaction with the Earthlings is of great concern to me. These humans are very lonely fucks. They sit and stare at each other and wait for what they call "Pocket Rockets". Let's just leave them alone and check on them in another 100,000 years. Except for Paul. We may need to subject him to the Vulcan Pinch. But we need to use caution. He may enjoy it.

End of Intergalactic Memo

WSOP Winners- Champions Forever

(or until a meteor hits the Earth and throws us out of orbit and spins us wildly towards the sun, melting all the winners and champions, including all their rings, bracelets and things)

We love lists. We all do. Nice, concise lists that give us all the information we are seeking quickly. Top 10 lists are always a favorite. They cut to the chase. They cut to the bottom line. It's the American way. We are in a huge hurry. The following isn't a top 10 list, but it is a list. It's a list of all the winners of the WSOP from the time it started. Since this book is about Hold 'em, I thought you would enjoy seeing the winners of the event and meeting them. I was going to have recent pictures of each winner, but a lot of them are dead. As we all know, the dead don't photograph well. Some of the past winners that are alive, **look** dead, and they don't photograph well either. Then of course there's the bullshit release forms, family approvals, and the negotiations and lunches that my people would have to have with their people. That would mean I would have to hire people since I have no people. I'm a leader with no followers. And we all know what we call a leader with no followers: Just a guy out taking a walk. I was going to make this list of just the second or third place winners. They are so forgotten. And that is so unfair. The winner gets his name immortalized and the second and third place guy gets rivered again. Just like he did when he got beat by the winner. But if I did the 500 hours of research it would take to find out the second or third place winners, no one would care. Just like with this list of winners. I don't think anyone really cares. But it saved me a lot of fuckin' time. I only had to copy it from another book. So without further adieu (whatever the fuck that means), I present to you the winners of the World Series of Poker from 1970 to the present. Well, maybe not the present. I just realized that the 2006 WSOP has just been completed, so if you are reading this in 2008 or 2009, it would not include the present winner. So I am going to put some responsibility on you, the reader, to help me out. I have dates that say NYD and that means Not Yet Determined. I need you to fill in the names of the winners so that when future generations read the book, my original statement will be correct. From 1970 to the present. Thank you for your help. Kind of makes you feel warm and fuzzy when you help doesn't it? Just like family. No one has ever done this before. This is really exciting, ground-breaking shit.

1969: Tony Korfman- If this award had been available in 1969, I know deep in my heart I would have won it. I just know it. I would have been in my twenties and just reaching my sexual and intellectual prime. I would have been an overwhelming favorite. Oh well. Shit happens.

1970-1971 (and 1974): Johnny Moss- First to win a Main Event. He and Stu Unger are the only two players to win 3 WSOP Main Event titles. With the huge fields of today, I don't see this ever happening again. The odds would be fuckin' astronomical.

1972: "Amarillo Slim" Preston- He was on the Tonight Show about a dozen times.

1973: W.C. "Puggy" Pearson- Elected to the Poker Hall of Fame in 1987. Died in 2006.

1974: Johnny Moss- Nice Guy "Johnny".

1975: Brian "Sailor" Roberts- A former member of the US Navy. Died from sclerosis in the late 1980's.

1976-1977: Doyle "Texas Dolly" Brunson- Born and raised in-where else? Texas. He has won a record 10 WSOP bracelets. That many bracelets is waaaay beyond a Mr. T Starter Kit. His books Super System and Super System 2 are must reads for every poker degenerate in the country. My guess is they will be textbooks in public schools in the next few years. Unlike the book you are reading now, which will be available in finer liquor stores and garage sales in better neighborhoods.

1978: Bobby "The Owl" Baldwin- Called one of poker's most brilliant minds. Or was it mimes? I get mixed up. Anyway, I love Baldwin pianos.

1979: Hal Fowler- A former Los Angeles advertising executive. He decided to turn pro after his win. According to my secret sources (not sauces- that's McDonald's), that didn't work out too well. Can we all spell bustout?

1980-1981 (and 1997): Stu "The Kid" Ungar- Very talented. Very respected. Very addicted. He died broke at the age of 45. Very tragic.

1982: Jack "Treetop" Straus- Kind and generous. Known as "Treetop" because he was 6'6''. He died in 1998 while playing poker.

1983: Tom McEvoy- He was the first one to win his way into the big event by winning a satellite.

1984: Jack Keller- Former US Airforce member. At the age of 51 he was voted into the Poker Hall of Fame. He died in 2003. I saw him once at the Las Vegas airport. He nodded at me.

1985: Bill Smith- Another tragic figure of the game. Died in the early 1990's. Was a very heavy drinker.

1986: Berry Johnston- Very quiet champion. Inducted into the Poker Hall of Fame in 2004.

1987-1988: Johnny Chan- Tied with Doyle Brunson at 10 WSOP bracelets.

1989: Phil Hellmuth Jr.-Called "The Poker Brat". Appears at speaking engagements all over the world to talk about himself.

1990: Mansour Matloubi- The first non-US resident to win the WSOP Main Event. He owned hotels before winning the WSOP and does not claim responsibility for the smell of incense in hotel and motel lobbies.

1991: Brad Daugherty- He won the event at the age of 40. Originally from Idaho. I love their baked potatoes.

1992: Hamid Dastmalchi- The second of two Iranian-born WSOP Main Event champions in 3 years.

1993: Jim Bechtel- Had 3 cashes in various events at the 2005 WSOP.

1994: Russ Hamilton- Since he won the 25th Anniversary edition of the WSOP, they also gave him his weight in silver. From the picture I saw of him, he must have gotten a lot of fuckin' silver.

1995: Dan Harrington- Known as "Action Dan". No one knows where he got his nickname from. Local hookers deny any knowledge of it.

1996: Huckleberry Seed- A very quiet Cal Tech electrical engineer dropout. He must have loved role call throughout his entire school career. I named one of my kids Huckleberry, but it was because I didn't like him.

1997: Stu "The Kid" Ungar

1998: Thuan "Scotty" Nguyen- Nicknamed "The Prince of Poker". Charming, playful, approachable, smells good. Has more jewelry than my wife.

1999: Noel Furlong- Born in Dublin, Ireland. Parents named him Leon, but the nurse that wrote out the birth certificate was dyslexic. So Noel was born. Not Leon.

2000: Chris "Jesus" Ferguson- Born in 1963 in a manger in front of the Bellagio card room. Able to cut fruit in half with playing cards and feed crowds of people with just one banana. He has 5 bracelets and could easily turn them into 50 of them if he felt like it.

2001: Carlos Mortenson- Known as "The Matador" because of his

Spanish heritage. I love his Spanish rice. It has just the right amount of spice. I love rice when I feel like eating 2,000 of something.

2002: Robert Varkonyi- An MIT graduate who incorporates most of the most unpopular letters of the alphabet into his last name.

2003: Chris Moneymaker- A former accountant for a restaurant chain. He got tired of yelling at the help for giving the customers too much butter with their rolls. He took 40 bucks and ran it into 2.5 million. He ran a toothpick into a lumber yard or a pat of butter into a dairy farm. Just depends on how you want to look at it. If you wear Depends.

2004: Greg Raymer- He beat 2,576 other players. He's a former patent attorney and when he's not involved in tournaments, he's suing the people who knocked him out of them. He's very approachable and talked to me at the WSOP last year when I accidentally bumped into him. He said, "Expect a subpoena, fat boy."

2005: Joe Hachem- This guy is a former Australian Chiropractor. He won $7.5 million and can now afford to hire people to break anyone's bones he chooses. He beat a field of over 5,600 players and then offered to adjust their backs. Happy endings were extra.

2006: Jamie Gold- Excuse me. I have to go to the bathroom and throw up.

2007: NYD (Not Yet Determined)

2008: NYD

2009: NYD

2010: NYD

2011: NYD

2012: NYD

A Title is the Beginning of a Relationship

I lost count of how many boxes of Oreos and gallons of chocolate milk I consumed while pondering the title for this book. Is it humorous? Is it offensive to some? Is it too offensive to many? I needed a resounding "Yes!" to all those questions. I even thought of having **you** choose the title when you buy the book. You would have numerous choices and you would just slide in a gold plaque (I like gold- not the Jamie kind) that would have the title engraved on it. That would have been fuckin' neat! And talk about "out of the box"! Everyone would have talked about it. Probably even Howard Stern! But then gold shot through the fuckin' roof. It's over $600 an ounce. Each book would then have to be $614.95. I think I would have priced it out of the market. I think. The following titles were considered for this book:

-He Rivered Me Without a Trojan or His Horse

-He Rivered Me Without a Condom (this was the title for about a month)

-He Rivered Me Without a Thin Rubber Sheath

-Rivered- Without a Trojan or His Horse

-The Mother Fucker Rivered Me Without Penetration

-He Rivered Me- No Condom, No Penetration- It Was Fuckin' Terrible

-Viewer Discretion Advised

-A Book to Move Your Bowels By

-A Good Bathroom Read

-For a Boy Named Timmy

-Tournaments, Cash Games and Ghoulash

-Tournaments, Cash Games and Quiche

-Tournaments, Cash Games and Green Meatloaf

-Tournaments, Cash Games and Casserole

-Tournaments, Cash Games and Breastfeeding Etiquette (this was almost the winner)

I'm the kind of guy who can admit my mistakes. Well, kind of. I bet my son David a dinner at Todd's Unique Dining, in Green Valley on Sunset Road, that I made the right choice. It had to be a humorous yet marketable title. Log on to Dr. Phil's website and tell him which title you prefer. He will tabulate the results and keep them in a mayonnaise jar for me and break the news slowly to me during our next therapy session. I can handle the truth. I know I can. I just know I can.

Jesus Christ

Jesus was not the first choice of names when the Christ Child was born. It seems that the 3 Wise Men were bringing the newborn gifts of gold, silver and other gifts that kids like to play with from one of the most popular outlets of kids toys and apparel, back then called "K-hrist Mart". As they were approaching the manger, one of the wise men stepped in some camel shit and lifted up his foot and looked at it and yelled out, "Jesus Christ!" Mary turned to Joseph and said, "Gee, Joseph, that sounds like a better name than Clyde." And she was right. Women know these things. "Jesus Saves" sounds a lot better than "Clyde Saves". Chris "Clyde" Ferguson just doesn't have the same ring to it. Thank God for camel shit.

Random Thought

During a recent tournament, I'm sitting next to a very nice, very friendly guy from Atlanta. We seemed to hit it off and the dinner break was coming up in a few minutes and neither of us had eaten since the tournament had started. He asked me if I wanted to have dinner with him at the snack bar during the break. I told him, "I need to tell you two things before we have dinner: I'm not cheap and I'm not easy." I knew he understood. He took his hand off my knee. We went our separate ways.

The Box

There is a small box that is under every poker table, every craps table, every blackjack table and every other type of gaming table in every casino in the world. It is out of sight of the public and gets changed every 8-hour shift- 7 days a week. It's called the "drop box". That's where all the money goes from the buy-ins or "rakes" from each of the tables. I have seen people's houses fit in those boxes. And businesses. And life savings and families. We have an old saying in the casino business- "God bless them when they win, as long as they play. Eventually, everyone winds up in the box." And everyone does. No matter how good you think you are. No matter how much you think you have. If you have the "bug" and are addicted to playing, you will wind up in the box. Take my word for it.

Random Thought

A guy asked Hemingway one time, how he went broke. He said, "Slowly at first. Then it went very quickly."

Don't Somersize- Summarize

As you breeze through this literary piece of work, there are many many moneymaking suggestions that will immeasurably help you on your quest to become not only a better poker player, but a richer, fuller humanoid. I know what you're thinking, "If I don't underline or highlight these informational, educational and wealth-building ideas, then I won't be able to find them when I review this complete work." And then, of course, your follow up thoughts would be, "This would be one of the greatest books ever written on Hold 'em if the author would take some of his valuable time and show his appreciation to the reader by summarizing all of his tips on how we can become better players and wealthier players in life, as well as in poker. All he would have to do is take a page or two at the end of the book, and by summarizing his tips and suggestions, we, the reader, would be able to fully enjoy the book without trying to highlight or underline valuable tips and information." I myself have thought this numerous times as I read a book on poker or some other form of gaming, especially when it was written by an expert in his or her field. Based on my thoughts on this subject, I set aside some of my time to ensure that the reader could enjoy the book and I would condense all of the information he would need to become a much much better player. But I used that time to do something else. Yep, ran out of fuckin' time. So get out the highlight marker. There's not that much to highlight anyway. Maybe next time I'll manage my time better. I'm putting that "summary" crap on my list of things to do in my next book.

Random Thought

*If you happen to be **under** the gun in a poker game in your **underwear** try not to think of other words that have "under" in them. That could be one of the first signs of poker madness.*

Ram and Scam

Downtown Las Vegas is different than the Las Vegas Strip. It has more people carrying cardboard signs that say "Will work for food and a tournament buy-in". My wife and I were in our pickup waiting for my daughter who was buying some shit in K-Mart. A guy walks up to our truck with a thick fan belt in his hand and said, "My fan belt broke- they're $24.95 and I've only got $10. Can you help me?" (Oh, and I almost forgot, he said his 3 kids are waiting in the car and they haven't eaten in 4 days) He actually said he had his kid in the car and just didn't know what to do. He'd never asked for money before and was embarrassed and humiliated. I reached in my pocket and as I'm pulling out my money, I remembered a guy that came up to me at Binion's Horseshoe about a month before with the same story. I had given him a 20. I looked a little closer at this guy, and wouldn't you know- same fuckin' guy. I like a guy who thinks out of the box as well as anyone else. So I had him arrested for leaving his kid in the car on a hot day. Fuck him and his fan belt.

Dogs and Cats

Dog and cat lovers of America were shocked to find out the most popular pets owned by Americans were giraffes and gazelles. This distortion of the pet population is mainly the fault of Siegfried and Roy. Mainly Roy. Siegfried hasn't been in part of the house in many years and this is where Roy stashes them all. I guess he'll know now after he reads this.

It's About the Bracelet- It's About Bragging Rights- It's About Pride

It's <u>Not</u> About the Money

I actually heard an announcer narrating a poker tournament say that. And I had to fully agree with him. Well, almost fully agree. So I wrote this. If I could just win one World Series of Poker Main Event, I would be the happiest man alive. The happiness would, of course, come from the bracelet. The solid gold bracelet with the gold inscription of my name, forever etched in history. And if I could just win one World Series of Poker Main Event, I would not only have the gorgeous gold WSOP Main Event bracelet with my name etched in history forever, I would also have bragging rights. Every time I played a game of poker, everyone at the table- everyone in the room- everyone in the building- would know I was the best poker player in the world. And if I could just win one WSOP Main Event, I would have tremendous happiness from the magnificent, gorgeous, solid gold bracelet with the gold inscription of my name forever etched in history, bragging rights, which is so important because of the respect you get, and tremendous pride. Pride in the accomplishment of winning an event so few ever win. My family and friends would be so proud of me and tell me on a daily basis how they are so happy I am here with them. And if I could win just one WSOP Main Event, my happiness would be eternal because of mainly that crap about the bracelet that I know they get wholesale and will probably turn my wrist green, the tremendous bragging rights that go with such a prestigious award, the pride my family and friends would have when they discuss my every meal, my every bowel movement, and of course, lastly, the most unimportant thing of the tournament- the money. It's never about the money. Or is it? How the fuck could it not be about the money? Millions and millions and millions of dollars. That's like saying I play the lottery because first and foremost I want to keep the clerks at 7-11 working; second, I enjoy looking at the perfect symmetry of the ticket; third, the excitement of watching someone take out ping pong balls and call out numbers; and yes, I almost forgot, the fuckin' money. Give me a fuckin' break. The poker community should just "come out" and admit it. It's about the fuckin' money. Always has been. Always will be. Give me the fuckin' money and I'll buy my own fuckin' bracelet. I'll buy a fuckin' bracelet factory and give a bracelet to everyone I know. And I would then have "bragging rights". I could forever brag that I bought everyone I know a fuckin' bracelet. And pride? Please- I'm getting chest pains. I'll hire 10 people to call me 20 times a day and tell me how proud they are to know me. You think all these poker fucks sit around poker tables for 10 hours a day, 6 and 7 days a week for their health? You think it's about comraderie? You think it's about male bonding? It's all about the fuckin' money. Always has been. Always will be.

Random Thought

Poker players sometimes have really outrageous jewelry. The rage right now seems to be "giant face" watches with diamonds and white gold and platinum. And I mean huge faces. Fuckin' huge. One kid had a watch on that I swear was bigger than Big Ben in England. I know it was bigger than my grandfather clock in my living room. This kid was really over the top. He had a huge cross around his neck with a gold chain that could tow a small vehicle. And the cross was really authentic. He had a real guy hanging from it. But I guess everyone needs to work. Even guys that hang from jewelry.

T-R-O-U-B-L-E

When I was at the WSOP, a lady walked by me who had one of the biggest asses I have ever seen. It was fuckin' huge. She was wearing a pair of the tightest Levis known to mankind. Across her ass, in great big letters, she had embroidered "Here Comes Trouble". There was enough room left over to embroider the Declaration of Independence, the Constitution and still have enough room left for the complete works of Shakespeare in lower case. But "Here Comes Trouble" was what the message said. And she was eating the biggest fuckin' bean burrito this country (or Mexico) has ever seen. The message was loud and clear to everyone. We were witnessing a WSOP first. It was the first time that a human weapon of mass destruction was walking across the room. And I guarantee you that no one in their right mind was going to fuck with her. No one.

Random Thought

Always keep your words soft and sweet. Just in case you have to eat them.

Has the Federal Witness Protection Program

Invaded Poker?

When I watch televised poker, I noticed that the lighting around Todd Brunson is not very good. Plus he sits on his chair backwards with his face buried into the back of it. It makes me wonder if the producer isn't scrambling his identity much like they do with the televised witness in the dark room with the distorted voice. You can never make out who it is- unless, of course, the janitor accidentally comes in and flips the light switch on. If you watch closely, Todd does get very nervous when someone enters the room. Especially if they have a mop.

Flawed

We are all flawed. No one is perfect. Eulogies always talk about the good the person did. Some eulogies are very short. But for the most part everyone is doing the best that they can. It's not easy on this planet. For anyone. No matter how wealthy a person is. No matter how many tournaments he has won. No matter what kind of car he drives. No matter how big his penis is. Character flaws, physical flaws, health flaws, mental flaws. We all have flaws. There is no perfection. Everyone is fighting a tough battle. So be nice.

Fan Mail

Dear Author,

My 15 year old son Gus is a Hold 'em fanatic. The title of this book at first gave me some reservations about him reading it. I read it from cover to cover as he anxiously awaited whether I would allow **him** to read it. I was sorry I waited so long to give him a decision, but I wanted to complete the entire book before I gave Gus my approval. Let me put every parent's concerns about their kid reading this book to rest. Don't agonize like I did about the decision to let them read this based on the title or its content. Whatever you do, **DO NOT** let your fuckin' kid near this book. Gus is not even allowed in the same room where we keep it. It's under lock and key in our gun cabinet.

Frieda Gold

(No relation to Jamie Gold. You think I'd admit it if I was?)

Random Thought

The thing about tournaments is you only need to win one or come close to winning one. Then the hook is set. And you get reeled in. You are hooked big time. Which brings us back to the quote by Hemingway when someone asked him how he went broke. "Slowly at first," he said, "Then it went very quickly." Be careful of tournaments. They cast a big shadow. A big, expensive, addictive shadow.

Snake Oil For Sale

In the days of yore, a wagon would pull up in a small western town and a guy would get out and sell a liquid to the towns folk that was meant to cure all their ailments. And make them feel better. And you know what? A lot of the people felt better. And when the guy came through town 3 months later, they bought more. Nothing much has changed 200 years later. The Snake Oil is just packaged differently. It's all about packaging and selling the "sizzle". If you sell enough product, whether it's a juice or a belt you strap around your testicles or a painted light bulb you stare at for an hour, a percentage of people will swear they felt better or were "cured". Just remember, all of these salesmen have one goal- to get into your fuckin' wallet. That is the prime objective. None of these juices or exotic treatments are cheap. Show me someone who doesn't charge or charges very little to help the masses, to help the sick, to help the elderly, and he'll have my vote. Until then, I don't see any Edgar Cayces on the horizon. Many years ago there was a man named Edgar Cayce who helped a lot of people. He never charged anyone. People would give him eggs, cows and anything they could afford because he literally saved their lives. He saved many many lives. Many books have been written about him. The younger generation doesn't buy into the Snake Oil salesmen. It's the elderly they attack. The ones with ailments. The tired and the weak that are looking for an answer to being tired and weak. Years ago, P.T. Barnum said it best, "There's a sucker born every minute." And with 50% of the population over 50 years old, there are tens of millions of them. I've been a sucker and chances are you've been one too. Just beware. And be very careful. Hold on to your fuckin' wallet. Tightly. There's a lot of pricks out there selling snake oil.

Random Thought

Between tournaments and cash games- between Limit Hold 'em and home games- lies a shadow. Sometimes that shadow causes anguish. Sometimes that shadow causes bankruptcy. Sometimes that shadow causes homelessness. Be careful of that shadow. Be very careful.

Fly Like an Eagle (Scout of Course)

My dad came home from work one day and all through dinner talked about some guy at work whose son was working his way to becoming an Eagle Scout. I could see this one coming like a Sumo wrestler barreling towards a buffet. Three weeks later I had my 3XL scout shirt, my fuckin' 10-way pocket knife and a 400 page scout book that I still have in my bookcase and still haven't opened. My dad was proud, my friends were appalled and my switchblade was alone in my underwear drawer, replaced by a knife that had more fuckin' tools on it than my dad's workbench. I was actually a Boy Scout for about 3 months. Until our scout hall burnt down. Unfortunately. You know how hard it is to get a 12x12 beam to catch on fire? Right before I ran out of matches, I remembered some valuable information I had learned in my Arson Merit Badge class. I had actually gotten 3 merit badges before the "accident": there was the Arson Badge, my favorite- the Uncovering People in the Federal Witness Protection Program Badge, and the one that helps a lot when you live in the desert, Shallow Grave Digging. To become an Eagle Scout, which is one of the highest honors known to mankind, you have to become proficient in many different fields. I think a lot more kids would get involved in scouting if the merit badges kept up with the times. I have the following helpful suggestions for merit badges, which I would like for the Boy Scout Association higher echelon to consider:

-Creating Subway Odors at Home

-Hiking with Michael Jackson

-A Study of Things Found in a Wadded-up Kleenex

-Counting Cards

-Chalk Body Outline Designs

-Making Your Gym Teacher Cry

-Stray Bullet Research

-Smoking, Drinking, Sex and Incredible Farts

-Identifying Animals by Their Waste

-Barbecuing During Pandemics

-Bedding Cocktail Waitresses

-Paperboy Extortion Techniques

-Soul Crushing Comments After You've Rivered Your Opponent

-Opening Act Tribute Badge

-Bobbing Corpses and Small Tippers (Is there a correlation?)

-Mites and Crotch Itch

-Using Your Webcam After Mom and Dad Have Gone to Bed

-Eczema and Cyst Identification

-Proper Things to Say to Your Parole Board

-Crack Pipe Repair

Merit badge courses like those would triple enrollment in the scouting program. If there are two things that I really respect in life, it's guys that can clear out an entire room, including the dogs and cats, with a fart or a series of farts, and of course Eagle Scouts. And their proud parents. Who forced them into scouting. But that's another diatribe. In another dimension.....

Final Table

The final table of any tournament reminds me of the bar in Star Wars, of different creatures drinking their favorite elixir. At the final table of Hold 'em, the elixir is poker. Every seat a different creature. The final table always has a very distinct odor to it. A combination of pungent smells. 10 people brought together by this game of chance. This game of luck. This game of patience. This fuckin' game that will drive you fuckin' nuts if you let it. Which seat will lady luck smile on? Which seat will the poker gods bless? It's anyone's guess. The air around the final table is filled with anxiety. It's filled with excitement. It's filled with the smell of an incredible fart I laid around 4 or 5 seconds before I sat down. It must have been from the rancid cheeseburger I ate about an hour before while on a break. The fart was actually starting to wrinkle the shirt of the guy sitting next to me. I looked at the guy next to **him** and said "nice one" (shifting the blame has always been one of my strong suits).

Final tables are very unique. Everyone strives to get to them. Not many make it. It doesn't matter how big the tournament or how small the tournament, how cheap the tournament or how expensive the tournament, there **will be** a final table. To prove the rarity of achieving the final table status in any given tournament, get the results from your local casino or card room for its past 10 tournaments. If you look at the top 10 winners of each tournament, you won't see many duplicates. 95% of the people are different each time. There are so many tournaments and so many people playing them that even the pros have a difficult time making the final table with any consistency. That, in a nutshell, is the attraction of the game. Anyone can win on any given day. Most final tables I have been at have resulted in chopping the money when we got down to 2 or 3 players. Sometimes 4. When I get to the final table, the first thing I try to do is assess my opponents. The last final table I played I was in seat 1. The kid in seat 2 smiled and winked at me when I sat down. I'm not a winker, but I winked back anyway. He said, "How are you doing?" I said, "Not bad." I told him I had just eaten a tuna melt and I wasn't going to be responsible for the outcome. The tuna melt had settled in me and was screaming to get out. The scent of tuna was in the air. I thought I also smelled chicken. That's when the kid told me he had a chicken wrap about an hour before. It smelled like the chicken had died a natural death. It was definitely not slaughtered. It probably collapsed from old age. Seat 3 was a salesman. He never shut up. Yakitty yak- on and on. He was an insurance salesman. They are one of the lower species on the food chain. You know- "You're in good hands," until they have to write you a fuckin' check. Then good fuckin' luck. My wife and I took out big life insurance policies on each other last year. We felt it was time. We're both getting old. Now it's just a waiting game. Seat 4 was a big fuckin' guy. I'm a big guy. But this guy was huge. He said his name was "Titanic". I'm thinking, if I'm on a fuckin' ship with this guy and we hit an iceberg, I'm getting on his stomach. There was enough room to save half the passengers and part of the crew. He kept talking about just getting back from the beach and having a bad sunburn on his back. The image of him on a beach towel was overwhelming. Seat 5 was a really old guy. Older than me. Really fuckin' old. He looked like he had a lot of money. I can sense these things. One of the tells was that his wife looked to be about 25. Her role model, she said, was Anna Nicole Smith. She took good care of the old guy while he played. She cut his meat, adjusted his shawl and emptied his drool cup. Whatever she could get from him she deserved. God bless the young wives of the very old. They provide happiness and sloth for the few years the aged have left. God bless them. Seat 6 was a teacher. He was a real idiot. He would ramble about the solar system and then mid-stream switch to Doyle Brunson's Super System. As a teacher, I believe he was able to find a way to make a living and pass the time, and trick his students into thinking they were getting an education. He said he named all his children after the Marx Brothers. Even the girls. I guess that's better than the Baldwin Brothers. But not by much. Seat 7 was an economist- whatever the fuck that means. He was talking about the rich, the middle class and the poor, and trying to define each category. I said to him, "Listen Pal," (I usually start off with "Listen Pal" if I don't like you- even a little bit), "the definition of rich, middle class and poor is very fuckin' simple. Monday, when you go into work, if your name is on the building, you're rich. If your name is on your desk, you're middle class. And if your name is on your fuckin' shirt, you're poor." Seat 7 didn't open his fuckin' economist mouth again. Seat 8 was a very young girl who looked like she was 22 or 23. And I think she was a hooker. She avoided any subject that had to do with careers and employment. Very nicely dressed- no excessive jewelry. The reason I thought she was a hooker is she mentioned it was slow where she worked and she had an increase in business with her Yankee Baseball special. For $50 she would let you get to third base. Whatever the fuck that means. But I gave her $50 anyway. Seat 9 was a really disheveled looking guy. He had a 4 or 5-day growth on his face and looked like he probably kept track of his relatives through his police scanner. I nicknamed him Norman Bates from the movie Psycho. But I don't think this guy would go near a shower. At least he looked like he hadn't had a "shower encounter" for a long long time. He had the massage girl shave his back. He looked pathologically miserable. Pure fuckin' miserable. Misery exuded from his bodily pores. I felt it. I smelled it. But that could have been the incredible fart I had just exuded. I do exude award winners occasionally. Seat 10 was an Asian kid. Clean cut (aren't they all?), nodded a lot (don't they all?) and smelled of cigarette smoke (what else is new?). He had no charisma reading on his dipstick. None, zero, zilch, zip. The final table was in place. It could have been a final table anywhere in the world where Hold 'em is played. It just happened to be in Las Vegas. At the Bellagio.

Things To Look For At the Final Table

♠ Look for the headphone and sunglasses to the gay participants ratio. It's almost one to one.

♠ Look for the complete disregard for the safety of others when cards are tossed into the muck following a bad beat.

♠ Look for the intensity of the participants when they drink their bottled water. Before and after the all-in bet. Before and after the tipped over chair. Before and after the "finger" to the guy on the winning end of the bad beat.

♠ Look for the really heavy, sweaty guy that licks his fingers before he looks at his cards. He announces to everyone that he did not wash his hands after going to the bathroom on the last break. The question on everyone's mind- did he go number one or number two? (At this point I don't think the number matters).

♠ Look for a copy of the New England Journal of Medicine and Hold 'em Strategy under the seat of at least one player that is young, has a 3-day growth on his face and has a small penis. I hate these young punks that think that life is all about poker and money. Someday they will find out- it's just about money.

♠ Look for the player with the Dr. Phil lunchbox. Don't try and bluff this sick fuck.

♠ Make sure to look for these "tells" and adjust your game accordingly. Getting to the final table probably means you've been playing for 12-15 hours, which also means you're probably going to have to adjust your underwear accordingly also. No one said this fuckin' game was going to be easy.

Deal or No Deal

Deals are very common at the final table. Deal making or chopping becomes very common when the final table gets down to the final 3 or 4 players. Sometimes final tables have been known to chop the prize money before they even deal the first hand. This is not real common since everyone is eyeing the person with the least chips- the short stack. When he loses, everyone moves up a notch in the winner's column. Sometimes the short stack gets lucky and doubles up a few times so he becomes part of the deal. When you are a short stack at the final table, you are the target. You are fresh meat and the vultures are circling. Each player eliminated means more money for the survivors. Many times you see a tournament played out on television until the end, but a deal has already been made. People want to see a winner. They demand it to satisfy their poker appetite. The television producers know this and tournament play is played til the end. They may have made a deal for the money and agreed that whoever wins all the chips wins an extra amount of cash or the bracelet or plaque or whatever. If the tournament is a regular one that is in a casino with no TV coverage, then usually once a deal is made, everyone gets to go home. Including the floor people and the dealers. After 12-15 hours of intense play, everyone is tired, exhausted, strained, constipated and smelly. It affects everyone. The young, the old, the feeble, the very feeble. Everyone gets tired. Even the degenerate tournament players are tired and want to go home by then. But sometimes, someone doesn't. And if that happens, everyone keeps playing.

There have been a lot of articles written on chopping the prize money. Most of the major casinos have a computer program that will compute prize money payouts based on your chip count at the time. If there are 5 players left in the game and all agree to chop or at least look at what the computer says you will receive if you do chop, the floor person comes over and counts all of your chips. With 5 people left, everyone receives 5th place money since the next person out would get 5th place money anyway. Then the rest of the prize pool is divided up based on chip count percentages. If you have 50% of the chips on the table, you would get 50% of the prize pool that's left after everyone gets 5th place money. The computer calculates the payouts rather quickly and the game is only held up for a few minutes while this is done. When everyone sees how much they will receive, they either decide to chop or continue playing. If just one person doesn't like the deal, then play continues. When that person is eliminated, the possibility of a chop is brought up again. Many deals are made in tournaments. When you get down to the final stretch of a tournament, the blinds are usually huge, the antes are very big and it's basically a crapshoot as to who will win. And no one likes to shoot craps for a million bucks. So deals are made. And there's nothing wrong with that. It's at this point in the tournament when any two cards can win any given hand. Forget waiting for a premium hand. The fuckin' blinds are too big. And the antes keep climbing. You **have** to play. There's nothing worse than getting blinded out of a tournament and going out without a fight. So remember, next time you make the final table, you can roll the dice or you can chop the pot. The choice is yours.

Psych 101

I knew a guy who was addicted to gambling and at the height of his addiction, he was playing Hold 'em 15 hours a day. We were chatting one day after he got out of rehab, and he said it was a very enlightening time for him. Every time he thinks about playing again he thinks of his options. Back to the 15 hour a day addiction habit that was destroying him and his family, a bullet in his head or going forward with his life. So far he had chosen #3- going forward with his life, but he was having moments of weakness and he needed some advice and support from me. I told him I've played with him numerous times and he plays just fuckin' terrible. He throws his money away. I told him his wife is a really really bitchy person with a lazy eye, and I don't know how he can stand to be around her, let alone go to bed with her. I told him I didn't think he was giving Option #2 enough consideration. It's times like these I'm glad I didn't put my psychology degree to use by becoming a counselor. I know when I worked as a volunteer on the Suicide Hotline I didn't do well. The Hotline standards and I didn't exactly see eye to eye.

Random Thought

70% of the time an over card will flop when you have pocket 10's.

Boys Town-

I'm Not Father Flannigan, Spencer Tracy Was

The Hacienda Hotel and Casino sits nestled in the mountains outside Boulder City, which is about 20 minutes from Las Vegas. Every year we sponsor a dinner, including entertainment and gifts for the kids of Boys and Girls Town in Las Vegas. Our banquet room seats about 120 and it was filled to capacity this year by the kids and alumni from Boys and Girls Town and the folks who run the entire Boys and Girls Town facility. It's really really hard not to be impressed with these kids. Every one of the kids has suffered a bad beat. We suffer bad beats on the river when we play Hold 'em and then talk about them and shrug them off. These kids have to live their bad beats. Some have been abandoned, some are orphans, some are in transition while the family tries to become a unit again and some are there because the family has been fractured by drugs, alcohol or both. All sizes, shapes, races and religions were represented. It was obvious to me that Boys and Girls Town was doing one Hell of a job raising these kids while they were in their care. And I'm sure many of them will be the Hold 'em stars of tomorrow. Every girl and every boy who came my way introduced themselves, shook my hand and looked me in the eye. It was a very impressive event held for very impressive kids. I was impressed by the way the kids looked after each other and helped each other. I was impressed with the interaction between the adult supervisors and the kids. It was obvious to me that there was mutual respect between them. The youth of today represents 28% of our population and 100% of our future. The kids that I met during this function, and other functions we sponsor, makes me think that the future of this country is in good hands. Hug your kid tonight and tell them how great he or she is and that you appreciate them. And be thankful there are organizations like Boys and Girls Town that are there to pick up the pieces if Humpty Dumpty does accidentally fall off his perch. Because once in a while he does. No matter how hard he tries to keep his balance.

Random Thought

You may be only one person in the world, but you are the world to at least one person.

Poker Ed 101

The education of a poker player is perpetual. It ends the day you die. Even then, you might be able to play a hand with St. Peter in order to get into the Pearly Gates. You never know. Peter is the maitre 'd of Heaven and I've never known a maitre 'd who turned down a chance to make a buck. When we had maitre d's in the Vegas showrooms, you use to be able to get closer to the stage for a twenty dollar bill. It was quite humorous to watch people at the Las Vegas Hilton line up at 5 A.M. for the Elvis concert being held at 8 P.M. that night. They thought that if they were first in line they would get a front row seat. First in line guaranteed you only one thing- a seat. Not a front row seat. Not a middle row seat. But a fuckin' seat. That's it. And if you didn't give the maitre 'd a little something to help him make his Mercedes payment, your seat would be behind one of the numerous supporting posts that were throughout the showroom. The more of the Mercedes payment you helped the maitre 'd with, the closer to Elvis you would be. For enough fuckin' money, you could be in the show! Or close to it. When Elvis was in the Hilton showroom, it didn't matter who you knew or who you blew. Your fate was in the hands of the maitre 'd. He was the fuckin' man! Nowadays it's all about tickets. And of course the scalpers. Want good seats? They're still available at a very high price, but instead of a maitre 'd and the showroom staff making a few bucks, we have scalpers and ticket agencies that buy huge blocks of tickets and resell them at much higher prices to the tourists and the locals. It's nice to see that Las Vegas has jumped on the technology bandwagon with all the various ticket outlets and the accessibility by phone and computer to fill up the showrooms up and down the strip. It's nice to see that Las Vegas has joined the 21st century and showroom personnel are no longer needed and personality doesn't have to play a part in the showroom experience. It's nice to see the computer has replaced the courteous welcome at the showroom door. And of course it's nice to see how we've managed to save the public money by not having to deal with a maitre 'd or his staff. But have we? Have we really saved the public any money? If there is a St. Peter at the Pearly Gates and he has his hand out, I'll know we've come full circle.

Random Thought

Comps are tough to get in the poker room so I was surprised to get 2 tickets to the Elton John show at Caesar's Palace. The gesture was nice- the seats weren't. I was so far away from the stage I couldn't tell if I was watching Elton John, Olivia Newton John, Pope John or John The Baptist. But the comped popcorn was fresh. Hail Caesar!

Suggestions For Life-

I Hate Fuckin' Rules, So I Call Them Suggestions

I was asked a while back to speak at Boulder City High School in Boulder City, Nevada- the town I live in and raised my family in. I spoke at 3 separate Careers classes and came up with the following suggestions for those kids for a successful life. That was about 10 years ago, so most of those kids who didn't follow my suggestions should be on parole by now. The suggestions apply for everyone- the old, the young, no matter your race, your religion or your girth. The first part of each suggestion is the one I gave the kids. The second part is reality as we poker fucks know it.

1) Say "please" and "thank you" a lot. This really creates a "nice person" image and you can fool a lot of people.

2) Look people in the eye. Once in a while **glance** at their bankroll when they pull it out to buy into a game. Glancing over a urinal could be construed as poor etiquette at a minimum and gay at the maximum.

3) Always show respect for dealers, police officers and firefighters. A lack of respect to a dealer can cause you to get a bad beat. Disrespecting a police officer can get your ass shot off, and dissing a fireman can cause your house to burn down, but the nice thing is, even if you piss them off, they will save your foundation.

4) Don't mess with drugs and don't associate with those who do. Unless of course they want to sponsor you in a big tournament. Then all bets are off.

5) Choose your life's mate carefully. From this one decision will come 90% of your happiness or 90% of your misery. Which of course always begs the question, "Why shouldn't gays be allowed to marry?" They should have the right to be as miserable as the rest of us.

6) When you have kids, tell them how terrific they are and that you love them. Even if you don't. And even if they're really ugly. Stay on good terms with them. Someday they'll be adjusting your shawl and emptying your drool cup.

7) Avoid negative people. This may mean never playing in a poker tournament again. So you might want to ignore this suggestion and skip to number 8.

8) Be kind- everyone is fighting a tough battle. Like you give a fuck. Don't these people realize you're trying to raise an entry fee into the WSOP?

9) Become the most positive and enthusiastic person you know. Have a great attitude. That should be really easy surrounding yourself daily with people in poker rooms who want to crush your soul. And juggle your testicles.

10) Measure people by the size of their hearts, not by the size of their bank accounts. Let's see how much food you can buy with a big heart when you get to the checkstand. Most guys measure people by the size of their penis.

11) Write a 5-year plan and 1-year updates. Read it every day. Then throw it away. It's never going to fuckin' happen.

12) Always dress up for an interview. And wear cologne. You never know when a girl will be the one interviewing you and she might want to blow you.

13) Read the business section at least once a week. It's only a few pages long. Then read the obituaries. If your name's not in it, read the rest of the paper.

14) Choose the right friends and be the right friend. Always pick people who have a ton of fuckin' money and drink a lot. They won't remember how much you borrowed from them.

15) Be there when people need you. At least fake it. Or send

someone else to be there who looks like you.

16) Happiness is not based on possessions, but on relationships with people you love and respect. It's hard to write this shit when you are laughing convulsively.

17) Keep a pen and pad next to your bed. Sometimes million dollar ideas come at 3 in the morning. And sometimes calls from your favorite hooker come at 3 in the morning and you need to jot down her new cell number.

18) Show respect for everyone who works for a living, regardless of how trivial their job. When I think trivial I think trivia, and when I think trivia I think Jeopardy, and when I think Jeopardy I think Alex Trebek, and when I think Alex Trebek I throw up. And then I have to call one of those people with trivial jobs to clean it up.

19) Buy a Christmas gift for a kid who has less than you do. If you can't find a kid with less than you have, then fuck it- buy yourself a nice gift.

20) Take care of your reputation. It's your most valuable asset. Besides of course your house and your stock portfolio. If you fuck up your reputation, there's always the Federal Witness Protection Program that allows you to start over. Sort of like a Catholic confession.

21) Never give up on what you really want to do. Dreams start to become reality when you're in school. If your dreams haven't become a reality by the time you're 25 and you're playing poker for a living- you're fucked.

Have a nice life. Good luck to all.

Random Thought

Some of the proceeds of this book will be used to fund scholarships for high school students planning to go to college or rehab. The book isn't that good so there probably won't be too many proceeds. Oh well. At least my intentions were good.

Sit N Go's

I like Sit n Go's. Basically it's a one table tournament that pays three places out of the ten spots at the table. A sit and go can be played for any amount. Some casinos have $60 buy-ins, some $100 buy-ins, and if you have enough interest from other players, I'm sure a casino would do a $250 or $500 Sit n Go. As long as they make their entry fee of about 10%, they could care less about supplying you with a table and a dealer. The blinds go up very rapidly in Sit n Go's just like they do in satellites. And as we all know blinds drive the action. Once the blinds start climbing, you need to play **less** than premium hands. You have no choice. If you don't you will get blinded out. You should investigate Sit n Go's at your local card room or casino. I think they are the most overlooked source of a supplemental income that is in the poker room. A Sit n Go is like making the final table in a tournament. So for a small buy-in, you get a final table experience, and better than that, you get short-handed experience when the field narrows down to 6, 4 and finally 2 players. And most of us lack a very important part of tournament play- final table play. Especially heads-up. Heads-up is a totally different animal than any other form of playing. Just having an Ace takes on new meaning. A pair is dominant. Aggressiveness is imperative. And it's only through experience that you can get good at heads-up play. And heads-up play is hard to come by. But in Sit n Go's you can get heads-up experience just by outlasting 8 other players. You don't have to outlast 500 other players like in a big tournament. Check out Sit n Go's in your area. You could be pleasantly surprised and more importantly pleasantly rewarded.

Random Thought

There are days when the cards will not cooperate. On those days, no amount of skill will help you. Go the fuck home!

Nicknames of Hold 'em Hands

We all like nicknames. When I worked at the Dunes there were plenty of nicknames for the dealers. Big Al, Starvin Marvin, Ray the Rug, Skid Rowe, the list went on and on. Hold 'em hands also have nicknames. These are the ones I know. I'm sure there are plenty more.

A-A	Pocket Rockets
A-K	Big Slick (I call A-K "No Pair")
A-8	Dead Man's Hand
K-J	Kojack
K-9	Canine
QS-JD	Pinochle
Q-7	Computer Hand
J-5	Motown
5-10	Woolworth
10-4	Highway Patrol
10-2	Doyle Brunson
9-8	Oldsmobile
3-9	Jack Benny
9-5	Dolly Parton
7-6	Union Oil
5-5	Speed Limit
7-4	Paul Bania- Paul plays at our private Boulder

City game every week and always plays this shit.

5-7	Heinz 57
4-5	Jesse James
2-2	Quack Quack or Ducks

Thank You Ernie- Thank You Grant

I would like to publicly thank Ernie Cabral for taking the pictures in this book. I will never forget how he begged me and begged me to take the pictures and I am sure he will never let me forget he took them. Never ever. Ernie's wife Connie is a lovely creature that somehow tolerates him, much like most of us tolerate diarrhea- hoping that soon it will go away. But Ernie doesn't go away. If he has your cell number, you're doomed. If he has your email address, you're double doomed. If he knows where you live you are totally fucked. Ernie is like the crazy uncle you hope soon gets committed. Like the brother you never wanted. To those 10 or 20 thousand people who Ernie calls his "close friends" there is only one answer. Only one escape from him. Death. Sweet fuckin' death.

PS- I would also like to thank Grant Turner- the boy next door- for typing this shit. He's shaken his head and rolled his eyes at me more times than my wife has. No one understands me. No one thinks the therapy sessions have helped. But Grant is beginning to come around.

You're Great

I was just reading an article by Jeff Simpson who was reflecting about some Stardust memories as the Stardust Hotel and Casino heads for destruction to make way for another monster Las Vegas strip project. He talks about Larry Vance, a long time Stardust employee who worked at the casino for 600 or 700 years. Then a little sentence that followed that statement triggered my thought process. That is always dangerous. When something triggers the bowels of my brain I go on a tangent. I start to fantasize. I start to visualize. I start to circumcise (I couldn't think of any other word that rhymes with fantasize and visualize and I needed 3 for balance- it's a feng shui thing). So the sentence said that Larry Vance was the son of baseball "great" Dizzy Vance, not to be confused with baseball great Dizzy Dean or trumpet great Dizzy Gillespie. Or a not so great Dizzy Izzy who I dealt craps with at the Dunes in the early 1800's. So I was pondering about this "great" guy Dizzy Vance and wondered what made him so great.

There are a lot of people in our country who should be called "great" but we never hear about them. People who do their jobs with love and enthusiasm every day. People who make guests feel welcome, who serve in restaurants and who drive their rigs through dangerous ice and snow so we can get our favorite product on our grocer's shelves. People who deliver our mail and our newspapers every day without fail. So I am proposing a "You're Great" campaign. Every town, every village, every city, every county will nominate people that they think are great. Every month. All year long. Every year. A committee will choose the ones they feel have exuded the most "greatness". One person will be chosen from each area for the "You're Great" award, which of course comes with a nice prize. All runners up also receive a plaque and a dinner for 4 at a local restaurant, which will be donated by that restaurant. The money will come from our taxes. Finally, our tax dollars at work for something positive. This kind of campaign could have a profound effect on the attitude of our country. So many people are great, but never get recognized. A black lady in the Bellagio was very kind to my son and me a few months ago. I was asking about the game "Casino War" and she was busy doing her pit boss duties, but with a smile on her face and a song in her heart, she took the time to explain the game and seemed to really really enjoy her job. As opposed to the dealer who dealt the game who was an ex-Gestapo agent.

We have a local restaurant in Boulder City called "Evan's Grill". Evan comes out from the kitchen and shakes peoples' hands and thanks them for stopping in whenever he can. He genuinely appreciates his customers and shows it. Evan is great! Greatness is everywhere. My dad Arthur Korfman Jr. was a great Pacific Gas and Electric employee for 35 years. When he brought home the company car, it sat in the driveway the whole fuckin' weekend while we drove around town in a junker. No amount of coercion by me could convince him to use the shiny new station wagon. And when I suggested to him that I be allowed to siphon some gas from his gas tank into my clunker, it was met by a backhand that even Andre Agassi would be jealous of. My dad was as dedicated an employee of PG&E as anyone could be. He was great. So greatness isn't all about being a sports figure or a famous singer or actor. Greatness is everywhere. There are a lot of great people who go unrecognized for their greatness. With this program, they wouldn't anymore. Now that would be great!

Random Thought

One of my favorite Neil Diamond songs is kind of an obscure, left field kind of song. It's called "Captain Sunshine". Everyone needs a "Captain Sunshine" in their life. Everyone. Whenever I hear it I think of my dad. He was my Captain Sunshine. Thanks Neil.

George Clooney- Watch Out!

This year's "Sexiest Men Alive" list has just been released and once again, as in years past, I'm not on it. I contacted *People Magazine* because I've really been working on my table image and I was sure that I would make the cut. I was told by the editor that I was close and I shouldn't give up my dream. He said they pick the top 100 men and I was 120th sandwiched between Todd Brunson and Kathy Liebert. I despise working out, but this may force me to reconsider.

Fan Mail-

I Love Fan Mail

When I read a book by Tony Korfman I get chest pains. His short, staccato like sentences affect my digestive juices and I have been known to have bowel obstructions by Chapter 4. I think readers should file a class action suit. He must be stopped from writing any more books. Please, for God's sake. Help me stop him.

Linda Korfman
His wife

Tournament Death-

A Preparation for the Real Thing

I think Hold 'em tournaments were created by a guy who feared death as we all do. He wanted to lessen his fear by creating situations in life that would prepare him for his ultimate death- the big one. And so tournaments were born. And so was tournament death. When you are eliminated from a tournament, you have experienced tournament death. And everyone in that room will have that experience except the winner. No matter how big or small the tournament, the winner is the only one who doesn't experience tournament death. One minute you're alive, the next minute you're fuckin' toast. It's sudden, it's final, it's bone crushing, soul crushing and testicle crushing. You're dazed, confused, shocked, bewildered, stunned, numb, perplexed and dumbfounded. Other than that, you're fine. As you walk out of the tournament area embarrassed and humiliated, you don't want people to know you were knocked out- a loser- a failure- so you hold your balls making believe you just have to run and pee, but you'll be back. But the people at your table know you're not coming back. Ever again. And those of us who play tournaments with some frequency have experienced tournament death over and over. And so did the inventor of tournaments. Until his final tournament. But before his final tournament, he gained national prominence by coming up with the slogan "Got Milk?". His final words, unfortunately, had nothing to do with tournaments. They were "Got Chest Pains".

Random Thought

No one is ever safe in a tournament. Your tournament life is always at risk.

The Truth-

Can You Handle the Truth?

The numbers I am quoting have been rounded off. 1 in 26.42 hands has been rounded off to 1 in 26. If it were 1 in 26.57, I would have said 1 in 27. If that bothers you, please make a fuckin' appointment with your therapist immediately- and remove all sharp objects from your dark, dingy apartment. If you are already seeing a therapist, increase your visits. If you are living in your car, you probably borrowed this book or stole it. So if something from a borrowed or stolen book bothers you, and you can't afford therapy, the only alternative would be to slam your head in the car door. Let me know if these calculations, which have been checked by some of the world's leading mathematicians, help you. They've never done anything for my game. Maybe it's because I made them up.

Pre-flop Probabilities

Pocket Aces- 220 to 1- The average dealer deals 30 hands an hour on a full table. This means you should get pocket Aces about once every 7.5 hours. Is that fuckin' depressing or what?

Pocket Kings or pocket Aces- 110 to 1

2 Kings, 2 Queens, 2 Jacks- 73 to 1 (any of the 3)

Pair of sixes, sevens, eights, nines or tens- 43 to 1

Pair of twos, threes, fours or fives- 54 to 1

Ace-King suited- 331 to 1

Ace-King offsuit- 110 to 1

Any Ace-King- 82 to 1

Ace-Queen or Ace-Jack suited- 165 to 1

Ace-Queen or Ace-Jack offsuit- 54 to 1

King-Queen suited- 331 to 1

King-Queen offsuit- 110 to 1

Ace with a card less than a Jack suited- 36 to 1

Ace with a card less than a Jack offsuit- 11 to 1

Any Ace before the flop- 6 to 1

Any pair- 16 to 1

Any two cards suited- 3 to 1

Any two suited connectors- 46 to 1

Any two connectors- 15 to 1

Chances of Flopping

A flush- 118 to 1

Quads off a pocket pair- 407 to 1

Quads after being dealt unpaired hole cards- 9800 to 1

A Set after being dealt a pocket pair- 8 to 1

A Full House with a pocket pair- 136 to 1

A Straight with 6-5 - 76 to 1

A Straight with 7-5 - 101 to 1

A Straight with 8-5 - 152 to 1

A Straight with 9-5 - 305 to 1

A Straight with 2-7 - Priceless

And Finally

♠ Your hand will have no Ace 85% of the time.

♠ 42% of the time you get pocket Aces you will have crotch itch.

♠ If you are playing heads up, the chances of you and your opponent being dealt pocket Aces is over 270,000 to 1. The chances of you or your opponent having bad breath is 14 to 1. The chances of you having sex with your opponent is 9 to 1.

♠ The chances of never receiving an Ace as one of your hole cards for the rest of your life is 47,343,691 to 1. Unless you are really really fuckin' old. Then the odds can drop as low as 2-1.

Poker Etiquette

Not a lot has been written on poker etiquette. There is usually one asshole at every table. If you have poker etiquette you are able to identify him. If you can't identify him within the first 15 minutes you are at the table, then it's probably you. Here are some helpful hints to become a respected player with proper poker etiquette. I thank Emily Post, the matriarch of etiquette, for giving me the courage to attack such a "sissy" sounding subject. But I knew it had to be done.

Critiquing: When critiquing another player's poor play, especially after he has suffered a soul crushing bad beat, try not to "needle" him too much while you are explaining to him what a fuckin' idiot he was to call the bet. Everyone at the table enjoys a good laugh at the expense of another player, but no one wants to watch another player who just suffered a bone crushing defeat be abused too much. It makes everyone uncomfortable and sometimes causes menstrual cramps.

Dealers: Dealers are just trying to do their job. And feed their families. And pay their car payment and rent. So making them beg for a tip is disrespectful. Unless it's a big tip. Then it is usually humorous and entertaining for you to make them beg, kneel and even offer various sexual services, all in the name, of course, of good clean fun. Dealers are there for servicing you. Tip them big. And enjoy them. Make them beg- but do it respectfully.

Stalling: Most people understand how stalling irritates everyone. Deliberately playing slow has a way of aggravating the other players, the dealer and of course the management who depend on the "rake" which is taken from each pot. Less pots means less money for the house. The house has plenty of money. Fuck em. The players should appreciate a good staller. He's saving them money. And the dealer should also appreciate him- he doesn't have to work as hard. Stalling is good and bad- depending on your perspective.

Table Space: It is common courtesy not to infringe too much on the table space of the people sitting on either side of you. I say not to infringe too much because I, for one, am a rather large humanoid and need more space. Plus I have a lot of stuff I put in front of me when I play. I usually have at least three card covers, the largest one being an urn that has my great grandmother in it. We haven't gotten around to cremating her yet, but we plan to soon. The final bid is suppose to be in next week. Cremation is costly. I put it out to bid. It's a very lucky urn. A huge lucky urn. She was a very big woman. She had a huge ass. Whenever I took her shopping it was always very humorous because security would always stop us as we were leaving the store because they thought she was shoplifting throw pillows. We would always laugh hysterically as they made her take off her spandex in the parking lot. And of course, then there were the apologies as a gesture of "security kindness". So as I was saying, this lucky urn takes up quite a bit of room. By the time I order my coffee, my bottle of Perrier with a large glass and 3 ice cubes, open my bag of snacks and set down my pair of glasses, I have already infringed on the table space of the opponents on both sides of me. When the double cheeseburger with an extra order of onion rings arrives, it kind of launches table space etiquette to a new level. I found out that once you invade another person's table space by 50% or more, they get fuckin' testy. They have no fuckin' etiquette. None at all.

Leaving the Table: When leaving the table for a quick cigarette or just to cool off after a bad beat, you should courteously let everyone know you have counted all your chips and if anyone puts their slimy fuckin' hands on them you will put their balls in a vice and crush them. The players will appreciate your honesty and candidness.

Peeking: You should never peek at another player's cards unless you can do it without causing suspicion. That is the primary reason to wear sunglasses. No one knows what you are looking at, unless you try to adjust your opponent's fingers so you can get a better look at his hand.

Verbalize Your Action: You should clearly verbalize your action especially when making a huge bet. Unless, of course, you can take advantage of a situation by mumbling. Then, by all means, mumble.

Abuse: Abuse of spectators, dealers and other players is usually never tolerated, except when a dealer delivers a testicle crushing, bone crushing, soul crushing river card and then gives you a little smirk the way dealers do when they have completed the delivery. Then it's no holds barred- the gloves are off. Never tear the cards in half. This is really bad etiquette and also impossible to do since the cards are plastic. Plus you might break a nail. It's more sensible to fling them in a playful manner across the room or towards the dealer's eyes. This is sometimes looked upon as a playful gesture and not subject to the penalties that assault and battery usually bring.

Slowrolling: This is when you turn your cards over one at a time during the showdown phase of the hand, and you do it slowly, showing the insignificant card first and then the card that you know in your heart will be the winner. When this is done correctly, if you listen closely you can hear your opponent's diaper burst. Emily Post says this type of behavior is unethical, dishonest, unfair, wrong, immoral and underhanded. I say it is a lot of fun. I highly recommend it. Fuck Emily Post.

Farting: We all pass gas. Even runway models. And sometimes the urge to pass gas comes at times that are not conducive to passing gas. As you can tell by now, I love saying "passing gas". So if you're at the poker table and the tremendous urge comes to pass gas, I think you need to evaluate certain things just like you would evaluate pocket 10's against a tight opponent:

1.) If the person sitting next to you is a complete asshole, then the decision to fart is a no brainer. If it's a really hot looking chick that you want to ask out but you don't have a chance in Hell with her accepting the invitation, that's a no brainer too. Fart away, bucko. The louder the better. Then look down at the ground like you have your dog with you and yell, "Rover!" Everyone will laugh hysterically except for the people who don't know the Rover joke- like the bitch that won't go out with you.

2.) You need to remember what you ate for lunch or dinner to evaluate the impact that the odor of the fart will have on the game and especially the dealer. If you had chili or tuna, the smell could cause the dealer's eyes to tear up and he could misdeal the cards, which could cost you a ton of fuckin' money if you were finally dealt pocket Aces. Normal farts like those from Cheerios, Corn Flakes and Wheaties are usually pretty mild, but Raisin Bran and Shredded Wheat scrub your colon clean and the end result of a clean colon is usually a cleaned out poker room. Farting can be tastefully accomplished when proper etiquette is used.

Eulogies: When asked by family members to provide a eulogy for a fellow poker player, the following phrases might not be acceptable to some members of the family:

-Life is Motion- He's not motioning anymore.

-He bit the big one.

-He's failed the freshness test.

-He's fish food.

-He was dealt 2-7 off.

-He missed his big blind.

-He got rivered with embalming fluid.

-He was literally blinded to death.

-The cocktail waitress called him a "stiff".

-He Puggy Pearsoned.

-He was laid out like a 6-foot party sub.

-He perfected his exit strategy.

-He flopped- He got turned- Then he got buried.

Breastfeeding at the Poker Table: I know a lot has been written about breastfeeding. Well, maybe not a lot. Actually not at all in a poker book. But I felt it had to be addressed in this book. Why? Well, to start with, it's in one of the working titles. The title of this book has changed more times than Michael Jackson's nose. Or the place on his face where his nose use to be. For a while, it was "Texas Hold 'em- He Rivered Me Without a Condom". Then after much pressure, the tamer version- "He Rivered Me Without a Trojan or His Horse". Then I made a complete left turn. It was "Texas Hold 'em- Very Humorous- Very Informative" for almost a week. Then "Texas Hold 'em- Tournaments, Cash Games and Casserole". Then for almost a month it was "Texas Hold 'em- Tournaments, Cash Games and Breastfeeding Etiquette". Proper etiquette dictates that breastfeeding should not be done at the poker table. That's because no kids are allowed at the poker table. But that begs the question- What about breastfeeding pumps? And if that's OK, that begs a bigger question to a lot of guys- what about penis pumps? There was actually a judge in Las Vegas who was busted for using a penis pump under his robe while he was sitting on the bench. He had been doing it for a long time and his only "tell" was the euphoric look he would have on his face at times. And sometimes he would yell, "Fuck me you bitch," three or four times while court was in session. And yell, "Yes! Yes!" which would disturb the court stenographer because she had no exclamation point on her steno machine. So when you hear someone yell, "Yes! Yes!" at another table, it's probably because he just put a bad beat on his opponent. Unless the guy happens to look like a judge…..

One Small Step

There are certain earth shattering events that everyone remembers where they were when that event happened. I can name three of them real quick. The first one was when Doyle Brunson won the World Championship with 10-2 suited. Wow! And when the first Krispy Kreme store opened in my hometown. Double fuckin' wow! And of course the event that made all the papers- Neil Armstrong's walk on the moon. I loved the landing, the bounce in Neil's step, and his immortal words that I still use today, "One small step for man," and then some crap about mankind. It still sends shivers down my spine. I know it's hard to believe, but some people still think that the whole moon landing thing was faked. Something about Armstrong bitching about how hot it was on the movie set with all the lights, that big heavy suit and having a pebble in his boot. And of course, let's not forget about the reflection of the catering truck in the visor of his helmet. Doesn't Hollywood know by now that reflections are going to be the downfall of mankind if they aren't more careful? Well, at least I know that Doyle's 10-2 was real and there was no doubt in my mind about the Krispy Kreme store. A dozen Krispy Kremes can overcome any reflection. Man, they are fuckin' good!

Random Thought

There is a 60% chance that an Ace or a King will appear on the board by the river card.

Poker Cruises

I noticed that among the more popular events that the poker marketing department has come up with are the poker cruises. I've gone on regular cruises, but never on a poker cruise. A cruise is a floating buffet. The food is incredible. You barely finish one fantastic meal and you look at your watch and say, "Holy fuck- It's almost time to eat again." The cruise lines do this repeatedly until it's time for you to leave the ship and go home to microwave dinners again. I envision poker cruises to be different. The focus wouldn't be on food. It's on poker. The menu would be designed like playing hands. 3 of a Kind- 3 eggs, 3 slices of bacon and 3 pieces of toast. A full house would be huge. Two pounds of bacon, a loaf of bread, a dozen eggs and your own lifeboat if the ship gets in trouble. The buffet would be a poker player's dream buffet. Paper bags with sandwiches, an apple, a banana and a bottle of Fiji water in them. You just pick one up and take it to the poker table with you and you feel right at home. Cruises are designed to give you that feeling. If they would put a microwave in my cabin, I would consider a poker cruise. I really would.

Random Thought

There is nothing more beautiful or more compelling than A-K suited- especially in Spades. And then the flop comes Q-J-10 of spades. Now that is beautiful. And your opponent has pocket Aces. And an Ace comes on the turn. Now that is pure fuckin' beautiful. Absolutely a thing of beauty. Plus, you're drunk. Life is fuckin' good.

The Meter is Running

Life is short. And fleeting. So there's not a lot of time to accomplish what it is you want to do. And whatever that is, you need to try it. And usually, more often than not, if it's something you really, really want to do, you will be good at it. And being good at it means that you will be successful at it. Because people who have a passion for what it is they do are good at it. Very good. And even if you fail, you will have failed at something you wanted to do. Life is short. And fleeting. So go for it. You'll be fine. I promise.

Dreams Can Come True

We live in a country where you can follow your dream, no matter your religion, no matter your race, no matter your age. My grandfather always wanted to go to medical school but couldn't. At 82 he finally got his wish. His dream came true. He just entered the University of California Medical School. He's a cadaver.

Image

Image is very important. People talk. Rumors abound. There is one high profile Internet star who hopes people never find out about his sexual exploits. With midgets. And the exploits involve leather- and thongs. I won't tell who. He's sworn me to secrecy. Plus he loans me an occasional midget.

Cash Games:

To Play or Not To Play- That is the Question

Cash games do not have anywhere near the intensity that tournaments do. You very seldom ever hear a roar from a cash game. There's never a fuckin' idiot standing on a chair screaming "I am the King" at the top of his fuckin' lungs at a cash game. No high fives. No hysterical young players needing a diaper change because they just rivered someone. No hugging people in the audience. Cash games are more subtle. Earthlings surround a poker table sometimes for 10-15 hours and try to win each others' money before the house gets it all. Because eventually they will. If you play long enough and no fresh money comes into the game, the house rake will grind everyone into total and complete submission. But we all know that before we play. At least I think we all know that. Cash games come in all shapes and sizes. They fit every bankroll. There's an ass for every seat. Sometimes an asshole. I play cash games and tournaments. But I'm beginning to like cash games more and more.

When I first started playing cash games I didn't like them because I didn't do well. I didn't do well because I tried Limit Hold 'em and I played every pot because it was cheap. Then I tried No Limit Hold 'em but I played 1-2 No Limit and 2-5 No Limit. Same shit. I'd throw $2 or $5 in the pot every hand to see the flop. Then I found the level of No Limit that was meaningful to me. It's $10-$20 No Limit. I usually buy in for $2,000 and that's **my** limit that I will lose. I don't put a limit on my winnings, but I definitely put a limit on my losses. There are some days that the deck of cards does not cooperate. If you play with any frequency at all, you will have days that will stun you so much that you will consider going to church. Or calling Dr. Kevorkian the famous suicide doctor. And going to church with **him**. It's days like those you could possibly lose your entire poker bankroll. That's why you must limit your losses. It's tough to get up and walk away from a game a loser, but you have to learn to. You have to get use to walking away when you lose **and** when you win. It's very tough to do because the game is never over. The casino or card room never closes. No windows- no clocks. They have us by the fuckin' balls. That is about the only thing I can say for tournament players that lets them lead a more normal existence than a cash game player. When they get knocked out of a tournament, they're out. No rebuys. No reloads. They either go find another tournament or they go home and watch tournament poker on TV and think about how they misplayed their final hand and then keep dreaming the dream. And everyone who plays tournaments dreams the dream. If someone is an occasional player, a tournament might be the answer for them. But if someone is looking for a steady income, they should play cash games. You will no doubt have hills and valleys, winning sessions and losing sessions, ups and downs. But at the end of the day, at the end of the week, at the end of the month, you should come out a winner if you play a solid cash game.

People who play tournaments have been known to go busted unless they cash with some frequency, and that is difficult to do in today's tournament fields. Usually 10% of the field gets some semblance of cash. The bigger amounts of money are awarded only if you place 1st through 4th. In a field of say 250, that's not easy. In a cash game, if you get ahead after a few hours, you can go home. In a tournament, you might play 10 hours and go home empty. You need a bigger bankroll to play tournaments. Tournaments can get real expensive when you don't come in the money. In cash games, you can pick your spots and play whenever you want. I like to play cash games when a corresponding tournament is in its 4th or 5th hour. When guys are getting busted out of a tournament, they usually come into the live poker room area and want to play in a cash game. Their adrenaline is usually running from the bad beat they just took in the tournament, and they're looking to win their tournament entry money back plus plus. Tournament players tend to overplay their hands when they sit down in a cash game- especially if they're steaming. Cash games have a much lower luck factor than tournaments. That's because the blinds always stay the same and you can play your hand as you see fit, not as the blinds dictate you to play it. All-ins are very common in tournaments, and the escalation process of raise, re-raise, all-in comes very quickly. This happens very rarely in cash games. Cash games do not have the grueling intensity that tournaments have. A steady tournament player has a different mindset than a steady cash game player. A cash game player is more relaxed. His stress meter is a lot lower. Most cash games I've played in are fun. People chat. They "kibbitz" (they kid each other). When a pot is developing, everyone gets quiet out of respect for the people in the pot who need to make expensive decisions, and then when the hand is over, everyone starts chatting again. Everyone at the table is there to win, but the atmosphere is totally different than a tournament table's atmosphere. Most people play poker to have some fun and forget about life for a while. To the younger generation, it seems that poker is the answer to fast money with no heavy lifting. They can work whenever they please and they hope to be a celebrity someday. Or see a celebrity. Or go to bed with a celebrity. But many just wind up jerking off to a picture of a celebrity. That's as close as they'll ever get. That's poker.

Random Thought

I look at some of these lonely fucks playing poker for a living, and I can see the wheels turning in their heads as they're sitting there with their sunglasses and headphones on and a snarl on their lips. They're thinking, "Here I am sitting here playing poker day after day, month after month with each dealer slowly sucking the life out of me. I've been playing for 5 fuckin' years- my clothes are wrinkled, my skin is pale and I smell. There's not a day that goes by that I don't think about the sweet release that death will bring." Other than that, I can tell they're having fun.

Cash Game Overview:

♠ The nice thing about cash games is you can change your seat. I always like to position myself with the guy who has the most chips to my right.

♠ In a loose game- play tight. In a tight game- play loose. In any game- be observant. When losing- tighten your play.

♠ Playing bad cards leads to bad beats. Playing bad cards and playing badly are different. Either way, the results are the same- you go home broke.

♠ At the end of the day, everyone at the table gets the same cards- good and bad. But at the end of the day, only a few players are winners. And of course the house. They always win.

♠ No Limit cash games = 80% betting, 20% cards.
Limit cash games = 20% betting, 80% cards.

♠ Don't try to bluff a loose player. He'll call you every fuckin' time.

♠ If I raise before the flop, I will make a continuation bet after the flop. A man needs to know where he's at and a continuation bet lets you know in a hurry.

♠ If I'm bluffing, I like to bet $100 bills at you. Most Las Vegas casinos allow you to keep $100 bills on the table in No Limit games. Cash money has more impact on people than chips. If I want you in the pot, I'll bet $100 chips. 3 or 4 chips doesn't seem like a big deal.

♠ When I go to the bathroom, I always wash my face. It refreshes me.

♠ People have a tendency to play much tighter at the game when they're eating. They don't want to be bothered when they're eating, so they only play premium hands. Remember this.

♠ People who read at the table, like the guy I played against last week (he was reading a fuckin' novel!) tend to also play very tight. If a guy is eating or reading, and he opens under the gun- call the Ghostbusters because he has a fuckin' monster! If a guy is eating, reading and getting a massage, call Dr. Phil. He needs fuckin' help.

♠ If you want to have a few drinks, go to the bar. Do not play poker and drink. Do not drive and drink. Either one is very dangerous.

♠ Don't loan money to a player to play against you. If you loan him money, tell him to play at another table. Don't loan him any more than you can afford because it's 8-5 you won't get it back. No matter what he says. In fact, make that 9-5.

♠ Hold 'em is about betting and position. I came in 9th in a tournament of 60 people and never looked at my hole cards until after the turn. Or was it after the flop? Or was it before the flop? Fuck, I don't know. I'm old. I can't remember. But I came in 9th. Not looking. I just relied on betting and position.

♠ Any time I win a nice size pot, I'm in the next one. I believe in rushes. Sometimes you go on a fuckin' rampage for 3 or 4 or more hands and tear everyone at the table a new asshole. I love it when I win a pot and can't stack the chips fast enough before I win the next one. That can't happen if you don't play consecutive hands. Card rooms should employ "chip bitches" to help you stack your chips. Large breasted chip bitches with tight asses. They would do very well. Actually, they probably do very well already. Never mind.

♠ There are 1,326 possible hole card combinations. 85% of the time, you will have no Ace. 85% of the time, you go to bed without having sex. Poker is a lot like sex. I just proved it.

♠ Listen to your gut- your intuition. Your brain has accumulated a ton of information you don't even realize you have. Your first "read" of a situation is going to be right 80% of the time. So what if the fucker bluffed you. You've still got your chips and you'll nail his ass next time.

♠ 30 Seconds is a long time. Just sit there right now and count to 30. Not real fast- just regular-like. It's a long time. If I told you I was going to squeeze your balls for 30 seconds, you would realize how long it is. My point is, if you have to ponder for more than 30 seconds, throw your fuckin' hand away. 45 Seconds tops. Well, maybe 46 seconds- but that's it. Not a fuckin' second more. Once in a while you will throw away the best hand. All good players do. The best players do. So it's not a big deal when you do it. The important thing is that at the end of the day, you have more money than you started the day with. That is the goal.

♠ What you have put into the pot is not yours anymore. It's in escrow. People make decisions based on what they have in the pot. That is fuckin' nuts. If you think you're hand is a loser, why put more money in so that you can say the most fucked up sentence a poker player can say, "I knew you had me beat. But I had to call."

♠ Never criticize an opponent's play. Why would you want to educate a weaker player? If anything, praise his play. You want him to continue it and not change it or play differently. There are enough tough players out there. Leave the weak ones the fuck alone.

♠ Moans, groans, sighs and whiney calls usually indicate strong hands. This game is all about analyzation and dramatization. We analyze and dramatize. I'm surprised many of us don't have Oscars on our mantels.

♠ When you're in a pot, watch your opponents' faces when the flop comes. Sometimes you can pick up information. And many times an opponent will only look at one hole card before the flop if he sees an Ace. Then he checks his hole cards a second time when the betting gets to him. Watch for this. A lot of people do it and it's a great fuckin' tell that the guy has an Ace. I have to be careful because I've been guilty of this move. I'll see an Ace as my first card, wait for everyone to act, then look at my second card. You see this especially when someone is on a short stack. Look for it.

♠ In home games, beware if anyone helps you rake in the pot. No one should have their fuckin' hands in the pot except you, and of course the dealer if you have a designated dealer. Home games are a haven for cheats. I know they're your buddies. Your teammates. Your office pals. If your gut tells you that something smells fishy, check the garbage disposal. If there's not a rotting salmon in there, you've got a fuckin' problem, Bucko.

♠ In No Limit cash games, I hate calling fuckin' bets. Especially big bets. I'd rather put you in a position to have to call and be puckering **your** asshole than you puckering mine. If I think I have the best hand, or if I think I can make you lay down your hand, I'm coming at you. If you've got big enough balls and you call me and win the pot, God bless you. I like guys who have the balls to call.

♠ The flop is the time for major decisions. You have seen 5 out of the 7 cards in the hand. You've seen over 70% of the hand. At this point, you decide to either fold or continue based on your assessment of your opponent's hand and whether or not the flop helped your hand. Most of the time flops do not help a hand. If I raised before the flop, I always make a continuation bet and most of the time win the pot. I like continuation bets. They usually let you know in a hurry where you stand. I know I've said this before. I repeat myself. I'm old.

♠ You win money at poker by betting. I like to bet. Passive people who check all the time or just call all the time don't do well in the long run. If you're afraid of losing your money, you shouldn't be playing. If you are constantly afraid of the nuts or you only like to bet the nuts, you are playing the wrong game. Play Monopoly with your kids. It'll be more fun for you and less stressful and much less costly. Once I identify that you only play the nuts, I own you.

♠ You will have soul crushing, bone crushing bad beats. You just will. We all do. Do not ever lose your temper when these bad beats show up. If you feel you are losing control, get up from the game, go to the parking garage and slam your nut sack in a car door. Mike "the Mouth" took my advice and hasn't lost his temper in two months. But he does have a lot of car door imprints on his nut sack.

♠ Practice guessing what a player's hole cards are, even when you're not in the hand. I know a few people who can do this with amazing accuracy. What a tremendous advantage they have when they play!

♠ Losing streaks will be part of your poker playing experience. I reduce the amount of money that I am willing to risk until I turn my luck around. I normally take $2,000 with me to a 10-20 No Limit game. If I'm on a losing streak, I'll lower my game to 5-10 No Limit and take $1,000 with me to the poker room. If that doesn't work, I'll drop it to 2-5 No Limit on my next trip. Until my losing cycle is over, I'll drop as low as 1-2 No Limit with a $300 buy-in. You can adjust your numbers to suit your bankroll. You cannot allow a losing streak to wipe out your poker bankroll.

♠ Never show your cards if your opponent hasn't called your final bet. Why give any of the guys at the table free information? That's fuckin' nuts. By the time they figure out how you play, you might be a 2 or 3 thousand dollar winner. Any tiny bit of information you give your poker opponents will be information they will use to get your chips. Sometimes all of them. On the other hand, I am always probing what they had during conversation. Most hands do not go through until completion, so getting good "reads" on people is difficult. In a cash game, you might be playing with many of the same people for many hours. Any information on their play is valuable. Very valuable. And conversing with them sometimes reveals what they had in a hand they didn't have to show.

♠ I like to play J-10. It has immense possibilities. It can produce 5 nut straights among numerous other hands. And if it is J-10 suited, there are even more possibilities. Like I said, I like J-10. I don't love it. I wouldn't marry it. I don't want to have kids with it. But I do like it.

♠ The most common mistake players make is to stay too long at the game when they're losing. "Stuck and Steaming" is a term commonly used in the gaming industry. Most people know they should quit, but they don't have the discipline. That's probably the number one reason most poker players are losers. Maybe they have nowhere to go after the game. That's why you **must** get Tivo.

♠ In cash games, play position, play the player, play the situation. Fuck pot odds. I don't play pot odds. If my fuckin' hand is beat- it's beat. When you run into a brick wall, who gives a fuck if one of the bricks is a little loose. You are still all fucked up from hitting the wall.

♠ Limit games take more patience because you can't run anyone out of the pot. The strong, the mediocre, the weak, all stay in the fuckin' pot once they make their first bet. So you need real strong hands to start and big lungs so you can hold your fuckin' breath for the rest of the hand.

♠ When playing in any poker game, but especially in cash games, position will win you more money than any other single thing. When you have good position, it gives you the advantage of seeing the actions of all the other players.

♠ When things aren't going well in a cash game, you have a lot of options. You can quit and take a walk for 20 minutes and see if things will change. You can change your seat when another one becomes available. You can change tables or just go the fuck home. Tivo awaits you.

♠ Much of your earnings in No Limit Hold 'em come from setting traps effectively and avoiding traps that are set for you. In No Limit, when someone checks to you and you bet and they go all-in, you are faced with a huge decision you won't face in Limit Hold 'em. Therein lies the difference between the two games. And the challenge. And the fun. And we all like to have fun.

Random Thought

Poker. It's grueling- It's grinding- It's intense- It's suspense- It's pretense and it's fuckin' expensive if you play shitty cards.

Absolutes- Not the Vodka

I assume you're reading this book to either become a winner or become a bigger winner. There are some absolute "givens" when you play. They are absolutes. The game isn't easy. We all know that. And we want to have fun. And what better way to have fun than to walk out of the game a winner. Maybe not every single time. But most of the time. So here are the absolute "nuts" to put you on the path to being a winner. It's just a start, but it's an important start.

1) No alcohol while you're playing- drinking dulls your senses. You'll make bad decisions and they will be very costly.

2) Drink a lot of water, Perrier, soda- any type of fluid that's not alcoholic.

3) Be well rested when you play. If it's going to be a late night session, try and take a nap in the afternoon. When you get tired or sleepy while playing, either drink a cup of coffee or go home. There's always tomorrow. If you're in a tournament, chances are your adrenaline will keep you from getting tired.

4) Don't play when you are upset. You need all your faculties to be sharp when you are playing, whether it's a cash game or a tournament. If you are preoccupied because of an argument or something that's weighing heavily on your mind then you will be at a complete disadvantage at the poker table.

5) Be healthy. If you are sick or not feeling well, forget about playing. You cannot play your best when you're sick.

6) Money management- Volumes of books have been written on this one element of winning. I'm an aggressive player so I have to be very aware of money management because it can go quickly. My personal rule of thumb is that I have the money I'm going to play in one pocket and my other

money in another pocket. My other money is for another day. If I'm playing a $1-$2 No Limit game, I'll buy in $200 and have another $200 for backup. And that's it. I don't care if I've got $5,000 on me, I won't rebuy again. I figure it's not my day. And you will have days that are not your days. So why cripple yourself over one bad day? Go do something else.

7) If you're going to play poker- play fuckin' poker. I play with these guys who have big bets on football games or basketball games and they're watching the games on TV and not concentrating on the poker game. Then they lose the games they bet on and go on tilt at the poker table. That's fuckin' nuts. If you are a good poker player- play fuckin' poker. Forget the sports on TV. You have to lay 11-10 plus points, and believe me, at the end of the day, at the end of the month, at the end of the season, the sports books will have you for lunch. They won't buy you lunch- they'll eat you for lunch.

8) Walk out a winner. There's nothing wrong with walking out of the poker room or the casino a winner. Accumulate your chips and be aware of how much you have. Don't limit your winnings, because you might be on an incredible rush. But when you get ahead a good amount, mentally set aside an amount that you absolutely, positively know you will leave with. If I buy in for $200 and I get to $500, I know I am going to walk out with at least $300, which would make me a $100 winner. If I get to $1,000, I know I'm leaving with $700. Playing No Limit sometimes presents you with a tough decision of whether or not to call an all-in that will substantially reduce your chip stack. But like I said, why not walk out a winner? It's a great feeling, and chances are if someone goes all-in for a large bet in a cash game, he owns you. And soon he will own your hard earned chips. Take my word for it.

9) Be nice- be kind- be careful of traps. Always be respectful of the other players and the dealer. Sometimes traps are

unavoidable. Just beware of them. They can be bone crushing and very difficult to rebound from. A large raise after an opponent checks or an aggressive large river bet after an opponent has been passive for the hand could be big huge red flags that something is terribly fuckin' wrong. If he puts a huge bet into the pot and you don't have the fuckin' nuts, he probably does. And on the off chance he is bluffing, so what. So fuckin' what. You still have most of your bankroll and you'll get him next time. I promise.

10) Make them pay to draw. If you put your opponent on a draw, make them pay for that card. The goal is to put enough in the pot to make your opponent twist and turn in their chair and pucker their asshole. Like I said, play aggressively. Unless you want your opponent to make his hand.

Everyone Loves A Parade

We have a traditional Christmas parade every year in our small town of Boulder City, Nevada. This year was no different- except it rained. And let me tell you, nothing smells worse than a wet Santa. Nothing. He frightened all the small children. And half of the adults. I just thought you needed to know this. In case you run out of conversation at the poker table. You never know.

Poker Pals

I like being with people who make me laugh. And I make them laugh. Bobby Hitchins is one of those people. His dry, sarcastic wit cracks me up. My buddy Dan Young and I laughed a lot. Dan's not with us anymore. He was my poker buddy for a ton of years. So was Jack Lukow. I came to town with Jack a lot of years ago. We both started as dealers in downtown Las Vegas. We laughed a lot. I love to laugh. I love to make people laugh. Life is good when that happens. I miss Jack and Dan. They can't be replaced.

I Now Pronounce You...

As a poker player you need to stay healthy, and to stay healthy you need to eat healthy. Many foods are bad for you and cause long-term problems. Of all the foods and all the food groups, the one you should avoid, that causes the most grief and suffering, is..... wedding cake.

Location, Location, Location

The key to being successful in Real Estate is Location-Location- Location. I would rather have a tent in Beverly Hills than a mansion in a slum area. It's all about location. The Beverly Hills location- you got something. A lot of something. Even though it's a fuckin' tent. But the mansion? Unless you're Donald Trump and can rehab the entire area, you don't have much. The intent of this book is to entertain, have a few laughs and make fuckin' money. A lot of it. And Real Estate is one of those streets that can get you to your destination. If you're a player, you will occasionally get lucky and make a score. What you do with that score can and will make a difference for your entire life. Everyone dreams of winning a million in a tournament. That's great. And people do win a million. The problem is that it runs through their fingers like water. Right off the top is 35% for taxes. There is no getting around that- unless you have big write offs. And if you don't pay the taxes, you will at some point pay the consequences, which could be a ton of penalties, fines and possibly jail. So if you do get lucky and make a score, the first phone call should be to a tax guy. A certified public accountant. You need guidance- immediately. Then call me. Not really. I'm just fucking with you. Call my daughter. I'm looking for a guy for her with no earring and a lot of money. If he has enough money, I'll relax my requirement on the earring. Anyway, after you chat with the CPA, he will probably advise you to set aside your tax money, which will be due on April 15th. Now you've got about $650,000 left from each million. Let's assume you won $1 million. If you pay off mom and dad's house, take care of your hangers on, buy a car, put a healthy down payment on a house, take all your buds on a vacation, loan a few bucks to some relatives and to every degenerate you know, stake a few close pals into tournaments, set aside money for the tournaments you want to play in for the next 6 months, figure on travel and hotels and meals to go to those tournaments, and buy a few pair of underwear- you, my friend, will wake up busted a month later with a huge fuckin' headache because now you have a mortgage on a house you bought that's way bigger than you fuckin' need.

I believe the time to make a plan- and write it down- is before you win the money. Make a list and update it periodically until it comes time you need it. If you play in a lot of tournaments and you play well, it's probably only a matter of time before you make a score. So take some time out of your busy day and spend a hundred dollar bill and make an appointment with an accountant- NOW! It will be the best $100 bill you ever spent. He will help you put a plan in place that will probably include keeping receipts and a diary way before you win the tournament. Because anything you spend on tournaments before you win one is deductible from your winnings. But the time to establish all of the allowable expenses is before you win. If you win a tournament in December and you haven't kept track all year, you're fucked. Suppose you spent $80,000 for the year and didn't keep records. Recreating all of your expenses accurately might be tough to prove. If you are playing tournaments with any regularity, even if you have a full time job, the tournaments are your part time business. If you play poker for a living, then poker is your **full time** business. Either way, treat your business as a fuckin' business, which involves a little bookwork and for sure a fuckin' accountant. A good accountant could probably keep track of you for maybe $200 or $300 a month. Or less. Most of you guys piss $300 in the morning. But let me tell you, Bucko, if you happen to make a score, you will kiss the guy. Maybe not on the lips. But for sure you'll give him a hug.

That million dollar score, or less, even if it's 200 or 300 thousand, would be spent differently if it was my score. If I made a mill- after taxes $650,000- automatically I spend $350,000- $400,000 on a small apartment building. A 4-plex or a 6-plex. Get a small mortgage if you have to. The realtor that sells it to you can manage it also. They charge about 10% of the rent. No big deal. But it will turn out to be a **huge** fuckin' deal for you. Every fuckin' month, a check in the mail. And when the mortgage is paid off, a much bigger check. Plus appreciation of usually about 10% a year on the building. Plus higher rents as time goes by. Plus a nice write off every year. Plus-Plus- Plus. If you have 6 units and are getting $700 a month from each tenant, that's $4,200 a month. The realtor gets $420 for managing it. You do the math. Now if you buy one of these every time you make a score and are able to accumulate 4 or 5 or more of them over a 10 or 15-year period- Bucko, you hit it out of the fuckin' park. Patience is the key in tournament poker and Real Estate. Real Estate is a fuckin' winner- big time. Especially rentals. People have to live somewhere. And the areas that are sunny are the most popular areas people are moving to. My favorite areas are Las Vegas, Southern Arizona, including Phoenix, Scottsdale and Bullhead City, which is a **real** sleeper. Laughlin, Nevada is only 5 minutes away from Bullhead City and they have 10 casinos there and people love casinos as much as they do the sun. Another great area is Kingman, Arizona. Very up and coming. You buy a 4-plex or a 6-plex in one of these places and I will sleep better knowing that you will wake up someday having a nice monthly check roll in to take care of all your expenses whether you cash at the next tournament or not. So if you pay the IRS $350,000 and buy a 4 or 6-plex for $400,000, you still have $250,000 to fuck away any way you wish. Put $100,000 aside for future tournaments, cash games and expenses, and have a ball with the $150,000 that's left over. Take care of the family, give a little to friends, help some people out and get ready for the next tournament, which I'm sure will be right around the corner.

I Like My Eggs Over Easy- Not Over Burnt

The words "My compliments to the chef" abound in many of Las Vegas' finest restaurants. I'm not a guy who's into 3-hour meals. You can only twirl that fuckin' water glass for so long. When I go to a restaurant, I go to eat. Then I want to go home. On the way home in the early morning from a late night session in a Hold 'em tournament, I decided to stop at a Denny's. It's fast and pretty good. If you've never seen a Denny's menu, it's a sight to behold. The pictures are fuckin' gorgeous. They are designed to make you want to order everything on the menu. Anyway, I ordered bacon, eggs, hash browns and pancakes. The eggs were runny, the bacon was raw and the pancakes were burnt. Totally unlike the gorgeous pictures. On the way out, I told the cashier, "My compliments to the photographer." She didn't laugh either.....

Random Thought

There's a ton of tournaments everywhere. Hooters in Las Vegas was holding one so I called for information. It took forever to get someone who sounded human. Up until then it was a series of recordings. And the usual "Press 1", "Press 2", "Press 3" bullshit. You know the drill. I suggest to marketing departments of phone companies, utility companies and government agencies, that they get more creative with their recordings. I suggest the following as an example to at least entertain and amuse the person calling. We all like to be amused.

"Thank you for calling Hooters. Your call will be answered in the order in which it was received, by the first available human being. Our humans are presently helping other customers like yourself who have a fuckin' problem. Or

*think they do. Press '1' to hear this message again or press '2'
to hear enjoyable alien sounds while you pleasure yourself."*

I think most people would press "2". I know I would.

911

I got rivered in a tournament last night by TJ Cloutier or whatever the fuck his name is. He seemed like an OK degenerate. There was a guy at the table who kept telling TJ what he threw away- like TJ gave a fuck. Neither one was in the pot, but it always amazes me how people are fascinated and attracted to any type of celebrity just because they have been on TV. Like in the scope of things, a guy on TV is going to make a fuckin' difference in the world. Especially a poker fuck. The people who really and truly make a difference usually go unnoticed- Teachers, doctors, cops, firemen just to name a few. If my house was on fire or someone was breaking into my home at midnight, I doubt very much if I would call TJ Cloutier or Mike Matusow. Well, maybe I would call Matusow. He could talk the burglar into committing suicide. He's like Dr. Kevorkian without the med cocktail. At least he could save me the price of a phone call to 911.

Random Thought

I was playing a tournament at Caesar's and I'm sitting next to this kid that every fuckin' hand is spewing out these incessant numbers and percentages. I'm thinking- there's 40 fuckin' tables in this joint and I have to be sitting next to Rain Man. I'm actually looking around for Dustin Hoffman.

Online Poker

I don't play online so I'm not going to spend much time on this online poker chapter. Why don't I play online? Well, first of all, I don't like it. I don't think it's good that you can wake up in the middle of the night and 20 seconds later be losing a lot of money. "Yes," you say, "but I can be making a lot of money too." Yeah sure, Bucko. That's the problem. That kind of thinking can get you in deep shit. It's too easy to get addicted. At least with a real poker room you have to get dressed. Well, not dressed. But you do have to put a shirt and pants on. And drive there. And park. And walk into the room. So at least you're getting some exercise- and fresh air- and the feel of clothing in case you ever have a date. I think we are becoming more reclusive if we never have to leave the house or our room because our pleasure is right there- all 17 inches of it. In the form of a computer screen. My, how times have changed. The second reason I don't like to play online is that I don't trust the game. The sites are offshore and not regulated by our government in any way. If I go to a casino, I have a very high expectation of being protected from cheats and scam artists. All bets are off with online sites. They can talk the talk all they want- my problem is I don't know if they can walk the walk. There is so fuckin' much money involved and a lot of smart Internet fucks out there, so it makes me wonder if card manipulation is involved. And can anyone see your hole cards? A book called "Dirty Poker" by Richard Marcus opened my eyes to a lot of Internet shit. Do the sites themselves fill up a game with a robotic type player that is programmed to analyze your play and crush your ball sack? Are robotic type programs used by other players to crush your ball sack? Is there widespread collusion among players to crush your ball sack? Does your ball sack need crushing? These are questions you need to answer yourself.

Marcus is a self-proclaimed cheat and seems to know what he's talking about. He highly recommends that if you are going to play, play in the evening when there are millions of people playing so you are less likely to fall victim to cheats. That makes sense. Because let's face it, you're going to play. Even if you knew for sure you were going to get fucked. One kid told me, "Even if they cheat, they probably cheat at the higher limit games- not the games I play." Reminds me of a guy I knew years ago who was going to a poker game that he knew guys cheated at. I said, "What the fuck are you doing? You know that two of those guys are cheating!" He said, "I know, Tony. But I feel lucky." Oh well. Nothing I write or say or what Richard Marcus writes or says is really going to make a difference to online poker. They will continue to grow and flourish even with the new law recently passed that makes it illegal for banks or credit card companies to transfer money to offshore accounts. There will still be ways around that law and the game is in a "feeding frenzy" stage that is sure to be with us for a long time. It's the new drug of choice. "Come into my website" they cry out. And the name "website" is appropriately named. Just like a spider spinning a web to catch its prey. The web is spun, the prey enters and gets caught and fights to get out and to live, but to no avail, and the spider has his prey for lunch. There is no difference with a poker site. You're the entrée. And you're playing against other entrées that are faceless, heartless and humorless. Now, can anyone think of a better way to spend a fuckin' evening? Many of today's youths are caught up in online playing and are without plans, goals or a destination for their life. That worries me. And there's one final reason I don't play online. Not a big reason to some, but to me it is. It's fuckin' illegal! And more importantly, I don't have a computer.

Random Thought

Online poker players often complain about frequency of bad beats more than live table game players. I think there's a number of reasons for this. Hands are dealt very rapidly online so there are more hands per hour and thus more frequency of abnormal occurrences. Also, more amateurs play online to get experience and they play more mediocre hands and junk than a more seasoned player would play. This in itself leads to more bad beats. I just recently stood a raise from the small blind to play a 4-5 offsuit in a Bellagio tournament. I knew if I could hit I would crush my opponent and become the chip leader and the table captain. The flop came Q-4-5. I checked, he bet, I raised, he went all-in- about 30,000 in tournament chips. I had about the same amount and called. He turned over K-Q and didn't help. He said something very nasty and stormed away from the table. I think he missed his last anger management class. Oh well, I had junk and got lucky. I got very lucky. I normally don't play junk, but I got involved because I was the big blind. Playing junk usually leads to a reduced chip stack. The more you play bad hands or junk, the more you will get bad beats. Plain and simple.

Rivered by Frist

The Unlawful Internet Gambling Enforcement Act of 2006, or the UIGEA, was rammed down the American public's throat in the middle of the night by Senate Majority Leader Bill Frist, much like another Bill, Bill Clinton, rammed little Bill down Monica Lewinsky's throat in the middle of the night. The law was designed to ban most forms of online gambling in the United States, especially targeting poker sites. It aims to do this by requiring banks and credit card companies to stop processing transactions if they are related to any form of online gambling, which of course, poker is a huge part of. Basically, the bill makes it a lot more difficult for players to deposit money into poker sites. The bill makes it illegal for banks and credit card companies to transact business and transfer money into online gaming sites. Banks that don't comply can face severe fines and punishment. It does not criminalize playing the game of poker. The poker sites are all offshore so our laws do not affect them. A huge part of their players come from the good old USA, and believe me, they are not going to walk away from the 12 billion dollar a year cash cow they created in this country. And for that very reason, actually 12 billion reasons, I don't understand why we wouldn't want to legalize, regulate and tax online gambling in the United States. Regulation, not prohibition, is the reasonable and responsible solution.

By legalizing online gaming, a system could be put in place that has safeguards for age and identity verification, and sets high standards to ensure the game is fair and square. It is absolutely fuckin' idiotic for our government to allow 12 billion dollars a year to go overseas. It's nuts. Many countries, including Australia, the United Kingdom, Caribbean nations and European countries license and regulate online operators. If not legalized on a nationwide basis, I think we will have individual states looking at legalizing Internet gaming. Gaming in this country has always been a states rights issue. Almost every state has some form of gambling now. Race tracks, casinos, lotteries, poker rooms- so what's the big fuckin' deal? If a state legalized online gaming, they would have to keep people from other states from gambling on their site. Once a state legalizes online gaming, the other states will see the tremendous revenue they are missing out on and jump on the bandwagon. Quickly. Just like they did with land based casinos. A wise old man once said, "No man's life, liberty or property is safe while the legislature is in session." There may be more truth in that statement than humor. The Internet story for playing poker is far from over. The numbers are too fuckin' big. And no one ignores big numbers. Huge numbers. It aint over til the fat lady sings. And she's not even humming yet. She's just barely cleared her throat.

Random Thought

Timing is everything. In life. In investing. In poker. The slightest alteration of an occurrence, and I mean the slightest, can change the outcome of the total event completely. You can go fuckin' nuts trying to figure this out so the easiest thing is to make carefully calculated decisions for every occurrence and then hold your fuckin' breath and hope the outcome is right for you. Of course, whatever the occurrence, whatever the event, no matter how strange or bizarre it is for you, it's good for someone. If you get rivered, it was good for the guy that rivered you. If your house burns down because you left the coffee maker on, it's good for the building contractor. If your timing is off and you get run over crossing the street, it's good for the funeral home. Last week at the Bellagio I had a kid all-in. About 24,000 chips in the pot. I had K-Q, he had a pair of nines. The flop came K-Q-7. Turn was a 3. River- you guessed it- a 9. One tiny riffle changes the outcome of the hand. He goes home. Three hours later at the final table we are down to 4 players. The same kid busted me. The outcome of the event would have been totally different if that one fuckin' 9 hadn't shown on the river hours before. Of course, I caught a river card hours before that to survive an all-in or I wouldn't have been at the final table either. The important thing is, in the scope of things, in the scope of the big picture- life and happiness- nobody got hurt or killed and we all went home to our families. Maybe he didn't, but I did. He looked like a lonely fuck.

Cheating

The word "cheat" is probably one of the worst words in the English language you can use to describe a person or their behavior. When your friend says he or she "cheated on me", you know it's not going to be a good conversation. You can call someone a scam artist, a conman, a flimflam artist or a fraud, but the word "cheat" takes in so much more. It covers a lot of territory. Cheats are found where money is found. Just like all the other words I used to describe a cheat. Having an edge in a proposition bet is not cheating. But some can argue that there is a fine line there. At the end of the day, the money will go to the guy who has the biggest edge. I have been in the gambling business all my life. Even before I turned 21. I hung around a rickety old card room in San Bruno, California called Artichoke Joe's. Joe didn't put up with any shit. If he knew about it. But shit went on. There was money involved. I played in the section where 5-card draw was played, and the other section was 5-card lowball. Many times on the way to the bathroom, I would stop at the lowball area rail and watch for a few minutes. Lowball players were the "high rollers" back then. That was the action game. No limit lowball. Most players held their cards up to see them so it was pretty easy to see their hands when you were on the rail. There was a standard set of signals that all lowball players used, to signal a hand if they saw someone else's hand. You only need to signal one card, the top one, to your friend, confederate or just another guy who plays at your local place all the time who you want to help out. There was a huge pot by the standards of "huge pots" back in the 60's. At least a few thousand. A drunk was involved in the pot with this real smooth kid that everyone liked. The drunk had gone all-in and the kid had a big call to make. When I got to the rail, the railbirds were already buzzing. The kid was staring at the drunk and the drunk was staring at the kid. The drunk did something then that caused him to lose a lot of money. He picked up his cards to check them and didn't protect his hand. He had an A-2-3-4-10. I scratched my chin and went to the bathroom. I didn't know if the kid picked up on it or not. It wasn't 2 minutes later the bathroom door opens. I'm washing my hands- the kid hands me a matchbook- says "Thank you" and walks out. The matchbook had a hundred dollar bill in it. The kid had a rough 9, which is not a real good hand in lowball. It was a 9-8-7-5-4. I found this out later from one of the railbirds who watched the hand play out. The kid and I never spoke to each other. Once in a while he would give the appropriate "hello nod", which many of us do to this day in the poker room. What happened should have never happened and could have never happened if the drunk had protected his hand. Of course, drinking and driving and drinking and playing poker do not mix. At all.

The absolute best book on cheating and cheating techniques is Steve Forte's "Casino Game Protection". It covers everything. It should be in every school in America. High schools should teach a class on cheating and various scams so people could recognize when they are being fucked. There are numerous con artists that operate all over the country. When an opportunity presents itself, it's hard for them to resist. But that's what separates the men from the boys. When you can see the guy's hole cards sitting next to you because he is not protecting them when he looks at them, how many people would tell him? I would like to think 50%. Setting out to cheat someone is a different story. The friendly, private poker game is probably the most common place where cheaters operate. Whenever I play at a poker game, my antenna is up. That doesn't mean I can't get fucked or haven't been fucked. I've been fucked numerous times. Sometimes I suspect it after the fact and sometimes I don't. The cheat doesn't call me the next day and say, "Hey Tony, remember that hand you lost with $600 in the pot? I hand mucked* (see number 5 below) a card in and fucked you." It would be nice if they did that so you could be more aware next time. But the cheat is not going to tip you off. To the cheat, we are all "marks". Here are some suggestions for you no matter where you play:

1) You can trust everyone if that's your nature. But **always** cut the fuckin' cards. Many times, private games have a rotating deal. Everyone gets to deal. This is the most dangerous form of dealing in a private game. So much shit can happen when 10 different guys are dealing. You only need one guy to be able to manipulate the cards. Just one. Believe me, Bucko- you will never know it. He may look as clumsy as the rest of you, but it's just a cover. At our private game, we have a center deal. He works for a few of us doing chores and on Thursday night he deals poker for us. It gives him a chance

to make extra money, plus we don't have to fuck cards.

2) Change decks periodically. If someone holds out just one card, he can dominate the game. You should have 3 or 4 different type decks and rotate them. All this does is slow down a cheat. If a person is at your game with the intent of cheating you out of your money, he will figure out a way to circumvent every obstacle you put in his path.

3) Good players will win more frequently than mediocre or bad players. Over the long hall, this is true. We all get the same amount of good and bad cards, so hand selection and how you play the hand will dictate that some people win more often than others. The cheat will win almost every time. **Especially** late in the evening. That's when the most cheating occurs. And everyone's guard is down. And people are stuck. Sometimes a lot of money. This is when the cheat is at his best. The players are tired, been drinking all night, not paying a lot of attention to the cards being dealt and just ripe for the picking. It's at this point that the cheat usually likes to raise the stakes. Beware of the guy who suggests raising the stakes towards the end of the evening. This "move" is clearly designed to take advantage of the players who have been drinking. Maybe it's time you look a little closer at your "friendly" home game and see how "friendly" it really is. Unless you're the cheat. Then of course, you'll leave it alone. The home game I play in is a tournament format. It's No Limit Hold 'em, and just like a tournament, you buy in a set amount and get a set amount of chips. We play $50 buy-ins with a $10 high hand pot. You get 100 chips and we designate the chips at $10 each. The blinds start at 10-20 and go up every 20 minutes. One tournament takes about an hour to an hour and a half. The highest hand in each tournament gets the high hand money- the buy-ins are split 80-20. First place gets 80%- second place gets 20%. So if 8 guys are playing, the high hand money is $80 and the prize pool is $400. The winner gets $320 and the second place guy

gets $80. We play 4 or 5 tournaments when we play. Some guys leave after 2 or 3 tournaments. The buy-in could be any amount. If $50 doesn't satisfy your urges, make it $100. Or if $50 is too much, make it $20. This entire structure doesn't mean you won't be cheated. It just minimizes the possibility of you losing all the money in front of you- late in the evening, on one hand. The absolute worst thing you can encounter in any poker game is a cooler. You hear guys throw that word around when you watch tournaments on TV, but the cooler is the equivalent of your wife cutting off your penis while you're sleeping, shoving it in your mouth and having your faithful pitbull bite off your balls at the same time. That's a fuckin' cooler. A cooler is a pre-arranged deck that is brought into a game usually towards the end of your "friendly" session. Just because you have a center dealer doesn't mean this can't be accomplished. If the dealer is in collusion with a player, your balls are in a vice. It's just a question of whether or not the dealer and his buddy want to cause extreme pain or crush your balls completely. A cooler is also known as a "cold deck". The cards haven't been handled, so they are a little cooler to the touch than the cards that have been in the game. Unless the move is caught right when it happens, no one will pick up on the fact that the cards were a little cooler. Like I said, this move is done towards the end of the evening, when the stakes have been raised and the awareness levels of most of the players has dropped considerably. When you look down at your hand and see those pocket Aces, and another player has pocket Aces and maybe even another player with pocket Kings, and maybe the guy who's going to win the pot has pocket Queens, all of the fuckin' money in front of these guys is going to be in the pot before the flop. And the guys with the most money will have the pocket Aces. And a miracle river card will probably produce the winner of the hand. And it's not going to be the Aces, Bucko. This pot will not be chopped. But that's poker- right? Not if you've been cheated, pal. That's not fuckin' poker. That's larceny.

4) Many times people will want to make proposition bets while you're playing. I tell them all the same thing- "I've got enough trouble playing poker, pal." People who want to make prop bets seldom take the worst of it. In fact, they never take the worst of it. Even if they have a 5% or 10% edge, they are going to grind you out. If they try to lure me into a prop bet, I know fuckin' well they are going to have the best of it. I don't do prop bets. My kid asked me why I don't do prop bets and I gave him some very simple advice. I said, "Son, if a guy comes up to you with a sealed deck of cards and wants to bet you that he can make the Jack of Spades jump from the deck and squirt cider in your eye, don't bet him. Because, I'm telling you kid, you're going to wind up with an eye full of cider." If some guy wants to make any kind of side bets with you during the game, I can almost guarantee you are going to wind up with an eye full of cider. And an empty wallet.

5) Hand mucking will also produce a profitable evening for a cheat. Hand mucking is the art of bringing one card in and out of the game with an almost undetectable move. It can be done a number of ways. There is actually a device that can be used that goes up your sleeve, but most hand muckers are proficient enough to muck a card in and out of the game by "palming" it. The device would be "slam dunk" evidence, whereas the palming method gives the cheat an opportunity to just drop the card on the floor if someone gets suspicious. Just the manipulation of one card in and out of play can produce a tremendous profit for the cheat. The cards should be counted periodically. When you deal, there's nothing wrong with counting the remaining cards in the deck. Just add them to the cards already dealt once the hand is complete. If there's not a total of 52 cards, you have an obvious problem. Knowing you count the deck when you deal will slow down anyone at the table who is hand mucking or thinking of it. Hand muckers usually don't have their cards lay on the table when they make the card switch, like most Hold 'em players do when peeking at their hole

cards. They have an extra card on their person and to do the card switch they usually pick up their hand and "cup" their cards in their hands so you can't see what's going on. We all know how players normally look at their hole cards. We all do it basically the same way. When someone does it differently, keep an eye on him, even if you're playing in a casino. I always try to be aware of what I term "suspicious behavior". Even though every casino has a huge surveillance department, unless something specific in the poker room is brought to their attention, they probably won't see it. The poker room is a low priority. Why? Because their fuckin' bankroll is not at risk. They're getting their rake. And it's player against player. There is definitely a certain element of protection you get in a casino that you don't get in a home game. Make no mistake about that. The casinos do have a surveillance department and home games don't. And if there was suspicious activity at a table in the casino and you brought it to someone's attention, they can play back the tape. Every game is taped. 24 hours a day. Cheats know this. But it still doesn't stop them from trying. Too much money is at stake for them not to give it a shot. And when they do get caught, they usually get a slap on the wrist from the court system. Cheating is very hard to prove in a court of law. Almost everyone on the jury has lost money in a casino. Now here's a guy on trial who won a few bucks and he's being prosecuted? Tough sell to a jury. I've seen sharp attorneys make casino managers look like idiots on the witness stand. Nothing is "cut and dry". Nothing is a "slam dunk". That's why most cases are plea bargained. And the cheat pays a fine and goes on his merry way. Looking for his next victim…

And remember- Steve Forte- "Casino Game Protection" and his latest book "Poker Protection". They're expensive, but you can probably get used copies from Amazon or Yahoo. Knowing how to play is one thing. Knowing what to watch for when you play is another.

I Always Shop at the Big and Tall Shop of Horrors

I've always been a big guy. I was into Roman numeral sizes long before most of the other kids in school. I blew by XL and XXL. I think by the time I was out of high school I was XXLCMV. Nothing on a rack would ever fit me. The fuckin' rack wouldn't even fit me. When my mom would take me into a store to do school shopping, the salesmen would hide. That's fuckin' embarrassing. Whenever my mom said to me, "You have to find a salesman," it took on a new meaning. Sometimes it meant knocking on the doors of the stalls in the men's room. And when I coaxed him back to his department, he would always ask the same fuckin' question- "What size are you, kid?" And my mom would say, "You'll have to measure him." That use to thrill the shit out of the guy. Most of the time they would just toss me the tape measure. But if some cute blond haired kid would come in, they would leap over each other to measure **his** inseam. That's when I learned that not being blond was going to be detrimental to my upbringing. Especially when I was shopping for clothes. To this day I hate shopping for clothes. Instead of my mom going with me, my wife comes along. But it's the same shit. The salesmen still hide. When I find them on the floor in the back seat of their car, it's the same fuckin' dog and pony show- "What size do you wear?" And my wife always says, "You'll have to measure him." But they don't throw me the tape measure anymore. No, I didn't dye my hair blond. The fuckin' tape is too big to toss around. Now they use one of those fuckin' things with the long handle and the wheel at the bottom that you use to measure driveways with. And it's always the same conversation after the measuring:

Salesman: Wow, you're a big one.

Me: Good eye, fuck face.

Salesman: What shirt did you have in mind?

Me: The white one.

Salesman: That only comes in S, M, L, XL and Oh My God.

I'm afraid none of those will fit you.

Me: Don't you carry any sizes for the big man? Your fuckin' store is called "The Big and Tall Shop of Horrors" and you're telling me you don't have big sizes?

Salesman: We don't have room to stack the larger Roman numerals. I'm sorry.

Me: How about if I was a blond?

Salesman: That would be a different story.

   I bring this up because it has nothing to do with Hold 'em. And once in a while you have to cleanse your mind of the game, if only momentarily. It's good therapy.

Random Thought

When I was a kid I use to go to birthday parties and we would play spin the bottle. The girl had a choice- she could kiss you or pay you ten cents. By the time I was 12, I had paid off my parents home. Then they asked me to leave. They said I was lowering property values.

All the Lonely People

As I walk around the poker room, I can't help but thinking- All the lonely people, where do they all come from? All the lonely people, where do they all belong? I wonder if Paul McCartney was in a poker room when he wrote those lyrics. It seems like the human race as a whole is very lonely. I'm no Dr. Phil, but even when you're surrounded by family, there's a certain point when you want them to go home. There's nothing better than a tight, close knit, loving family that lives in another state. Kids keep us busy as they're growing up. We keep busy at work. We look forward to vacations. Then we look forward to going home from the vacation. We can't make up our fuckin' minds. Anyways, back to the poker room. Lots of strangers with an occasional familiar face that you give the traditional "nod" to. But no one stays in your life for long periods of time. They come and they go. Some are nice. Some are assholes. All types- all colors- all dispositions. But it's a great way to kill time. We all try to find things that we like to do to kill time. We have hobbies, we work, we take vacations, we go to family gatherings, and of course, we play poker. All of these things are designed to spend time with other human beings and to kill time. Time is our enemy. And we measure our enemy constantly. What time is it? What time do we have to be there? What time does the tournament start? There is actually something called an atomic clock that measures time to the smallest fraction of a second. Of a fuckin' second! Like who gives a fuck? Our life revolves around time. What time was he born? What was the time of death? We're always in a hurry. Can't be late. Hurry up. Faster. Time is definitely our enemy. And it controls our life. Why? Because time is running out. For everyone. So we need to enjoy the moment. Wherever that is. And we need to do things we enjoy doing. And surround ourselves with people we enjoy being with. And if that camaraderie comes in the form of a poker table with nine strangers, so be it. For many, the poker rooms are the bar rooms of yesterday. Instead of sitting at a bar being lonely, the people sit at a poker table being lonely. Headphones- sunglasses- no conversation. It's fuckin' perfect. The art of conversation is almost becoming non-existent. It's iPods, text messaging, emails, instant messaging, Gameboys and a host of other electronic devices that keep us from conversing with anyone. All the lonely people, where do they all come from?.....

Random Thought

Maybe it's time to ask your doctor if Lunesta is right for you. Side effects include the urge to play 2-7 offsuit and the urge to operate heavy machinery. I have these urges often. God, I need help.

Etiquette Continued

OK, I'm not done with etiquette. There are a few more things that I thought of that just have to be addressed. Especially in home games:

1) **Profanity in Home Games:** There is nothing wrong with profanity in home games. As long as the wife and kids are in the other room or in bed, what's the big fuckin' deal? But there has to be a limit. The F word, or "F-Bomb" as it is called in commercial poker rooms, is actually the only word that comes under the heading of profanity. This should be discussed at the beginning of the game. My suggestion is that each person should be allowed to say the word a certain number of times. Let's say 5 times. After that, you have to talk like Jesus. That's where I came up with the 5-time rule. I believe Jesus dropped the F-Bomb 5 times in the Bible. Or he meant to say it. Have you ever seen the painting of Jesus and his boys at the Last Supper? You see the look on his face at the end when he got the bill? It had "Holy Fuck!" written all over it. The food wasn't too expensive, but the cost of the wine was fuckin' outrageous. We all would have reacted the same way. There were 4 other instances that I won't bore you with. Maybe someday we'll meet over a glass of wine and I'll tell them to you. So 5 F-Bombs per person, I believe, is a good number for a home game. Anyone who abuses this number is fined and puts a set amount in a kitty to be divided by everyone at the end of the night. I think a good fine should be half of their net worth, which would slow profanity down immensely. Also, F-Bombs can be sold. This could support those bad fuckin' beats you will probably get while you're sucking on a beer, playing mediocre hands. So you may want to keep 3 F-Bombs and sell 2 of them. Also, someone has to keep track. This person is known as the F-Bomb tracker and receives 1 extra F-Bomb for his efforts. You can't carry forward your F-Bombs. You either use them, lose them or sell them. No carry forwards. We're not putting up with that fuckin' shit.

2) **Illegal Substance Use:** To go into another person's home and use an illegal substance before, during or after a poker game is absolutely deplorable behavior. Absolutely fuckin' deplorable. Unless you are willing to share. Sharing and caring are the two most acceptable behaviors known to man. And who am I to dispute acceptable behaviors.

3) **Weapons:** Weapons at a friendly home game are forbidden. Well, not all weapons. Suppose a robber holds up the game- someone should be armed. Let's modify our rule to no automatic weapons should be allowed at a friendly home game. Automatic weapons are hard to control when you pull the trigger, and you might shoot the guy who's playing really really bad poker along with the robber. Then everyone would be pissed at you and then you'd be the bad guy after you saved everyone's bankroll from the robber. So, no automatic weapons at the game. Oh, and no weapons of mass destruction.

4) **Peeing in the Sink:** I know. We've all done it. We have to go really really bad. We run to the bathroom and there's a guy peeing in the toilet bowl. And naturally, this guy's house only has one bathroom. And right there is the porcelain sink. Fuck, it's **almost** a toilet bowl! It's porcelain, isn't it? It could have very easily been a toilet bowl instead of a sink. Same factory, different assembly line. The problem arises when there's already someone peeing in the sink. Then I guess you have to apply the same porcelain logic to the kitchen sink. Unless the host's wife is doing the dishes. Then show some class. Ask her to turn her back.

5) **Speaking a Foreign Language:** There is nothing wrong with speaking a foreign language, if you are playing in that country. If you are playing in Kuwait and everyone is speaking Kuwaiteeze, I don't think that's a problem. English should be the only language spoken if you're

playing in a country like Des Moines. Or San Diego. Unless the players all agree on a different language. And then everyone at the table has to speak it all night long. We had Pig Latin night one time. It was fuckin' hilarious. Nine guys full of beer, smoking dope, peeing in their pants and speaking Pig Latin. I guess you had to be there.

6) **One Player to a Hand:** That's a pretty standard hard and fast rule in any game. Home game or casino game. Unless, of course, it's obvious the guy has a severe vision problem. Like he's blind. Sometimes people who are vision impaired like to play poker. At that point, they realize that their walking stick doesn't help. And many times guide dogs don't play premium hands. So the person asks for help. We had a blind person who use to play in our home game many years ago. Really nice guy. He didn't have many tells. But the guy who helped him did. He use to turn the blind guy's hand towards us so we could see it. And the dog would growl. Good thing the blind guy had a lot of money. The important thing is that he had fun. And it was hilarious when we walked him to the bathroom and made a few turns and brought him to the kitchen where he peed in the kitchen sink. Even the German shepherd laughed.

You Can't Make This Shit Up

I just ordered the Marie Antoinette Action Figure doll. It comes complete with the "Ejector Head" feature, which means that when little Suzie presses the secret button- there goes Marie's head flying across the fuckin' room! Sure you can get the same effect with a steak knife and a Cabbage Patch doll- but that's a one shot deal. A box of batteries and the Marie Antoinette doll can mean hundreds of hours of fun for all the neighborhood kids. And if your daughter isn't the most popular kid at school yet- she will be. It might be time to get her an Email address for her fan club mail, and maybe an agent. And maybe an appointment with Dr. Phil. The Marie Antoinette action figure doll is available for $8.95 plus postage and handling from www.mcphee.com. You just can't make this shit up.

Random Thought

*There's a Sumo type wrestler playing at my table. Really, really big guy. Huge. His shirt was fuckin' tight. About 3 sizes too small. I'm thinking, if a button blows off this guy's shirt, it could put the dealer's eye out. Or kill him. Worse than that, it could put **my** eye out if it's a ricochet. It's tough enough to play the fuckin' game without staring at a guy's shirt button. And the thread that's holding it on. Very distracting. Very fuckin' distracting. Lay people don't realize what tournament players go through. When the dealer says, "You're on the button", I sometimes think about the guy with the tight shirt. I've got to find another hobby. And increase my meds. I need help. I know I do.*

Living Hold 'em to the Fullest

-I got nailed on the river.

-He nailed me.

-I got sucker-punched.

-He sucked out on me.

These terms all mean the same thing- you lost the fuckin' hand on the river. I guess if Hold 'em only had 4 community cards, then all of these sayings would apply to the turn card. Or the turn card wouldn't exist and we'd go straight from the flop to the river. Whoever devised this game had to be a sick fuck. The flop gives you hope. The turn gives you satisfaction. The river crushes your hopes, your satisfaction and your ball sack. It's fuckin' beautiful. That's probably why we love the game so much and it's played so often all over the world. Each hand plays out like so many of our lives play out. But sometimes the river card is **your** card, and it's a great ending to the hand. With a lot of money as the prize. Just like life sometimes plays out for some people. But with Hold 'em, there's another hand coming in a few minutes, unlike life. But who the fuck cares? We've got Hold 'em as long as we're here. That's what counts.

Random Thought

You make the best decisions you can based on the information you have, but remember- the cards do not always cooperate. If you play consistent, good poker, at the end of the day, at the end of the week, at the end of the month you will be a winner. Or the other guy will be. What the fuck. It's a coin flip.

Tournament Play-

Quick and Deadly

I was late for a tournament at the Bellagio. I got caught in traffic. The tournament started at 2 P.M. and I got there at 3:30. I settled in my seat and ordered a water. The second hand I get dealt is A-Q suited. Blinds are 100-200. I open for $600. One caller. Flop comes Q-Q-7. I am a happy camper. I bet $1,000. My opponent goes all-in. He has me covered. I have about $1,400 left. I'm already in the pot $1,600, which doesn't mean shit because if I know my hand is beat, I'm not going to give him my last chips. But I don't think it's beat. If he has a Queen, I have him dominated. He could have slow-played pocket Kings or Aces. He could have pocket 7's. I figure, if I'm going to lay down 3 Queens with an Ace kicker after just seeing the flop, I might as well not play ever again. Hang up my saddle and put my gun in the drawer. Of course I called. Of course he had pocket 7's. Of course I got no help. And of course I was out. Out of the tournament. Out in the cold. Actually it was about 150° outside. But I was looking for sympathy. And understanding. And compassion. Not for the fact I lost the hand. Not for the fact I lost all my chips. Not for the fact I just spent $540 to enter a tournament I lasted 5 minutes in. But for the fact that I wasn't even able to crack open my bottle of water and take a sip. Now that's fuckin' sad. And embarrassing. Thank you for your kind thoughts and your prayers.

Random Thought

Accept the fact that some days you're the pigeon and some days you're the statue.

Collusion

Collusion exists in cash games and tournaments. There is too much money at stake for it not to exist. On any given day, at any given game, you could be the target. Collusion is the act of players teaming up before the game with a plan. They signal each other so they know each others' hand. Then they play appropriately. If I'm under the gun with pocket Aces, and I raise to protect my Aces from everyone and their mother getting into the pot, I will probably lose most, if not all the players and win the small and big blind- two piss ant bets. If I'm colluding with a partner, and he's seated 4 or 5 seats from me, I limp in with my Aces and 3 or 4 other players might limp in also and I signal my partner to raise. Then, I decide when it gets back to me whether to call or re-raise. That type of collusion is very devastating to the players at the table. Sometimes a team of 3 or 4 players will be at a table, which means 3 or 4 players will be playing the rest of the table like a fuckin' violin. Sometimes in a game your instincts tell you that something doesn't smell right based on some of the hands you've watched being played. If that's the case, go to another table. Notate who was playing at the table so you can check your notes the next time you're in the poker room. If you frequent a room, it won't be long before you either recognize who the teams are or you become a part of one of them. When people make their living playing poker, they are always looking for an edge. They have to. The fuckin' rent and car payment never stop. Just be careful. Be cautious. Be aware. Your bankroll is at stake.

Random Thought

Moisturize- You can never be too moist.

Not Good for Business

I played in a tournament with this really really irritating, aggravating guy. And like most irritating, aggravating people, he never fuckin' shut up. He would analyze every hand out loud while the dealer was shuffling for the next hand. And it drove everyone at the table fuckin' nuts. His voice was very whiney. His wife tried to keep him away from beaches because porpoises and whales would beach themselves. His voice caused people around him to become suicidal. If you invited him anywhere or he showed up anywhere, you could expect at least one suicide. Or an attempted suicide. It was like inviting Angela Lansbury in "Murder She Wrote" to a function. You know when you see her in the room there's going to be a murder. Why the fuck would anyone invite her anywhere? She goes out to a restaurant and everyone in the room is hurrying to finish their dinner because they know one of them is going to die. She's just not good for business. Unless you happen to own a mortuary. Some people were born to be bad for any business they enter. This whiney mother fucker I had to sit next to for 3 hours was bad for the game of poker. Some people are like that.

Random Thought

There was actually a lady on Letterman that hypnotized a lizard by rubbing its stomach. Then she dressed the lizard in really cute lizard fashions she bought on Rodeo Drive in Beverly Hills. I'm not making this up. Well, not all of it. She put a pretty outfit on a fuckin' lizard. I'm thinking, "I wonder if this would work on the Unibomber-Phil Laak." I know a lot of people would volunteer to rub his stomach. I know I would.

Big Stack Poker

Why fuck with the guy with the biggest stack during tournament poker? At some point you will- but for the time being- eliminate the little stacks. Sure, the big stack can double you up, but if he gets lucky on you- you're fuckin' toast. MGM-Mirage and Harrah's are two of the biggest fuckin' stacks the gaming industry has ever seen. Both sides know that it's not in their best interest to fuck with each other. Besides that, there are plenty of smaller stacks up and down the Las Vegas strip- way way smaller- to compete with- to swallow up- to eliminate. The World Series of Poker at Harrah's properties and the World Poker Tour at MGM-Mirage properties are all about the same thing- Money. Huge amounts of money. Everything else is conversation. If we had a national food shortage, it would be about food. If our cities were being bombed on a daily basis, like in some countries, it would be about bomb shelters. But we are in a country where we keep score by green paper with numbers on it. Money. Of course, the companies tell us it's about shareholder value that they are concerned with- and they are. They are very concerned since most of the executives own a lot of shares. And there's nothing wrong with that. And there's nothing wrong with money. So why am I even going on about this diatribe if there's nothing wrong with money? I guess to fill up space. I do that well. And to make an important point. Don't fuck with the big stacks until you have to. Maybe it'll be at the final table. And you're in the money. And that's what it's all about. Isn't it?

Random Thought

A friend of mine gave up sugar, smoking, caffeine, drinking, poker and sex. He was healthy as a horse right up to the day he killed himself.

Let's Talk Turkey

No one is perfect. We all have strengths and we all have weaknesses. We always strive to get things right. All of us. A lot of years ago in a small town in Nevada called Carson City, I got something right. I got it real right. I married my wife. I didn't know it at the time that I got it right. Most guys don't realize it until later. I was one of those guys. I was looking for perfection. An imperfect guy looking for the perfect wife. That's pretty fuckin' funny by itself. But she was perfect. Perfect for me. The right balance. She is quiet. I'm not. She likes bland food. I like spicy. She likes to stay at home. I like to go out. She doesn't gamble at all. I like to play poker. She hates to cook. I love to eat. It's the perfect relationship. I make the living. She makes the living worthwhile. She never questions me or my late night poker sessions. When I tell her I'm writing about her cooking, she just gives me a loving glare that all husbands have been subjected to. An intense, long, loving glare. I thought when I married her I could change her attitude on cooking. I tried to do it subtly. I bought really nice cookbooks and put them in places where I knew she would see them. Like on top of her credit cards. And in the cookie jar. And I bought her really nice, small cooking appliances. Mixers, blenders, electric frying pans- you name it. Every payday, a new small kitchen appliance. Some have never been used to this day. They are still in their original boxes. Brand new. The cookbooks still have the original shrink wrap they came in. I'm sure they're collectors items. She thought cookbooks were a sign of weakness. So all of her creations were really creative. Some were more creative than others. Once she made the rice that the package guaranteed you couldn't undercook or overcook. She lost it. And I like rice. When I'm hungry and I feel like 2,000 of something, I go for the rice bowl. One time she made a carrot cake but didn't shred the carrots. She just baked them whole right into the cake. She left those green things hanging out of the side. She called them carrot cake handles. Actually, it wasn't that bad. When my son David took his lunch to school, it was a common practice to trade lunches with another kid. For variety. In order to make a trade, he use to have to throw in an article of clothing. He went through four jackets one winter before I figured out what the fuck was going on. David actually became famous once when my wife made a tuna casserole and he took it to school and entered it into the Science Fair. He won. She had combined tuna fish, cream of mushroom soup and potato chips and got electricity. 2nd Prize went to a Japanese kid who made a robot that ate the casserole. It died.

Holidays, especially Thanksgiving and Christmas, were always really really interesting meals. Somewhere along the line, and I'm not sure of the year or the month, my wife fell in love with another guy. Well, not actually the guy. She fell in love with his invention- the pop-up timer. And every Thanksgiving and Christmas she lived and died by the pop-up timer code. The code, in part, reads, "Under no condition, including threat of divorce, remove the turkey from the oven until the pop-up timer has popped up." I was actually happy to see the pop-up timer come into our lives. It meant that the turkey would be served at a reasonable hour of the evening. Before the existence of the pop-up timer, my wife was a firm believer in making sure the turkey was done so none of us would get the dreaded turkey flu. So, and I'm not making this up, she would get up at 11 P.M. and put the turkey in the oven so we could eat at 5 P.M. the next day. That's right. She would gently bake the turkey for 18 fuckin' hours. Mr. T says, "Pity the fool," I say, "Pity the turkey." Have you ever seen a turkey that's been baked for 18 hours? Have you ever heard a turkey banging on the oven door, begging to be let out? And screaming? And swearing? It's not a good, cheery, fuzzy holiday feeling when a fuckin' turkey that has never done anything bad to you is screaming swear words in your oven. It's hard to explain to the guests, let alone the kids. And their friends. It got so bad that one year the President of the United States actually came over to the house and pardoned our turkey. While it was in the oven. The Governor was too busy. I remember a conversation one year with my 7-year-old daughter Tamera that went something like this:

Tamera: Daddy, what's that noise in the kitchen?

Me: Nothing, honey.

Tamera: It sounds really loud, daddy.

Me: It's only the turkey, honey.

Tamera: The turkey is banging on the oven door?

Me: Yes, honey.

Tamera: Why is the turkey banging on the oven door, daddy?

Me: Your mom's trying to cook it. Go back to playing with your dolls.

Tamera: But it's swearing too, daddy. And loud.

Me: Try turning up the TV, honey. We're supposed to eat soon.

Tamera: Why does mommy keep the turkey in the oven for 18 hours, daddy?

Me: She wants to make sure it's done.

Tamera: My friend's mom cooks their turkey for 4 hours.

Me: I know, honey. But your friend's mommy doesn't give a fuck about her family's health.

Tamera: Is it legal to cook a turkey for 18 hours, daddy?

Me: Not in all states, honey. But we're OK in Nevada. What happens in Vegas stays in Vegas.

Tamera: Gee, daddy. That's a really good saying. You should trademark it.

Me: Sure, honey.

Tamera: Daddy, I don't hear the turkey anymore.

Me: I guess it's time to eat, sweety.

And then we would gather around the kitchen table and give

thanks to God and of course the turkey. After dinner, the adult males would gather in the game room to play a friendly game of poker so that the host (me) could recoup the price of the groceries and the retainer to hire an attorney in case there are any charges of turkey abuse filed by any nosy neighbors. I'm sure this scenario is played out in many homes across our great land. And of course, for weeks and sometimes months, there's leftover turkey for sandwiches, soups, and lest we forget, turkey casserole (for the first time in my life, I have used the word "lest" in a sentence). Christmas and Thanksgiving have changed over the years in our house. We now serve Honey-Baked Ham on the holidays. The sound of a ham baking in the oven is nothing like a turkey. We don't go through as many oven doors as we use to. The hams are already baked so we just have to heat them. We also eat out a lot. But whenever I go to a restaurant that has a sign that says "Home Cooking"- I leave. I miss the good old days. And so do the kids. But I'm sure the turkeys and their families are happier. Much happier. Happy Holidays everyone.

Random Thought

Sometimes things are going wrong. Everything is turning to shit. You're in a total freefall. It's at those times that you hope your family and friends are there to catch you. Or at least break your fall. If not- a couple of pocket Aces back to back will bring you out of your funk.

This Could Be Huge

    I play poker once a week with a bunch of local guys. One of them, George the Greek, constantly bugs me about being in the book. When people know you are writing a book, they want to be in it. Some writers I've talked to call that part of writing a book "a pain in the ass". I call it insured sales. George the Greek said that if I mention him and how good he plays, he would buy a copy. I've mentioned him twice so I figure that's two copies for sure that I'll sell. Actually, I've mentioned about 30 people so far. If I don't watch out, this could become a "hundred" seller. That would mean popularity **and** notoriety. I hate all that shit. Book tours, book signings, talk shows, lecture tours- I'm fuckin' exhausted already and I'm not done writing. I don't like people coming up to me and touching me. I'm like a big fat Howie Mandel (another book sale!). My name isn't even Tony Korfman and the picture of me on the cover isn't even me. Well, it doesn't look like me. Those fuckin' kids with an airbrush gun and a diploma that says "Airbrush Artist" are fuckin' amazing. The guy I see in the mirror every morning and the guy on the cover of this book don't look like the same guy to me. There's a difference of about 40 pounds and 40 wrinkles. Actually, I had a stomach operation called a lap band a few years back. Thank you to Dr. James Atkinson and Dr. Barry Fisher and the girls in the office- Susan, Melodie, Francis and Stephanie. That's at least six more cha-chings. I love this country. I really do. A hundred seller. I can fuckin' smell it.

Random Thought

The toughest thing you will ever do- Is to find a friend- or two.

"Tell" Me A Story

Tells are an important part of poker. Every nuance means something. Every twitch, every scratch, every burp, every fart- they all mean something. Basically, they mean that the person probably hasn't showered and is very uncouth. Most poker players don't care about being couth. They just want your fuckin' money. The greatest book on tells is called "Caro's Book of Poker Tells" by Mike Caro. I played poker with Mike recently. He's called the "Mad Genius of Poker" and that is a perfect description. He looks like his barber died 20 years ago and his battery in his Norelco took a shit about the same time. If he tried to board an airplane with a backpack on, the Homeland Security phone lines would all light up. When we played at a tournament at the Venetian, he had a small iPod in front of him and I kept thinking it was a detonation device. Mike was actually quite fun to play with, which is very unusual in a tournament. The intensity of a tournament doesn't usually provide much fun, let alone fun people. Mike's book on tells is an absolute must read for anyone who plays poker.

There are many ingredients to playing winning poker. Think of poker like you would a pie. Cherry will do nicely for now. Or chocolate cream. I love chocolate cream. Marie Callender's use to have great chocolate cream pie with really rich chocolate and tons of cream. But Marie sold to some big company that is probably being run by some skinny accountant fuck who doesn't think that we should have really rich chocolate or a lot of whipped cream in our diet, so the chocolate is now mediocre and they squirt some fuckin' cream in 3 or 4 spots to give the illusion of a chocolate cream pie. I would like to personally thank that asshole who made that decision to benefit mankind. I hope your pencil wears out and you go insane looking for a fuckin' pencil sharpener. So, poker tells is like one piece of the pie. Not a really big fuckin' piece. But a piece. Tells are especially important in home games. In home games you play with the same people every week and you have more time to study and observe their mannerisms. Tournaments are the toughest places to use tells because you're not with the people at the table that long. You should still pay attention because any information you can get, no matter how insignificant it may seem at the time, may help you before the tournament or your personal tournament life is over. Most players who play frequently don't have really obvious tells. One guy I played with quite a few times in tournaments was a real sloppy eater. Borderline slob. When he eats, he doesn't wipe his mouth so flies are constantly buzzing around his head. I kept looking at the flies because they could see his hand and I was going to call Mike Caro to see if he knew anything about "fly tells". I use to yell, "Thank you, Lord!" out loud to the ceiling whenever I missed the river, hoping my opponent would think I just caught my miracle card. Then I would bet. They always called. Always. I think the word got out that I was bluffing when I yelled at the ceiling. Once the word gets out, you're fuckin' doomed. So I'm changing my style. I'm going to yell, "Thank you, God". If that doesn't work, I'll yell, "Thank you, Jesus" (not Ferguson). I'll let you know how it works out. I've got a good feeling about it. There are certain things I've noticed that occur with a certain degree of frequency:

1) If I make a rather large bet and I'm bluffing, and my opponent checks his hole cards, I usually relax because 90% of the time he isn't going to call.

2) 90% of the time people who ponder a long time usually don't call. The other 10% of the time, you're fucked.

3) When the flop comes, watch the people that are in the pot. If they glance at their chips, chances are they hit the flop.

4) Bluffing is scary to some people. They have a tendency to sit straighter, stop shuffling their chips, put their hands in front of their mouth or face and hold their breath. If that person's breath is really bad, their neighbors are really thankful when they bluff.

5) Betting patterns are huge tells when they change. When someone on a short stack in a tournament keeps going all-in and then just makes a small raise, this should make your hair stand on end. Look for the strength and weakness of

how each player plays his hand. You need to capitalize on the players showing weakness in order to build up your chip stack.

6) Continuation bets are a big part of the game. If a player makes continuation bets frequently and then all of the sudden changes his pattern (checks after the flop), be careful of a monster in the closet.

7) Before the flop, look at the people who are going to act after you. How they hold their cards before the flop can give you an indication of what they are going to do. This is very valuable information if you are thinking about buying the blinds or not raising with a huge hand, knowing that someone after you is going to raise based on how he handles his hole cards.

8) Most of the time if a player makes a pre-flop raise and doesn't bet the flop, I will. Most of the time you will win the pot with this bet.

9) Players have predictable betting patterns. It shouldn't take you long to determine those patterns and remember them. You may even want to take notes so that when you play with that same person again, you'll be ahead of the game.

10) Listen to your opponent's voice when he says "check" or "call" or "raise". Sometimes you can pick up strength or weakness in his voice if he's not a real experienced player.

11) Watch carefully the amount of money a person bets. Sometimes players fall into a pattern of betting a certain amount for monsters and a certain amount for bluffs. If there is no showdown, many times you can extract information about a player's hand during friendly conversation two or three hands later when the player thinks it doesn't really matter anymore. It's always easier to

get this type of verbal information from the players on either side of you. Especially when they feel that they are not advertising their play to the entire table. Every bit of information gives you a little more insight to their play. At the end of the evening, this all translates into more success in your game.

12) If most of the players on the table are having a good time and chatting and laughing, chances are they are not real serious gamblers and will tend to make more mistakes and play weak hands. These are the types of tables you want to play at.

13) Always have the loosest players sit to your right. In a cash game you can change seats when they become available. I want the loosest player to my immediate right if possible. He's always going to act first and once he gets involved in the pot, he will probably call you to the river.

14) A player who looks away from the pot or seems disinterested in it is usually waiting for someone to bet so he can raise. Any time a player shows real weakness, he is usually strong. Heavy sighing and speeches like, "I have to go home so I may as well bet," are all bullshit.

15) Players who tense up or are literally shaking when they bet are so fuckin' excited about their hand, they can hardly stand it. They may as well just scream, "I have a fuckin' monster! My diaper is about to explode!"

16) When Mike "The Mouth" Matusow shuts his yap, he usually has a strong hand. That's usually the case with most guys who are chatting all the fuckin' time. Beware when they shut up. Beware when anyone around you shuts up. They're up to something.

17) When you have identified the tightest players at the table,

stay the fuck away from them. They have the most obvious "tell" you can have at the table- they never play a fuckin' hand. I played with a guy one night who sat in a live game for almost 2 hours before he played a pot. He wouldn't even call when he was the small blind with no raise before him! He's half way in the fuckin' pot already and wouldn't put in a few more bucks to see the flop. He finally opened a pot and I'm looking down at pocket 10's and I looked at him and said, "You haven't played a fuckin' hand since the Carter Administration." Of course, everyone chuckled and we all threw our hand away. He showed pocket Queens. I looked at him with surprise and said, "I'm shocked. I didn't think you played Queens." He was actually showing Queens trying to "tell" us he that he played inferior hands like Queens. When you watch a cash game on television you can see how many different types of players there are. The players like Daniel Negreanu and Gus Hansen like to see a lot of flops. There are some players that are incredibly tight. Like Jerry Buss and Bob Stupak. I don't think I've ever seen Stupak play a hand. Maybe he's just there for the free food. I don't know. But I do know that these type of players "tell" you real quickly what kind of player they are. When I play against a tight, tight player, I don't give him much action. I say, "Adios, Mother Fucker." I know I'm running up a very steep hill if I get into a pot with him. And I don't run well. Especially up steep hills. Identify your opponents and act accordingly.

Like I said, tells are important, but they are just a piece of the puzzle for you to play winning poker. Pay attention- so that your opponent can pay your rent. And be careful of your own tells. Remember, someone is observing you also. We are all being watched. By someone. Somewhere.

Random Thought

You must identify the players at the table- quickly. A lot of the time this can be done through conversation. As soon as you identify a tight player, you know you can play him more aggressively. And the loose player needs to be played tighter. Because chances are that loose mother fucker is going to call you. And call you. And call you.

Limit Hold 'em

I don't play Limit Hold 'em. I tried it, but my problem is that I play too many hands. I have talked to many really really good Limit Hold 'em players and they do very well at it. They highly recommend it for players who don't have big bankrolls because Limit Hold 'em will not cripple you in one hand like No Limit will. If you're playing a 4-8 game, the most you can lose on the river is $8 more. Position and starting hands are very important in all Hold 'em games, but they are especially important in Limit. Very seldom will you be able to bluff someone on the river in Limit Hold 'em so you better have the goods when you make the river bet. Once your opponent makes or calls the first $8 bet on the turn, it's almost a certainty he will call the $8 river bet. You know, pot odds, pot commitment and all that shit. I say "shit" because if you think or feel your hand is beat, throw the fuckin' thing away. Starting hands should be premium hands when playing Limit. You can expand the premium hands depending on your feel for the game and your position, but poker, in all forms, is a game of patience and position. In that order. It's a waiting game. And those who have patience and wait are rewarded far more often than those who don't. Recommended starting hands are A-A, K-K, Q-Q, J-J, 10-10, A-K, A-Q, A-J, A-10. I would pre-flop raise with all of these hands. Medium and small pairs are not raising hands. I would play a medium or small pair, but once the flop comes I would get away from the hand if I hadn't improved. Forget drawing to small straights and small flushes. Even if you make them you will probably suck eggs. Small or medium suited connectors in a Limit game are a drain on your bankroll. Remember, and I can't emphasize this enough, the goal is to walk out of the card room with more money than you came in with. This is tough enough to do without playing garbage.

You will go through periods of time where you become card dead for hours. Fortunately, the blinds don't climb and get crazy like they do in a tournament. If you're the big or small blind, your hand requirements are going to diminish considerably because you're already involved in the pot. Just be careful, because if you get a small piece of the flop, the hand could get very costly and all of your previous patience goes down the fuckin' toilet. Along with your

money. It doesn't seem like money because they're chips. That's part
of the hidden seduction of the game. Money only comes out of your
pocket during the initial buy-in. Then you use chips. And a $100 chip
is the same size as a $1 chip. Just a different color. Usually a black
color. No big deal. Just a few blacks here and a few blacks there. Or
greens, or reds. They're only chips. That's why in a No Limit cash
game, if I'm bluffing, I bet cash. And spread it out. $500 or $1,000
looks like a ton of fuckin' money and gets the guy looking at it to
realize, "Holy fuck, that's a lot of money." As opposed to 10 black
chips. I bet 10 black if I want him to call. At No Limit games, you can
keep $100 bills in front of you. In Limit games, it wouldn't make
sense because your betting range is structured. If you're at a 4-8 game,
the most you can bet is $8. Then each person can raise $8 until a "cap"
is reached- usually 4 bets. If it's heads-up, then the opponents can raise
and re-raise each other until they're out of $8 bets, which means
they're out of money. But at some point, usually after the second or
third raise, one of the players says to himself, "Oh shit, I think he has
the nuts." And just calls the last raise. And holds his breath. And
sometimes farts. But that's all part of poker my friend. That's all part
of poker. Whether it's Limit or No Limit, there's a lot of breath
holding and a lot of social gas. And that's why the game is so much
fun.

Holiday Cheer

Smoking has been banned in virtually every card room so now smokers have to make a mad dash between hands to a place outside the card room to take a few hits. It has been proven that every time someone lights a match to light a cigarette, they are adding carbon dioxide to the atmosphere, thereby accelerating global warming and helping to destroy all life on our favorite planet, Earth. Except for the cockroaches. You just can't kill those fuckin' things no matter how many cigarettes you smoke or how many matches you light. So, thank you smokers everywhere for doing your part to end the human race. Oh, and Happy Holidays to everyone. Even the pricks who smoke.

Random Thought

I played in a tournament and who sits down at the table? Probably the toughest fuckin' tournament player in our solar system- Alan Cunningham. Let me tell you- this kid is fuckin' quiet. Win or lose. I'm talking really quiet. I took his pulse twice to make sure he was O.K. I made him smile a few times. And I put my hand on his knee a few times. That's as far as we got. I got busted a few minutes later.....

Playing Hold 'em-

Ninja Style

There are 5 basic weaknesses in opponents that Ninjas are able to exploit when they are in confrontational situations. Those weaknesses are transferable to the game of Hold 'em. Think like a Ninja- Play like a Ninja- Win like a Ninja.

Laziness: The lazy often allow their guard to drop through lack of awareness. The boredom of being "card dead" allows these individuals to play hands they shouldn't be playing and thereby allowing their chips to be annihilated.

Anger: This volatile emotion causes a person to act irrationally and without thought. A person with a short temper stands little chance of success in Hold 'em or combat. His anger will dull his thought process and his vision.

Fear: The meek and mild-mannered are easy to defeat through intimidation. These people have no desire for conflict and can easily be raised or re-raised out of a pot.

Sympathy: Ninjas of the past have posed as beggars and cripples to put their adversaries off guard. Underestimating your opponent because of his appearance can be your downfall at a Hold 'em table. The original Ninjas were very compassionate and kind, but their opponents knew not to ever mistake kindness for weakness.

Vanity: A vain or over confident person usually thinks too much of himself to realize his faults. He has a lack of sensitivity to others and is in an extremely vulnerable position because others are working for his downfall. His ego allows him to lower his guard so that he is set up for a surprise Ninja attack or a surprise re-raise on the river.

The ability to perceive these levels of danger allows us to play Hold 'em on a much higher plane. Our sensitivity levels can be raised when we are aware of our weaknesses. We must learn to trust our perception and work to develop it as a skill. When we are in a potentially dangerous situation at a poker table, when a lot of our chips are at risk, we need to learn how to tune into a level of thought higher than our regular consciousness and utilize our sixth sense just as we utilize our other senses. This is the world of the Ninja. To free ourselves from the notion that we are victims. To free ourselves from the notion that we are helpless. And isolated. And have bad luck. Once we recognize that the Universe is an integral process of our life, and positive thinking is a part of that process, we can move forward to tap into that consciousness to gain knowledge and power. Power that can be used as a tremendous advantage at the poker table and at the table of life. This is good shit. Remember it.

Random Thought

Rumor has it that Mike "The Mouth" Matusow is coming out with a new clothing line featuring Mike Matusow Jeans. The only problem is they come apart at the seams.

Money Management-

I Can't Emphasize This Enough

Poker is cruel- It's unforgiving. If the poker gods are pissed at you and the deck is not even coming close to cooperating in any way, shape or form, you are fuckin' toast. That's why money management is so important. You need your bankroll to play again, and to blow it all in one unbelievably bad session is unforgivable. You have got to walk out of the poker room and go home no matter how fuckin' lonely your existence is. No matter how dingy your apartment is. That, my friends, is why you need Tivo. It's like man's best friend with no dog shit to clean up and no mouth to feed. Whenever you come home, Tivo will have something waiting for you that you want to watch. To relax you- to calm you- to take you to another place. And you can nurse your testicles back to health after they've been stomped on at the poker table.

Random Thought

One of the greatest voices of our century, or any other century, is Celine Dion. I just thought I'd mention that. Why? Fuck, I don't know. I'm just an informative bastard. So sue me.

Bluffing

Bluffing is s strategy used by many poker players to force out an opponent who you feel has a better hand than you. Especially when you have no hand at all- like a flush or a straight draw that didn't materialize. The most expensive bluff is when you try it after the river card. Now the pot is large and your opponent already has quite a few chips in it so it's harder to get him to lay his hand down. River bluffs usually work only when you are willing to put in a lot of chips. I usually like to make my moves after either the flop or the turn. If my opponent has called both of those bets, chances are good he's going to call my river bet. And the two words that get caught in my throat when that happens are, "Good call." If I'm drawing for a straight or a flush, I'll bet before the river. After the river card, I'm done unless I made the hand. Good players are easier to bluff than weak players. Most weak players will play their hand all the way, even with second or third pair. They are hoping to catch a three of a kind and the odds are highly unlikely that they will. If the board is A-10-9 and they have a pair of nines, they have trouble laying the hand down. They value their hands at a higher level than a strong player. Once you recognize and categorize each player in a cash game, you need to assess each situation when you are in a pot with them.

Weak players just cannot lay a hand down on the river. No matter how much they try. They twist and turn in agony and they eventually call you. Don't try and bluff a weak player, which is also known in the game as a calling station. When you make a big hand, you will get a big payoff because they will be there to call you. You should always bluff players who have lost quite a few hands because they become "gun shy". I actually played against a "chair" one night and did very well. Everyone who sat in the fuckin' 6 seat was going busted, and every time I got into the pot with the 6 seat I rammed and jammed. Sometimes things work like that. A seat gets cold or hot for a period of time. You should be very aggressive against scared money. If you sense that your opponent is playing scared, you should raise or re-raise when you're in the pot with him. Bluffing is usually best when you're only against one other player. The more people in the pot, the greater the odds that some asshole will call your bet. If you're on a hot streak, take command of the table, but as soon as you recognize the streak is over, go back to your normal play. Bluffing is fun especially when it works. Don't ever show your bluff unless you have an ulterior motive. Let the table try and guess when you're bluffing and when you're not. If they guess wrong, your chip stack will keep getting bigger. And size does matter. No matter what anyone says…..

Random Thought

When you step into the poker room- the arena- the square circle- the stadium- your frame of mind is important. Anyone, and I mean anyone, no matter how badly they play, can beat you. Your frame of mind must be positive. You can win. You will win. You are better than them. Your penis is bigger than theirs. You are the best. You are an animal! Now get out there and kick some fuckin' ass! And remember, little Jimmy needs that operation.

Let's Build a Better Mousetrap

Every casino you enter has a ton of side games. These are all higher hold percentage games for the house, designed by their inventors to get a bigger piece of the "Blackjack player" pie than the normal Blackjack game. Some have been successful, but most have not. Tournament Hold 'em has entered that arena. Binion's Horseshoe in downtown Las Vegas recently hosted a new format for a Hold 'em tournament. A guy I met, whose name I couldn't remember if you paid me, convinced Binion's to try this new tournament. The way it works is that you get reloaded with chips every level. For example, if you go busted in the first 10 minutes, you just wait for the next level and the dealer gives you $5,000 more in tournament chips. Everyone in the tournament gets an additional $5,000 every level. So no one busts out until level 6. And you play on the same table with the same 10 guys. Almost 6 hours with the same guys. The same irritating, smelly, sweaty guys. Even cash games have guys coming and going. In most tournaments, you are frequently moved as games break up and you are moved to other tables. But in this tournament you stay with the same guys for almost the whole tournament. Let's face it folks, we'd get tired of Jesus Christ himself if we had to spend 5 or 6 hours straight with him. Listening to him moan and groan about the bill for the Last Supper or how his dad didn't come to his soccer games when he was a kid and on and on. Every bad beat would be, "Oh my Dad! Oh my Dad!" And the slamming of the chalice on the table. That's how this was. Without the chalice. Guys recapping every bad beat story they could ever recall, criticizing every play and getting up and down and up and down checking the chip counts at other tables. But the best part was yet to come.

The top 10 chip leaders after level 6 would go to the final table. Therein lies the rub that even Ben Gay couldn't help. At least with the same aromas, the same body odors and the same bad breath that you endured for 6 hours there was a defense. I always carry a large spray can of Pine Sol for these special times. No one, though, was prepared for the last 15 minutes of the final level. Everyone realized at about the same time that you would need at least $100,000 in tournament chips, maybe more, to make the final table. Everyone else would go home.

So every hand was chaos. All-ins everywhere. People yelling at each other. The clock ticking down. Only the highest 10 chip leaders out of 150 survive. Players screaming at the dealers, "Deal! Deal! Don't worry about counting the stacks! We'll do it!" The dealers were frantic! Time running out! All-In! All-In! 3 or 4 all-ins for each pot. 4 Minutes left! Holy Fuck! What the fuck am I doing here? No one likes chaos more than me, but this was painful. Three all-ins- 2 minutes left- it's 2-7 vs. 4-5 vs. 9-3. Every table, all 15 of them, had the same thing happening. Screaming- Yelling- Dealers crying- Diapers bursting. Finally it was over. It was like the end of the War of the Worlds movie with Tom Cruise. The aftermath was a poker room full of exhausted, frustrated poker players with the inventor of the game curled up in a prenatal position in the corner. The film crew he had hired to document this historic event, that was going to change the face of tournament poker, were on their cell phones trying to find a good therapist for him. On the way out the door I stopped to see the tournament director and handed him a mousetrap that I carry. I said, "You know, this one has been working just fine for a long time." He said, "I agree." And he started taking names for his next regular "normal" tournament. And I went home. $330 poorer- but all for the greater good. To help someone try and build a better mousetrap…..

Random Thought

Las Vegas-   *A great place to visit*

A great place to live

A great place to be young

Keep One Eye on the Road- One Eye on the Book

and One Eye on the Guy You're Talking To

I am going to put this book on a CD so people who are driving back and forth to their local poker room can hear it without trying to read the book at traffic lights and stop signs. Or on freeways. There is nothing worse than some asshole passing you on the freeway reading a Stephen King novel perched up on the steering wheel. Actually, there is something worse than that. It's the person who's driving and fuckin' insists on looking at you while you are having a conversation with him. There is something inherently wrong with the driver looking at me and me looking out the windshield terrified- waiting for the inevitable crash that will instantly bring sweet death because this asshole doesn't have a passenger side airbag. I tell these people, "Look at the fuckin' road! I'm only one foot from you. I can hear you!" But they've been programmed. It's hard to get a habit out of your system when you've done it for so long. It's when they turn around and look at the person in the back seat and talk to them that sends me over the edge.

So, in the interest of humanity, I am going to put this book on a compact disc. Actually, it will take 5 or 6 compact discs. So there would be no reason for anyone to perch the book on the steering wheel. Unless they wanted to follow along to the CD. And look for errors. But they will be disappointed. Because number one, I am going to do the CD myself. Unless I'm barred from the studio. Like I have been from bowling alleys and golf courses. I am an aggressive bowler. And bowling alley owners don't like aggressive bowlers. They like to see the ball touch the ground before it hits the pins. They prefer an underhand bowling technique. That's not my style. And golf courses- I believe that you should be able to drive **anywhere** on a golf course. Anywhere. Including on the green. Tiger Woods **should** make every fuckin' putt he ever attempts- the green is perfectly smooth. There's not a fuckin' thing in his way. Nothing. How could he not make the putt? But let me drive my cart up there and it's a different story. When Tiger Woods sinks a putt that has to go over two sets of tire tracks, I'll applaud him. Then he's done something. And to get a penalty when you lose a ball is insane. Why should you be penalized for losing an expensive ball? You have just experienced the traumatic experience of losing a gorgeous, shiny, expensive ball, and now they're going to penalize you? That's fuckin' nuts! Haven't you gone through enough pain with the search for the ball? And the expense? And if it was your favorite ball- more trauma! So I say fuck golf, fuck golfers and fuck the golf courses that won't let me on the course to play. Oh, and fuck the funny pants that you golfers wear- you're adults for Christ's sake. Wear cutoffs and tank tops and sweaty sweat suits like manly weekend golfers wear. So as I was saying, the CD isn't going to be exactly like the book. It'll be the book plus other shit if I go off on tangents. Imagine! Me going off on tangents. I think the CD thing will be fun. If you want to order one, go to my website pokergas.com. Or call my people when I hire people. Or maybe I'll just call **you**. Boy would you be surprised. Especially if you happen to be driving and reading. Now that would be fuckin' funny.

Random Thought

When I use to play golf I would never lie about my score. I couldn't. Anybody could look back up the fairway and count the wounded!

Huge Deal for a Huge Name

It's hard to believe how big the deals have gotten in the gaming industry. It use to be a big deal when a joint was built for 70 or 80 million. Then Steve Wynn came along and raised the bar to 500 or 600 million to build big joints on the strip. Then it was a billion to build a joint that would emphasize the phrase, "Build it and they will come." And they did. From everywhere. Then Circus merged with Gold Strike Resorts and with that merger came Mandalay Bay and Mandalay Bay Resorts with Mike Ensign at the helm steering an enormous fuckin' ship. Then MGM-Mirage bought Mandalay Bay Resorts in an 8 billion dollar deal. While this was going on, Harrah's was gobbling up it's share of the Las Vegas strip among other gaming properties. When the dust settled, it was Harrah's Entertainment vs. MGM-Mirage- the two monster "stacks" in the industry. With everyone barely catching their collective breaths, here comes the mother of all fuckin' deals- the Apollo Group buying Harrah's Entertainment for a deal worth close to 30 Billion Dollars! This deal was so complicated that it took about 3 months to reach an agreement and will probably take another year to complete because of all the different jurisdictions that the Apollo entity has to be licensed in.

I'm sure Bill Harrah, the guy who started Harrah's, would be proud. He started with a small Bingo parlor and definitely ran a toothpick into a lumberyard. I remember him when I worked in Lake Tahoe in the late 60's. He was a mover, a shaker and an innovator even then. If Harrah's did something, you knew they had researched it and it was the right move. When someone suggested that his bus program was bringing people to his resort who didn't play because there was no money on the bus and people were just going for a nice ride in the mountains, Harrah had to find out for himself. It was an easy experiment. He just got on the bus and announced to the passengers that for every dollar they showed him, he would match it. People dug into every secret compartment they had, to double their money. It cost him a fuckin' ton, but he found out there was plenty of money on the busses. After he did this randomly three or four times, he knew the bus program was going to be part of Harrah's long-term strategy for revenue growth.

Harrah's went public in 1972 and looked to Wall Street for financing. The company philosophy was always, "If you stand still, you become stagnant." Harrah's was never stagnant. Bill Harrah died in 1978 and the company was bought by the Holiday Corp, which operated Holiday Inns. The company then entered the Atlantic City market with a major casino and got into the riverboat market in Joliet, Ill. Then they partnered with the Ak Chin Indian tribe outside of Phoenix, Arizona. Bill Harrah has two sons who live in Reno, Nevada, but have no part of Harrah's anymore. But they can still be very proud of what their dad started. A company that is still viewed by the industry as a mover, a shaker and an innovator.....

Random Thought

You have a lot of decisions to make when playing poker, as you do in life. You analyze the situation and you make your decision. The smart one. The best one. The right one- at the time. You're the one that will call the play. Good luck.

Back In Time- Yesteryear

These are excerpts from a Doyle Brunson interview that appeared in the February 1977 issue of *Gambling Times Magazine-* a magazine published by Stanley Sludikoff that was the gambling magazine of its day. The interview was conducted by Allen Goldberg on May 4, 1976 at 6:30 P.M. Some of Doyle's remarks were:

♠ "Concentrate- play hard."

♠ "When I win a pot, I play the next one. If you don't, how will you know you're on a rush?"

♠ "You need card sense."

♠ "You need courage."

♠ "Don't be in too big a hurry."

♠ "You push around a tight player. A loose player you don't."

♠ "I don't believe there is such a thing as a top-notch woman player."

♠ "If the game is loose- play tight."

♠ "If the game is tight- play loose."

♠ "Play until either the game gets bad or you get tired."

♠ "In No Limit- you've got to have position. I believe you can win and never look at your hand if you have position all night."

Back In Time- Continued

An article by Bob Ciaffone appeared in a short-lived publication called The Poker Devil, Volume 1, Issue #1, November 1985. Because of the space, time continuum that affects all our lives I will try to do it justice by paraphrasing the article. Actually, the article is pretty short so I'll just copy it word for word. Bob has gone on to write many authoritative books on poker including the billion seller "Robert's Rules of Poker", which is still available at Wal Marts, 7-11's and Swap Meets. Look for it at a garage sale near you. It'll probably be next to this book.

Quotes by Bob Ciaffone

The Future of Tournament Poker

"By any criterion tournament poker has undergone tremendous growth in the last several years. The number of major Nevada tournaments has increased from two to seven, with some new additions anticipated next year. The number of entries has expanded in nearly all events, with over three hundred entries in certain very popular categories. The number of entries in the Horseshoe $10,000 entry World Champsionship event has risen to one hundred and forty. Will the future years show a continued phenomenal increase in tournament poker?

A common mistake in thinking is to extrapolate trends on a graph into the future at whatever the rate of change has been in the past. It is usually more accurate to analyze cause and effect than to simply assume a trend will continue indefinitely. I believe the most important factor in determining the future popularity of any gambling activity is the state of our economy. Poker action has made good gains in the last few years because of a very healthy economic environment. However, when the economy does slow, poker will be even more hard hit than other areas.

Can we poker players do anything about the impending mortal blow to our bankrolls? The best way to improve our prospects may well be to get some outside money to enter the poker economy via commercial sponsorship of the poker tournaments. Players presently compete only for prize money that is taken out of entry fees. The amount of money that is circulating keeps dwindling because of the house cut and taxes. What we need is a commercial sponsor to add some big bucks into the prize funds. This will only come about when a sponsor is able to get something big in return, and that something is obviously good publicity. For the kind of money I'm talking about, that publicity must come from television exposure.

There have been some attempts to televise poker events, but the manner of presenting them has been of such poor quality that the big networks have not shown much interest. I certainly believe that lack of interest has been caused by poor methods of presentation rather than an uninteresting product. You don't need to be a professional poker player to feel the intense human emotion while watching World Champion Bill Smith and the runner-up T.J. Cloutier battling for 1.4 million in cash at this year's Horseshoe tournament. However, we need some changes in the format of big poker events to improve the attraction for television audiences.

Here are a few of the changes I feel are necessary to improve the presentation of poker tournaments for TV viewing:

1. We need playing cards that are designed for easy viewing. Existing cards are often unreadable.

2. In the late stages of a tournament both players should be required to show their hands when one of them is all-in.

3. The dealer should wear a shirt with the word "DEALER" printed in big letters. It would be helpful if players wore shirts or caps with their names or initials.

4. The audience should know what each player is holding at the start of a deal. Obviously this would make a live broadcast impossible but so what? A tape-delay could be used, but I feel that a broadcast several weeks after the event would be practical and desirable. There are too many dull spots in play to

show poker exactly as it is played and editing is needed to cut out those dull spots.

These are only a few ideas; I am sure you can come up with many of your own for improving the format of tournament poker for television. It is time for poker to join the ranks of golf, tennis, bowling, and other forms of competition that are bringing in outside money from sponsors because of their great television popularity."

Grand Prix of Poker
December 1-19, 1985

1985 GRAND PRIX OF POKER SCHEDULE

Date	Time	Event	Buy-in	Pays
Dec. 2	Noon	Limit Texas holdem	$ 525	18
3	Noon	Limit hi-lo split (8 or beter)	$ 1,025	16
4	Noon	Limit seven-card razz	$ 1,025	16
5	Noon	Lmit seven-card stud	$ 1,025	16
6	Noon	Limit Omaha holdem	$ 1,025	18
7	Noon	Limit ace-five draw (with joker)	$ 1,025	16
8	Noon	Pot-limit Omha holdem (re-buys)	$ 1,525	*9
9	Noon	Ladies limit seven-card stud	$ 525	8
9	1 pm	No-limit deuce-to-seven (re-buys)	$ 5,050	5
10-11	Noon	Limit Texas holdem	$ 1,025	18
11	4 pm	Limit seven-card stud	$ 2,550	8
12	Noon	Limit Texas holdem	$ 2,550	9
13-14	Noon	Irish Eccentric International No-limit holdem Championship	$ 2,500	9
14	2 pm	Pro-Celebrity Charity Tournament	_____	—
15-16	Noon	No-limit Texas holdem	$ 1,025	18
16	6 pm	No-limit holdem Media Tournament	_____	9
17-18-19	1 pm	No-limit Texas holdem	$10,000	*9

* If these events have at least 100 entries, the prize money from 10th - 18th will be 1% to each player.

End of Back in Time- Yesteryear

Me, Todd and Marie

I unveiled my newly acquired Marie Antoinette card cover with the ejector head at a televised game I played on January 11th 2007 at Binion's Horseshoe in downtown Las Vegas. The game included Todd Brunson, Dan Harrington, David Williams and Vanessa Rousso. I told everyone that the card cover was not a toy. It was not to be played with or fondled. It was for display purposes only. That didn't stop those animals. Williams liked it, Harrington loved it and Brunson wanted to bed it. Marie seemed to like the attention so I didn't intervene. The game took forever to play. The dealer couldn't deal **any card** unless the television director told him to. I'm thinking, "This is a fuckin' poker game, Bucko- not Masterpiece Theatre." We started at 3PM and ended at midnight. I think we played 12 hands total. But we all had fun. Especially Marie. I think she has a "thing" for Todd.....

Random Thought

I had World Series of Poker fever. It quickly turned into World Series of Poker nausea. You had to be there. You probably were. Everybody was there. Every fuckin' body. They came in trains, planes and cars. Cabs, shuttles and cycles. Many of the Las Vegas homeless hung around the Rio for the entire tournament. They blended in well. Plus they could get the Rio water and an occasional partially eaten pizza slice. Life was good for all.

Poker and the "A" Word

The poker world has many many smart people in its population. Some are plain fuckin' brilliant. It's ironic that the most these brilliant people will ever accomplish with their intelligence is to calculate pot odds. For some, poker becomes a "black hole", consuming everything in its path, including houses, businesses, families and lives. For others, it's a pastime that we use to pleasure ourselves publicly. The people close to us are the ones who first recognize which of the two apply to us. Part of the human spirit is to think we are in "control". "Addicted to poker?" you laughingly respond when confronted or questioned by a close friend or family member. But the word has been verbalized to you. The "A" word. Addict. Addiction. Not a nice word. Not a pleasant word. Addicts are addicted to alcohol. Addicts are addicted to drugs. Addicts are addicted to cigarettes. But poker? Poker for Christ's sake? "It can't be," you reason. You do well at poker. You make your living at it. The brain does not want to come to the realization you have a problem. It never does- until you reach the edge of the black hole and are being viciously sucked into the center. You fight it. You fight it with all your strength. You fight it like there's no tomorrow. You fight it like you are fighting for your life. Poker **is** your life. It's your destiny. You know it. Your poker buddies know it. Why doesn't your family know it? You're an adult. Why don't they respect your decision? Why are they worried. Maybe it's because they read my poem.

My Name is Poker

My name is poker

I will seduce and pleasure you

I will thrill, excite and challenge too.

For many hours I will bore

Then slam your nut sack in a car door.

I start you slow with the limits low

As time goes on- your bets will grow.

The Carrot- The Stick- The Tournaments- The Fame

The Big Entry Fees- The Usual Suspects- And Finally, the Game.

Remember, my friends- My name is Poker

I come in many forms- With or without a Joker.

Once I take charge- You don't have a prayer

To escape from my grip- Is extremely rare.

If you get under my spell- You may never be free

I will own you one day- Just wait and see.

Listen to me and please listen well

When you're addicted to poker- You're headed to Hell.

You will have many highs- You will have many lows

I'm looking to addict you- like I have many pros.

I'll create a hunger for action that cannot be matched

And an itch in your brain that cannot be scratched.

My name is Poker- To the core I'll be true

I'm so happy to meet you- So happy to meet you.

A Prelude to 1200 Sundays

When I was writing this book, I wrote what I thought was a really good and powerful piece called "1200 Sundays". I was inspired by the book "700 Sundays" by Billy Crystal. "700 Sundays" is a very excellent read. It's about the 700 Sundays Crystal got to spend with his dad before he died. The piece I wrote was a story about the ultimate bad beat that my family and I experienced about 1200 Sundays ago. The kid typing my book into his computer, Grant Turner, whose opinion I respect, convinced me that "1200 Sundays" shouldn't be in the book. He was probably right. "1200 Sundays" is from a very sad time in my life, when the randomness of evil entered it. It was a day the Angels cried. And I cried with them. There is pain behind everyone's eyes. Comedians seem to have more pain than most. There's a lot of pain behind mine. If I go on a book lecture tour, I might read the stuff that didn't make it into the book. Some of it's funny. Some of it's not. Maybe then I'll share "1200 Sundays". We'll see. We'll just have to wait and see.

Random Thought

Have a great day and know that someone has thought about you today.

Big Deal- And Beyond- Way Beyond

We all strive to do a good job in whatever career we choose.
That's why we chose that career. But perfection is not an inherent
human trait. We all make mistakes. Sometimes the dealer makes
mistakes. Even the good ones. If a dealer makes a mistake that costs
you a little money- that varies between No Big Deal to Big Deal. If an
airline pilot makes a mistake while landing or taking off- Big Deal to
Really Big Deal. If a dealer makes a mistake and costs you **quite a bit**
of money- A Big Deal. If a surgeon makes a mistake while he's
operating on you or a member of your family- Really Really Big Deal
to Really Really Big Fuckin' Deal. If you get knocked out of a
tournament- Big Deal. Your kid gets notified he's going to Iraq- Huge
Deal. You're the kid who's notified- Gargantuan Fuckin' Deal. There
are a lot worse things that happen in life than a mistake by a dealer.
Shit happens and a mistake by a dealer is just a fart in the scope of
things. Get on with life and don't make too Big A Deal out of it. Put in
proper perspective, it's No Big Deal compared to a Really Really Big
Fuckin' Deal- And Beyond- Way Beyond.

I Love Numbers- Just Not These

I'm not political. At all. I don't have a political bone in my huge body. I vote for the man. Not the party. Everyone who makes decisions makes mistakes. 1-2-3-4-5-6-7-8-9. I've made a ton of decisions in my life. I've made mistakes in some of those decisions. When I make a mistake, I reverse it. I recognize the mistake as early as possible. And I change it. I never ignore it. 10-11-12-13-14-15-16-17-18. Mistakes do not ever get better as time goes on. They never get better if you ignore them. The intention of a decision is for good. Sometimes decisions start out good then they turn to shit. Poker players make decisions every time they're dealt two cards. Sometimes we decide to play the cards and then realize after the flop, after the turn or after the river card that we made a mistake playing the hand. 19-20-21-22-23-24-25-26-27. We throw the hand away, gather what chips we have left in front of us and think about what we did wrong so we don't repeat our mistake. The leadership of our nation has a tough time with that concept. They should have looked at the file footage and film clips of the war in Vietnam before they voted to get us involved in Iraq. 28-29-30-31-32-33. The Iraqi war has had me upset for a long time. 34-35-36-37-38-39-40. The reason I'm counting is I'm trying to put into proper perspective what the number 3,000 means. That's how many troops from our country have died in Iraq. 41-42-43-44-45-46-47-48-49-50. They were from cities and towns from sea to shining sea. But it doesn't shine as bright when I think of 3,000 kids giving their life for a cause that we can never win. And 15,000 wounded. Let's not forget the wounded. Many of them lost arms. Many of them lost legs. I just can't imagine that. I broke my middle finger 4 weeks ago and believe me, it's a real bitch trying to function without one finger. One lousy finger. I didn't in my wildest dreams realize how important one fuckin' finger was to my healthy happy life. But to lose a hand, or an arm or a leg? Unfuckin' thinkable! And for what?? If a doctor said to me he would have to cut off my hand to save my life, I would say, "Go for it Doc." If I had to cut off my arm or leg to save a family member's life, I would say, "Go for it." If I had to cut off my arm or leg for some guy in Iraq who doesn't even want me there, I've only got 2 words, "Fuck You! Do you think I'm fuckin' nuts?" I guess that's more than two words. But you get the idea. 51-52-53-54-55-56-57.

The Mid-East has been a hotbed of hate for thousands of years. We're not going to change that. We got rid of Saddam. We did our thing. Now it's up to the Iraqi nation to do theirs. 58-59-60-61-62-63-64-65-66-67-68. We can support them with money. Support them with tanks. And guns. And whatever else they need. And give them an 800 number to call if they need advice. And we will promise to "man" the phone 24 hours a day. Seven days a week. 69-70-71-72-73-74-75. *Life Magazine* did an issue during the Vietnam War to try and put **that** war in its proper perspective. They put the pictures, age and hometown of every kid killed the week before in a yearbook format in their magazine. 76-77-78-79-80-81-82-83-84-85-86. It was fuckin' unbelievable. You were looking at 120 faces of soldiers who died the week before in the jungles of Vietnam. All races- all religions- all Americans. And all of them young. Too young. 87-88-89-90-91-92. There was a huge uproar. *Life Magazine* never did that again. I think they got a lot of heat from our government because America came face to face with a number. A number that we had seen every week in our local newspaper. A number that meant something to many of us, but it was just a number. But the faces. That was another story. Right now our number is 3,000. And every single number is a face and a life. A young soldier's life. A soldier with parents and siblings and friends and wives and girlfriends and uncles and aunts and cousins and co-workers. Every single number. All the way to 3,000. 93-94-95-96-97-98-99-100. Three thousand is a huge amount of anything. It's incomprehensible. If our government decided that they were going to send squads to our houses and take our favorite pet and kill or maim 18,000 of them randomly, there would be a revolt. An uprising. But not all of them would be killed. 3,000 they would kill and 15,000 of them they would just cut off their paws. People everywhere in this country would go fuckin' nuts. Even if they didn't have a pet. And a pet doesn't come close to being compared to an American soldier. But 3,000 dead soldiers and 15,000 wounded? I guess it's not enough yet for the country to go nuts. 101-102-103-104-105-106-107-108-109. You want a different analogy? Different than a pet? 18,000 Wounded and dead warriors? How many is 18,000? Can't get your arms around a number like that? How about if the local high school in your town has a graduating class of 300 this year. 300 Seniors. Young men and women who are all looking forward to the rest of their lives. And they tragically all died. Every single one of them. The star quarterback, the cheerleader, the future scientist, the prom Queen, the good looking guys, the cute girls, the nerds the jocks- all of them dead. But wait a minute. That's only 300. We have to do that every year for the next 10 years to get to 3,000. The next 10 years- every graduating class. That's just for the dead soldiers so far. Right now we are working on year 11. And the wounded? We would have to wound every Senior in that same school for another 50 years- after we kill **All** of the first 10 Senior classes. 110-111-112-113-114. Can you imagine that? Wound and seriously wound every Senior in your local high school for the next 50 years? Some would be unlucky enough to lose their arms and legs. I have a hunch the American public would not allow us to get past killing the first Senior class of 300. The Million Man March a few years ago would pale in comparison to the uprising in this country if we killed 300 graduating Seniors, let alone 3,000. Let alone wound another 15,000.

I know this is a poker book. About poker. Well, some of it. And it's about fun. And about farting. And about life. And if I can get enough people thinking with my ranting about this war, and I can make a tiny difference in ending the war 1 day or 1 hour sooner, I may have made the difference in just one soldier's life. And if I get real lucky and catch a miracle card on the river, I might make a difference in more than one life. I just know that this madness must end. It must stop. I think every newspaper in every city should print the names and pictures of every soldier who died that week in every Sunday paper. A perpetual memorial wall in paper form. It's too bad *Life Magazine* isn't still around to show the 3,000 faces so far, and update it every month. I'm sorry for the kids who died, but it's time for the ones who are still alive to come home. While they still can. And then they can play in the sun and raise families. And have fun. And enjoy life. Until our leaders decide to send them to some other God forsaken place that doesn't like us and doesn't want us. 115-116-117-118-119. All in the name of goodwill. And freedom. That's always the two buzzwords our leaders use to convince us they are doing the right thing. If it's so right, they should send their kids first. And their nephews. And grandkids. Then the 3,000 sets of parents who lost their kids might understand. And 15,000 sets of parents with wounded kids might understand. But I would still have trouble buying into it. I still can't get past the issue of *Life Magazine*. And I never will. 120-121-122-123-124-125-126-127-128-129-130. Keep counting- all the way to 3,000. And every number was a kid who lived next door to someone. But not anymore…..

Another Last Supper

Sheldon Adelson, the owner of the Venetian Hotel and Casino in Las Vegas, is a really, really lucky guy. He has a first class poker room with a first class staff. What three better guys can you have supervising your poker room than Anthony, Daniel and Timothy. They're all named after saints for Christ's sake. And the poker room manager is named Jésus. Is this the beginning of a re-creation of the Last Supper or what? This time though, they'll probably hold it in the Lux Café, right across from the poker room. They have the most fantastic crunchy Sourdough bread that is a border line orgasmic experience. It's truly "Oh My God!" Sourdough bread that belongs on any and every Last Supper table. Warm crunchy Sourdough with a soft doughy center and served with creamy butter with a hint of garlic and a dash of heavy cream. Incredible. Forget ordering a meal. The food's not that good. But the bread! And let's face it, the Last Supper was all about the bread. And of course the wine. And the DaVinci Code. So the scene is set. Just like it was a few thousand years ago. Only this time it's at the Venetian. So shuffle up and deal guys. Shuffle up and deal.

(P.S. The poker room manager's name isn't Jésus but I needed it to be, for this bit to work. Thank you for your understanding, your love and the kind words you are mumbling right now.)

The End-

At Last!

Tony Korfman

He Laughed- He Cried

He Cared- He Shared

He Lived- He Died

A simple epitaph for a simple guy. I laughed a lot when I wrote this book. And I cried. And I've always cared about the people of this planet. And I shared my thoughts, my humor and my life with you. And I've shared the money I've earned with many many people. Family members and strangers. Many strangers. No one leaves this huge rock we live on alive. No one. Howard Hughes didn't and neither did Elvis. So don't take things too seriously. Have fun, be safe and drive carefully. Say "please" and "thank you" a lot and tip generously. Be kind to others. Everyone is fighting a tough battle. We live a life of choices. We can choose to be kind, to love and to laugh no matter what the circumstances. Or we can choose to be grumpy and miserable. I'm hoping this book brought you some smiles and some laughter. It was meant to be humorous and informative. If it offended anyone, I'm sorry. I'm not sorry I wrote it, I'm just sorry you didn't see the humor in it. If I had my life to live over again, I would have more hilarious prat falls. And I would try to have more folksy charm. I like those two words. Folksy charm. And I wouldn't have wasted any precious minutes of my life watching Celebrity Poker on TV. I think that's something that can be added to "What no person has ever said on their death bed". Of course, number one is, "I wish I would have spent more time at the office," and now number two, "I wish I had watched celebrity poker more often." All that we are is a result of our past- our upbringing. How we act and how we treat people is how we will be remembered. If we want to be remembered differently, we must think differently. Starting right now. Change your thinking and you change your life. That's easy to say and easy to write, but tough to do on a continuous basis. There are always speed bumps along the way in life, and Lord knows- my family and I have had our share. Everyone gets their share of speed bumps. Some are a little bumpier than others. The main thing is that we land on our feet when we get over the bump. And if we don't, hopefully there's someone there to help us up. And if there isn't, then we have to get up on our own. And forge ahead. And it's important to remember, that somewhere, every day, there's someone who thinks about you. I promise you that. At some point you need to be at peace with your talent, yourself and your life. I hope you attain that peace. I really do. Until we meet again- Thank you for your time. I'm Tony Korfman. I'm glad to have made your acquaintance. I really am.

The Glossary-

Unlike Any You've Ever Read

Historically, glossaries are not funny. I'm not one to try to alter history. I've been known to alter financial statements, to alter my checkbook, I was an altar boy once- but fuck with history? Never. Well, not never. But almost never. So the glossary is almost funny. In some spots. It's impossible to make something funny in **all** spots. Maybe some people can be funny in all spots. Dave Barry can do it. Steve Allen could do it. I can't do it. I'm actually not even allowed to try. My $300 an hour therapist forbids it. After 4 months of intense therapy, I'll never forget the day we had the "break through". The moment of truth when everything "came together". He said something that still brings tears to my eyes today. After 4 intense months of me bearing my soul, my therapist looked me straight in the eye and said, "No habla Ingles." And I handed him another $300. That was a moment of truth for me. Another came when I decided to have a glossary in this book. A glossary is also known as a lexicon, a word list or a vocabulary dictionary, and it culminates any good literary work. I love using the word culminates. It reminds me of a spelling bee I saw on TV that made me ask the question, "Is my life getting so lonely, so fuckin' lonely, that I have resorted to watching spelling bees on TV?" And of course the answer was a resounding, "Fuck Yes!" So this nerdy little gnome-like creature takes center stage and he has his hands in his pockets. It was late in the day and it was obvious to everyone that the announcer was getting a little testy. Even Gandhi would start losing his patience 3 hours into a fuckin' spelling bee. The conversation between the nerdy little gnome-like creature and the announcer went something like this:

Announcer: The word is "Culminates".

Nerdy Little Gnome-Like Creature: Use it in a sentence please.

Announcer: As soon as this contest culminates, I plan on hiring a hooker and getting drunk, not necessarily in that order.

Nerdy Little Gnome-Like Creature: Origin of the word please.

Announcer: It's Greek. From the word "Culminanus".

Nerdy Little Gnome-Like Creature: Definition please.

Announcer: From the Greek- To stick it up your ass.

Nerdy Little Gnome-Like Creature: C-U-L-M-I-N-A-T-E-S, culminates.

Announcer: Correct, you nerdy little gnome-like creature with your hands in your fuckin' pockets. And the rest of the nerdy little gnome-like creatures twist their collective faces in agony when their opponent gets the word correct, much like poker players do when a "fish" in a cash game goes busted against the tightest player at the table. And so with that, I present to you my Glossary. My glorious fuckin' Glossary. For those of you who don't like glossaries, you can perform culminanus with it.

Antidisestablishmentarianism: One of the longest words in the English language. You have probably never seen this word in your life and will probably never see it again. So don't worry about it. It doesn't have a fuckin' thing to do with poker. But neither does most of this book.

Ante: a) A compulsory bet before the cards are dealt; **b)** The lady married to your uncle; **c)** If your ante had balls, she'd be your uncle.

Automatic Shuffler: A shuffler built into the poker table. This saves a lot of time and they are used primarily in cash games to speed up play so that more "rake" can be taken from the game each hour.

Backdoor: When a player makes a hand he didn't originally intend to make, usually on the river. For example, if the final two cards on the board are diamonds and you make a flush, you backdoored a flush.

Bad Beat: When a very strong hand is beat by a weak hand, usually on the river. Many poker rooms now come equipped with car doors so you can complete the bad beat and not make it feel so soul crushing by slamming your nut sack in one of the doors. When women encounter a bad beat, they simply stare hatefully at their opponent , and when they get home, they slam their **husband's** nut sack in a car door. Then they usually have sex with their boyfriend.

Bet Blind: To bet without looking at your hand. I wanted to do an experiment to test my theory that Hold 'em is 80% betting and 20% cards, so I entered a tournament and "made believe" I was looking at my hand but never did. I just played position. I was amazed at the results. I still lost.

Big Blind: a) A larger forced bet, two positions from the dealer; **b)** Ray Charles if he was 6'7'', 375 pounds.

Blacks: a) A term for casino chips having a value of $100 each; **b)** Anything I say referring to a race would be considered racist no matter how humorous it was, so I'm going to leave this one alone. Abe Lincoln came to me in a dream and says, "Big Guy, do not fuck with this one." And I won't.

Bluff: a) To raise or bet on a weak hand in the hopes that you do not get a call; **b)** A poker magazine.

Board: The community cards that are face-up.

B.R.: Your bankroll.

Bug: a) The Joker; **b)** When you have "the bug", you are addicted to gambling in one form or another.

Bullet: a) An Ace; **b)** The name of one of my dogs. He was a very confused dog. He was half German shepherd and half pit bull and he kept attacking blind people.

Burn: a) A card dealt face down that's put into the discards, for the players' protection; **b)** What a player does after a bad beat.

Bustout: A player who's broke.

Button: a) A plastic disk that usually says "DEALER" on it to indicate who is the designated dealer for the hand; **b)** What you find missing from your last work shirt after you put it on. Dry cleaner employees get sweet revenge by removing one button from a customer's shirt if he was an asshole to them.

Buy-a-Pot: To win a pot by the art of bluffing.

Buy-In: The original amount of money a player invests in the game.

By Me: An expression meaning to check.

Call: a) To put an amount into the pot that equals the bet or raise made by your opponent; **b)** What you do periodically to let your wife know you're coming home soon.

Calling Station: A player who virtually calls all bets. This person is impossible to bluff but I keep trying.

Card Protector: A chip, a good luck charm, an urn, a large pig, an Elvis doll, a spinner, an unused package of condoms. There are many types of card protectors all used for the same reason- to protect your hand- and give your opponents something to stare at.

Cards Speak for Themselves: Regardless of what you say your hand is, the cards always speak for themselves.

Cash Games- Ring Games: Unlike a tournament, real chips are used. The blinds do not escalate like they do in a tournament. Ring games are full cash games- in other words, an ass in every seat.

Change Gears: a) Adjusting your style of play. This is very important during tournament play; **b)** What I did when I drove my first car. It was a stick shift.

Chase: a) Trying to beat someone's hand who you know has you dominated; **b)** What a guy did to me when I stole a Milky Way candy bar from his lousy fuckin' candy store. He caught me before I could swallow the evidence.

Check: a) To make no bet, yet keep your hand; **b)** A casino chip; **c)** What your wife writes every fuckin' time she walks into a store.

Check Blind: To pass without looking at your cards.

Check Raise: To check or pass and then raise the guy who bets. You know- ram it in his ass. This is frowned upon in small, friendly private games, but I do it anyway.

Chips: I love all kinds of chips. Especially the ones that say "$100" on them. And potato chips that are "kettle" made. Like Vegas Chips- Salt and Vinegar. They're fuckin' great. Ask for them at your local grocer.

Chiprunner: My favorite chiprunner is Masood at the Bellagio. He takes good care of me.

Cold Deck (or Cooler): This is a pre-arranged deck that is used to bust the guy with all the money. I've seen it used a few times many years ago. It's devastating.

Collusion: Two or more players working together against the other players at the game. There is so much money involved in playing cash games or tournament poker that collusion is fairly common. You have to be aware of it when you are playing. Read "Dirty Poker" by Richard Marcus for a detailed explanation on this form of cheating. Also Steve Forte's new book "Poker Protection" is fuckin' great!

Community Cards: a) The face-up cards dealt in the center of the table that are part of everyone's hand; **b)** Women who live in the community that have sex with everyone. Wait a minute- that's community hookers.

Counterfeit: I just learned this term recently. It's when you think you have a winning hand and the board pairs and the pair on the board is bigger than the pair in your hand. And of course you get fucked. Again. The name "Hold 'em" should be changed to "Fuck 'em". No Limit Texas "Fuck 'em". If there is a way to fuck up a very nice day- this game will find it.

Covered: a) In a tournament, when someone goes all-in and you have more chips than he does, you have him "covered"; **b)** The word your grandkids will use some day when you're in a wheelchair with a shawl and a drool cup and one of the kids says, "I think grandpa's shawl fell off." And the other kid says, "I took care of it. He's covered." Then they empty your drool cup and your wallet and go play in a tournament.

Cowboy: a) A King; **b)** A very wild player; **c)** My wife's favorite, Roy Rogers.

Crying Call: To whine and whine when calling an opposing player while playing a hand.

Cut: After the shuffle, the cards are separated in half, and the bottom half is placed on the top half. No matter how friendly your home game is, it is absolutely imperative the cards are cut every time they are shuffled. If for whatever reason they are not cut, do not play the fuckin' hand. I will repeat that- DO NOT PLAY THE FUCKIN' HAND. Don't even look at it. You may have just been cold decked.

Cutoff: a) A seat that is one off the dealer button; **b)** When your Levi's get old, you cut off the legs and wear what's left. I never have, but my friends have. They didn't have fat legs like me. If you are over 50 years old, it should be against the law to wear shorts or cutoffs. And if you are built like a tank, you should not be allowed to wear tank tops. Very severe fines should be imposed.

Dead Hand: A hand that is fouled and no longer eligible to win the pot. It is your responsibility to protect your hand and your testicles at all times.

Dominated: a) A situation in Hold 'em where one hand is significantly better than the other; **b)** A situation at home where the wife is significantly better than the husband, so he plays poker 10 hours a day and tries to only go home when she's asleep.

Double Pop: a) When you immediately re-raise the raiser; **b)** When you have a dad and a stepdad; **c)** Double pop should not be confused with Double Fat, which is a double Fatburger- one of the greatest accomplishments of man in the wonderful world of hamburgers. Fatburger is one of my all time favorite hamburger chains. Better than In N Out.

Drawing Dead: Regardless of the cards you draw, you cannot win the hand. This is when you look for Dr. Kevorkian so you can order a med cocktail from him.

Drop Out (or Fold): a) To throw your hand away; **b)** To quit high school or college to play Hold 'em

Drop Box: a) A box under the table with a lock on it that gets filled with your money and then removed by a security guard who is guaranteed to bang the sharp edge of the box on your knee if you're in the ten seat; **b)** The box they put you in before they drop you into the ground.

Deuce: a) Cards with the rank of two; **b)** A coupe I had when I was in college.

Family Pot: a) A pot where every player at the table plays the hand; **b)** A pot that has been handed down from generation to generation so we would always have something to piss in. Many full time poker players don't have a pot to piss in. I usually loan them mine.

Floorman: A supervisor who is called upon to make a ruling whenever there is a dispute. They take a solemn oath when they are given this prestigious position to try to never make the same decision twice.

Flop: a) The first three cards turned up after the first round of betting; **b)** Most of the movies put out by Hollywood; **c)** What you do on your couch when you get home after a grueling night in the poker room.

Flush: a) Five cards of the same suit; **b)** What all caring human beings do after they've gone to the bathroom. People who don't flush are going to go to Hell. Take my word for it.

Forward Motion: To have chips in your hand and move toward the center of the pot.

Four of a Kind (or Quads): Four cards of the same rank. An orgasmic moment when it happens. Savor the moment. It doesn't happen very often. Like sex.

Free Card: A round where there is no betting and everyone gets another card at no cost.

Full Boat (or Full House): a) Three of a kind with another pair; **b)** When friends or relatives come to ride in your boat and then decide to stay in your house for a month.

Fuckin': The kid who's typing this shit for me, Grant Turner, has set a goal for me to use this word or a form of it at least 500 times. I'm proud to say that we easily exceeded our goal.

Go All-In: To bet all the money you have in front of you.

Heads Up: Just two players.

Hold 'em: A poker game with two cards dealt face down to each player, and five cards dealt face-up, known as community cards, that everyone uses in conjunction with their two face-down cards. The best five cards out of the seven are used at the conclusion of the hand.

Hole Cards: a) The two face-down cards dealt to each player; **b)** In the world of science, your hole cards are bacteria filled Petri dishes.

Kicker: An important side card to your pair. A higher "kicker"- like an Ace or a King is instrumental many times in determining who wins the pot. That's why a lot of people don't play an Ace-small. For example- A-2, A-3, A-4, A-5, A-6, A-7, A-8. If the board does pair your Ace, your "kicker" would suck.

Limp In: a) To come into a pot before the flop without raising; **b)** What I do when I enter a poker room on my crutch.

Local: A resident who plays in a poker game and is usually a good player.

Looking Out the Window: A player who doesn't pay attention to the game.

Loose Player: A player who plays almost every pot.

Maniac: A player who raises almost every time and plays like he only has a week to live.

Mechanic: a) A dealer who is able to manipulate the cards; **b)** What people claim they are before they fuck your car up. Most mechanics today are parts changers. They rarely "fix" anything.

Miss the Flop: When the first three community cards don't help your hand at all.

Money Management: The control of your money during the course of the game. This is especially important to people who try to make their living at playing poker. Money management should also be used by tourists. A phrase heard often is when a husband says to the wife, "Give me the money I told you not to give me if I asked you for it."

Move In: a) In a no-limit game, you bet all your chips; **b)** What relatives do when they first come to town. After they've been here for a year, then the term becomes "settle-in".

Muck: a) The discards piled in front of the dealer; **b)** A term just one letter away from "fuck".

Must Move Game: Usually a higher limit game that feeds the main high limit game. When a seat opens up in the main game, you "must move" from your game to the main game no matter how good your game is. You think you're confused now? I had to write this shit.

Nickels: Five-dollar chips.

Nuts: a) The best possible hand that can be made with the board that's showing; **b)** Where my dog landed when she jumped on my lap.

On Tilt: A term used when a player starts playing really bad after losing a big pot.

Open-ended Straight: A four-card hand that can turn into a straight by catching a card at either end to complete the sequence.

Outs: The amount of cards that you can get to improve your hand.

Paint: a) A face card; **b)** What my wife just did to our family room. What a fuckin' mess. Don't ever paint the inside of your house. Move. It's easier.

Pocket Rockets: Pair of Aces as your hole cards.

Pop: a) To raise the pot; **b)** The guy who humped your mom.

Position: Where you are sitting in the order of play. Position is one of the most powerful weapons in the arsenal of a poker player. God, I love the way I wrote that fuckin' sentence.

Premium Hands: The top starting hands in Hold 'em.

Quarters: Twenty-five dollar chips.

Rabbit Hunting: a) After the hand is over, running the cards out through the river to see if you would have made your hand; **b)** A sport that is cruel to rabbits and their families.

Railbird: A spectator watching from the rail that surrounds the poker table. Railbirds have been known to signal a hand to another player so you must protect your hand and make sure no one can see it.

Ram and Jam: To bet and raise very aggressively.

Rake: The part of the pot the dealer takes for the house. It's usually a small percentage of the pot with a cap. But let me make this perfectly fuckin' clear. It really adds up. Big time.

Reload: a) To buy more chips; **b)** What you do with your gun after you shoot it and miss your target.

Ring Game: a) A game with a player in every seat; **b)** No relation to Ring Worm.

River: The final community card dealt. Anyone who has played Hold 'em has had bad experiences on the river. Painful, gut wrenching, asshole puckering experiences. I need to stop. I'm going to be sick.

Rock: A consistent, tight ass player who is actually pretty easy to play against.

Royal Flush: a) The highest ranking hand without wild cards. A-K-Q-J-10 Suited; **b)** What the Queen of England does after she takes a shit.

Runner-Runner: The final two community cards that make your hand a winning hand.

Rush: a) A rapid succession of winning hands; **b)** What we all seem to do every day.

Satellites: Usually a one table mini-tournament.

Set: Three of a kind. A pocket pair and one community card that matches.

Sit N Go's: Simply put- a one table satellite where the top three players share in the prize money with the winner getting 50%- 2nd place 30%- and 3rd place 20%.

Small Blind: a) A forced bet by the player next to the dealer button. It's half as much as the big blind; **b)** Ray Charles if he was 4'9'', 75 pounds.

Straight: Five cards in sequence not of the same suit.

Straight Flush: Five cards of the same suit in sequence.

Suck Out: To have an inferior hand then to win the hand on the river. I believe the origin of the word is from the Greek "You suck", which Greek longshoremen said when they played with inferior players during their lunch break. Once in a while the underdog would win the hand and say to his opponent, "Suck me" and they would eat huge olives and laugh hysterically. This turned into "Sucked out" somewhere between 1047 AD and 1072 AD. The olive tradition was disbanded in 1964 when after consuming 450 olives, two opponents started throwing olive pits at one another and one of the players had his eye put out by an olive pit. That really sucked.

Suited Connectors: Two cards in sequence of the same suit.

Tapped Out: To lose all your money. To be busted.

Tell: a) A mannerism that gives away your hand; **b)** The last name of a guy who liked to shoot apples off peoples' heads with his bow and arrow. William had a tough time keeping friends.

Three of a Kind: Three cards of the same rank.

Throwing a Party: a) A player throwing his money away; **b)** What I did whenever my parents left town for a weekend.

Time Game: Instead of a rake, the house or casino charges you a set fee to play at the poker table. This fee is usually collected every half hour.

Top Kicker: The highest side card when two players have the same hand.

Toke: A tip or gratuity for the dealer. Many people in the casino industry make their living on tips because casinos usually pay minimum wage.

Trips: a) Three of a kind; **b)** What most people take on their vacation.

Turn Card: The fourth community card.

Two Pair: Two different pairs in the same hand plus one side card.

Under the Gun: The first player to act after the big blind.

Verbal Action: a) Action made verbally before you put your chips in the pot. Your word is literally your bond. If you say "All-in" you can't change your mind; **b)** When you mother-fuck the guy who is an asshole at the table. That is actually "Verbal Assault", but no one cares because the guy is an asshole.

Will Rogers: A player who has never seen a hand he didn't like.

WPT: The World Poker Tour.

WSOP: The World Series of Poker- a huge, giant, cash cow, money making machine, golden goose that lays golden eggs, that hopefully Harrah's doesn't fuck up with "Accounting" mentality.